CRIME, GENDER, AND SEXUALITY IN CRIMINAL PROSECUTIONS

CRIME, GENDER, AND SEXUALITY IN CRIMINAL PROSECUTIONS

Edited by
Louis A. Knafla

Criminal Justice History
Volume 17

GREENWOOD PRESS
Westport, Connecticut • London

ISBN: 0–313–31013–0
ISSN: 0194–0953

First published in 2002

Greenwood Press, 88 Post Road West, Westport, CT 06881
An imprint of Greenwood Publishing Group, Inc.
www.greenwood.com

Printed in the United States of America

The paper used in this book complies with the Permanent Paper Standard issued by the National Information Standards Organization (Z39.48–1984).

10 9 8 7 6 5 4 3 2

Contents

Preface

Volume 17 continues the new direction for *Criminal Justice History*. Each volume will center on a general theme or subject, which will include essays and reviews, and a title that reflects its contents. This volume highlights seven original articles on the history of class, gender, and sexuality in criminal prosecutions from late-medieval Europe to the British Empire in the nineteenth century. It also contains an extensive review essay on new directions in the history of crime in early-modern England, and book reviews of sixteen works on the history of crime in Europe and North America. An introduction outlines the articles and the themes that emerge from them, that will inform the social history of crime, a field that has struck the imagination of the historical profession in recent years. The book, as others in the series, concludes with a comprehensive index.

The following, succeeding volumes have been contracted and completed for publication to date: Volume 18: *Crime, Punishment, and Reform in Europe* and Volume 19: *Violent Crime in North America*. Future volumes will be announced as they are prepared.

Introduction

Louis A. Knafla

The three topics of this volume represent a major area of the historiography of crime and criminal justice in the 1990s. Indeed, class, gender, and sexuality have become hallmarks of the humanities and the social sciences. Much of the theory has come from the disciplines of anthropology, law, literature, and sociology. Much of the hard research has come from historians, from both the traditional and the new social or cultural history adherents. The chapters contained here comprise case studies of class, gender, and sexuality from late medieval Europe to early twentieth-century India. They address some of the critical questions of the historiography, and they are often written within the context of race, violence, politics, and the nation-state.

Trevor Dean examines how the statutes of the city of Bologna concerning vendetta, 1288–1454, were applied judicially between families and the state down into the sixteenth century. The statutes, by 1454, placed heavy penalties against attackers, which increased if revenge could be proved as a motive. Revenge taken quickly or slightly delayed brought swift prosecution when the evidence was readily apparent. While local nobles might find ways of lightly punishing or excusing vendetta, foreign judges who headed the civic judiciary prosecuted them regardless of past relations or conflicts between the parties. In addition, acts of pacification became legally required by the mid–fifteenth century before convicted offenders could have their bans lifted and return to the community, particularly with regard to male offenders. Reforming churchmen, noble patrons, and government officials keen to reduce the level of violent crime were prominent in shaping this policy.

The chapter raises many questions concerning the role of families, men, and women in the developing criminal justice system of Italian city-states in late medieval and renaissance Europe. Examining a full range of local court and governmental records, Dean is able to demonstrate that the city-state was not a weak institution, that it did not openly tolerate violent conflict but became prepared to handle it in decisive ways, and that it had a vitality toward dispute resolution that could override personal interests. Thus the "family ownership of injuries," which was so prominent in early medieval society, was giving way perhaps to the authority of the local municipality.

Female criminality has been an area of prominent research in the past decade. Where scholars once studied crimes against women almost exclusively, more recent work has focused on female disorder and crimes that women perpetrated. Andrea Knox provides an illuminating study of women's crime in an area hitherto unexplored, that of early-modern Ireland. She examines the widespread involvement of women in the antisocial behavior that developed in the era, as well as their active political roles in rebellions against the English. Using the evidence of women's testimony, she is able to portray their voices and explain the extent to which women became "knowing subjects of their own crimes" within their distinctive Irish experience.

On the social side, Irish women were generally well educated, and in cases of adultery and fornication their testimony was often constructive, creating defense strategies that convinced judges to set minimal terms of punishment. On the political side, however, Knox demonstrates how Irish women played a decisive role in political subversion at the cost of their own and their families' lives. Like men, they were tortured for their evidence and executed for their crimes. But their public statements, focusing on reputation, honesty, and morality, cut across the accustomed male voice that centered on masculinity, power, and class. Thus, they brought a certain dignity to the image of the criminal and raised the spectrum and level of debate on the causes of criminality in early modern society.

"Bridewell," the famous English prison workhouse, was founded in London in 1553. Housing largely vagrants and prostitutes, it constituted a new kind of prison that attempted to reform criminals through a regime of incarceration and hard labor that "constituted a revolution in penal practice." Spreading to Ireland, Scotland, and North America, it was used in London as late as the 1850s and in Chicago for its juvenile delinquents in the 1920s. Lee Beier's chapter explores the origins of the institution in the sixteenth century and Michel Foucault's work on madness that placed Bridewell as part of the foundation of Europe's movement to incarceration.

Beier finds that it was humanists who pioneered an interest in imprisonment; it was London Protestant clerics who created Bridewell out of their interest in, and zeal for, institutional reform. Arguments such as the use of forced labor to make better Christians of the poor overrode Foucault's cause of political power. But its creation as part of London's hospital reforms, and as a policing institution of young laboring apprentices and servants, placed it in the mainstream of humanist thought from Juan Luis Vives to Sir Thomas More. But bridewells never reached a pervasive nature. The records evidence reveals that most of them were small, sentences and stays were quite brief, and most paupers were never imprisoned. Nonetheless, Bridewell represented original thinking on crime and punishment and "established an institutional pattern that lasted until the birth of the modern penitentiary."

For most of the eighteenth century, blackmail remained a misdemeanor in English criminal law as a species of extortion. In the 1770s, one particular form of blackmail, extortion under allegation of homosexual behavior, was incorporated within the capital felony of robbery. This legal transformation initially occurred through case law, not by statute, and applied to this distinctive form of blackmail only. Antony Simpson examines the legal development and patterns of the capital prosecution of robbery as blackmail, together with its professional nature. It is suggested that antipathy toward homosexuality, as evidenced here by extreme hostility toward those who attempted to profit from its allegations, had strong origins in eighteenth-century popular culture. The chapter concludes that an examination of this legal development is a better indicator of popular feeling than the wave of capital prosecutions of homosexuals that began in England early in the nineteenth century.

Popular belief was an area that Henry Mayhew, a mid–nineteenth century writer on the English criminal classes, contested. Mayhew, an early sociologist, lived among them, had them in his house, studied them inside out, and classified them elaborately. As controversial today as he was in his own time, Mayhew defies characterization. David Englander sets out here to establish the basis for understanding Mayhew the man as well as Mayhew the bourgeois social investigator.

In 1861 the British proclaimed the India Police Act that established the formal police organization in the country. In spite of the success of the London Metropolitan Police, the British did not think that a similar police force would work with the Indian people. Instead, they devised an instrument to consolidate their newly established empire, one that would work for the hegemony of their imperial ambitions and operate to keep the large populace cowed at a minimal cost. Arvind Verma has examined the inspection notes of the Motihari Police Station in Bihar from 1865–1928, where Gandhi first began his nonviolent movement in 1919.

The evidence provides a glimpse into the working of the British police organization, the role and functions of the subordinate personnel and the phenomenon of crime and its control mechanisms. Senior officers strictly controlled the power of subordinates. Legislative provisions, which mandated police to mitigate social problems, were left in abeyance. Neither complaints against the brutality of landlords nor complaints against the police were entertained. Thus, planters were able to increase their control over the peasants as well as to prepare the foundation for civil disobedience and revolt. The police, adhering to the advice of Rudyard Kipling, became the bulwark for the Raj and used the force of the state to maintain him.

"Crime" and "colonialism" are two terms that reflected thinking on gender, race, and class in the age of imperialism. Examined with respect to prostitution, crime can be seen as an occupation bringing women either independence or ultimate submission to male stereotypes of women as property whose sexuality existed to satisfy male lust. Philippa Levine studies the traditional view of gender roles in nineteenth-century Europe with regard to the British Empire in Southeast Asia. Looking at the record from India to Hong Kong, local indigenous prostitutes "served principally and critically as racial markers." Her investigations reveal that the "white slave trade" was the dividing line between the active male and the passive female.

The white slave trade, based on race, was translated by Europeans to mean that women were totally passive because they did not work. Where European women who plied their trade in these colonies worked it as a profession—hardened and unruly people in control of their trade—the indigenous women were seen as articles of trade or barter stemming from mass slavery. Prostitution, while not criminalized by most Europeans, helped to shape female delinquency in Britain and gendered and racial expectations in the colonies. While the official records tell us little about these paradigms, the creation of a criminal class of women who were sexualized and racialized provides us with a more richly textured view of crime, and what it meant, in the Victorian era.

Essays on crime and justice are seldom written from single sources or from a single focus. While class, gender, and sexuality feature prominently as subjects in this volume, they are usually depicted within the institutions of the police, the military, the courts, and local and central governments. They are also highly affected by the dominant and marginal cultures and by the interplay of personal and group violence on the one hand, and by the forces of social control on the other. Here is where class has been a pivotal element in the historiography of who is tried and who is punished.

Until now, most of this research has focused on Europe and North America. We should not be surprised to see a future shift in focus to Africa and Asia. As Verma and Levine have shown, the study of crime and criminal justice in the latter continents can enrich the study of Europeans and neo-Europeans as well as discovering further the history of all indigenous peoples. What they all have in common is the problem of defining criminal behavior in legal terms, creating institutions to enforce it, and determining the role of the community in prosecuting and judging it. As readers will see, the line between official and unofficial practices can be a very thin one.

CRIME, GENDER, AND SEXUALITY IN CRIMINAL PROSECUTIONS

Violence, Vendetta, and Peacemaking in Late Medieval Bologna

Trevor Dean

In the rapidly developing historiography of Italian medieval crime and justice,[1] a settled view seems to have developed of the relationship between the criminal law and vendetta. There was not in Italy, it is now said, the rapid forward march of public penal methods of dealing with violent conflict, in which public punishment replaced private revenge or composition, but a lengthy period of coexistence of public and private, in which vendetta was overtly tolerated by the law and composition openly fostered by judges, lawyers, and governments.[2] This view is part of a broader trend that stresses the weakness, not the strength, of late medieval states, that redefines the distinction between public and private, and that presents states as forced to negotiate with a range of social and political bodies.[3] Among these bodies was the family: The vitality of private or semiprivate modes of dispute-settlement was sustained, it is said, by the persistence of a sense of family ownership of injuries. An injury done to one member of a family "belonged" to the entire family, could be avenged by any of them, could be forgiven only with the consent of all, and could be transmitted through inheritance to future generations.[4] The purpose of this article is to challenge this vision of the relationships between families and the state and between vendetta and the law by examining judicial practice in one late medieval city-state, Bologna.

Little need be said by way of introduction about the city of Bologna, one of the major centers of the Papal State with a large university, or about its disturbed and complex political history in the later Middle Ages.[5] The city experienced periods of rule by papal legates and governors, rebellions against the papacy in the name of *libertas*, and "tyrannies" of both foreign and homegrown origin. Throughout, the subsisting stratum of communal government consisted of a committee of eight *Anziani* (elders), two advisory colleges, and a legislative council (Council of Four Hundred), though from the late fourteenth century, real power was increasingly concentrated in a special executive committee known as the Sixteen *Riformatori dello stato di libertà* (Reformers of the Free State). Members of this committee, drawn from some two dozen families, formed the ruling oligarchy, that supported or sometimes fought with the emerging lordship of the Bentivoglio family. The judiciary was formed principally of a hired, foreign chief-judge (*podestà*), with a staff of subordinate judges, assistants, and constables. At various times, additional temporary law enforcers and bandit catchers were appointed. The *podestà* had overall civil and criminal jurisdiction in both the city and its dependent countryside (*contado*), but the major rural centers were also the seats of governors (*vicari*), drawn from the urban elite and holding limited jurisdiction in both civil and criminal matters.[6] The judicial system in Bologna had developed along lines common to most Italian city-states; successive compilations of statute law multiplied the defined crimes that were within the competence of the *podestà*; trials, based in the thirteenth century mainly on accusation by the victim, by the fifteenth derived from denunciation by district officials or on *ex officio* investigation; public penalties (fines payable to the commune or punishments inflicted by its officers) were first made irreducible, then increased (for example, for murder, moving from ban and/or fines, to public execution, then to execution and fine).[7]

It has to be admitted that the Bolognese statutes on vendetta are not among the clearest pieces of legislation in the civic lawbook. The aim of enactments in both the 1288 and 1454 statutes was to penalize the taking of revenge against anyone but the original attacker. The 1288 statute makes an initial distinction between penalties for those in custody and for those not but inserts its definition of what vendetta is, and how vendetta is to be proved, between these two sections, as if it depended on the condition of being in custody. The penalties at least are clear enough: "if anyone makes a revenge attack . . . on any person or persons other than the [first] attacker," then if he is in custody, he should be punished with death if the victim died, or with a fine of either L.1,000 or L.2,000, according to the seriousness of the wounds inflicted; if he is not in custody, he should be placed in perpetual ban, his houses and towers should be demolished, all his property should go to his victim, or to his victim's heirs. "And a crime is to be understood as done in revenge, that is by him who before had been attacked (or by his party or by another on his behalf), against someone other than the attacker, if he who is said to have been attacked in revenge can prove by trustworthy witnesses . . . that there is public repute that the said crime was committed in revenge, and, along with this repute, if there exists some circumstantial evidence or presumption."[8] This would seem to mean that anyone (except an original aggressor) who suffered a revenge attack could obtain the statutory penalties against his attacker by proving, through testimony of public awareness and other evidence, that he was indeed attacked in vendetta. In other words, a higher scale of penalties was available for vendetta victims if they could prove revenge.

This apparent dependence on private legal action by the victim disappears from the 1454 statutes, as one would expect given the general transition from a judicial system formed around private accusation to one formed around official inquisition.[9] In other respects, the 1454 statutes make essentially the same provision as in 1288: "if anyone attacks . . . in his revenge any person or persons other than him or them who is said to have attacked him," then the usual penalties for homicide apply (or a special tariff of fines for blows and wounds). "And an attack made in revenge is to be understood as proved when it happens thus, viz. he who is said to have attacked in revenge was attacked by someone other than he whom he had attacked . . . and he who is said to have been had attacked in revenge is an agnate or cognate relation of he who had attacked him who is said to have attacked later in revenge."[10]

Two points are especially to be noted in these legal texts. The first is that, by penalizing secondary or collateral revenge (against persons other than the first attacker), the statutes appear to tolerate, but only by implication, primary, direct revenge. The statutes penalize the extended development of vendetta; they do not explicitly allow the vengeance of victim on attacker. The burden of the statutes was to make heavier penalties available to secondary revenge, not to allow primary revenges to be excused. Their purpose was repressive, not permissive. The second important point is this: The concept of public repute or knowledge ("that there is *public repute* that the said crime was committed in revenge," "any person other than him *who is said* to have attacked him" emphasis added) seems to lie at the very heart of the definition of revenge. This becomes important when we consider two further problems that arise from these laws. First, how did witnesses and officials know when a revenge attack had taken place? How did they know how to distinguish vendetta from the countless other assaults and brawls that took place? Second, how was it intended that these statutes should work in practice? In answer to the first, we can say that it was publicity that distinguished the vendetta killing and that turned witnesses, as if at public execution, from active interveners into passive bystanders. "No-one moved," commented one contemporary of some political vendetta killings.[11] Making public the identity of the attacker was a key step in establishing an assault as an act of vengeance. Whereas ordinary murderers might try to hide bodies or to conceal their identity,[12] avengers needed their identity to be recognized. This is well illustrated in two contrasting sixteenth-century incidents: In 1552, murderers threatened a witness, who had recognized them, with death if she spoke and in 1583, avengers made sure that the father of their victim knew exactly who they were and why they had murdered his son.[13] In answer to the second problem, if vendetta was tolerated by the law courts, there would seem to be three moments when this could have effect: before trial, during trial, or after trial. Either local officials did not denounce crimes that they recognized as vendetta, or the *podestà* did not prosecute them to an outcome, or, if he did, the convict obtained remission of penalty on petition to the governing councils of the city. The first possibility would seem to be suggested in an obscure passage of the 1288 statute, but by the fifteenth century, when the judicial system rested more solidly on official denunciation rather than on private accusation, this would seem more unlikely (the passage disappears from the 1454 statutes). By then local officials dutifully were denouncing as crimes even accidents on building sites and chance woundings among boys at play,[14] and there was judicial action against insults including vendetta threats ("I'll pay you back/*io ten pagargo*" and so on).[15] As for the second and third possibilities, they will be examined below.

If the law was repressive, not permissive, with regard to vendetta, we may begin to search the trial record for prosecution of vendetta offenses. The results are surprising. There are occasionally prosecutions of assaults and killings specifically acknowledged to be motivated by revenge. Thus in 1324, Bono da Iesi confessed to stabbing a law student in his lodgings "to take his revenge" for the judicial execution, by the student's father (a judge in Iesi) of Bono's brother and uncle[16] and, a century later, Battista di Matteo, "considering himself burdened and injured by his brother Tommaso" as the result of a long legal dispute, "with the intention of taking vengeance on Tommaso," killed him in a shop on the piazza with one fatal knifewound to the spine.[17] Revenge was no excuse in such trials: Battista was beheaded.

It rarely was acknowledged in such explicit terms that the crime prosecuted was a revenge assault. More often in the trial record, we find the victim of an assault being prosecuted shortly afterward for an attack on his or her assailant, or on one of the assailant's relatives, in what have been called "criss-cross trials."[18] In January 1383, one Sandro di Guiduccio, a cleric, was tried for a bloody brawl with Giovanni di Domenico Albertuzzi. A week later, Sandro was seized at knife-point by Giovanni's brother, Pietro Albertuzzi, saying "Ha, rogue and rotten traitor, I shall kill you as you killed my brother."[19] Pietro was banned in L.100; Sandro, as a cleric, was remitted to the bishop's court. In May 1388, the "old and decrepit" notary Giovanni di Alberto and his wife Mata were prosecuted for a brawl with Imelda, wife of Stefano "Bonefidei." It took until mid-June for the trial to reach its inconclusive end (the named witnesses were unable to provide adequate proof). Only a week later, Imelda was charged with seizing Giovanni, dragging him into her house, throwing him to the floor and hitting him many times with her hands and fists.[20] Again, however, it seems that the witnesses' testimony did not prove the charge. In May 1473, Mariotto da Firenze was prosecuted for an assault in the street on Benedetto Ingrati, wounding him twice with a sword in the head and neck, and Benedetto and his brother Bartolomeo Ingrati were prosecuted for wounding Mariotto in their house by inflicting bloody wounds to his head and thigh. Mariotto was banned in L.200, and Bartolomeo in L.100. Benedetto was acquitted because the witnesses could not attest to having seen him hit Mariotto.[21] In the summer months of the same year, there were two prosecutions of armed assault in the rural center of Budrio. In one, Antonio Zambonelli, his two sons and numerous others were charged with attacking Paolo Marano and his sons in a meadow; in the other, Pietro di Paolo Marano was charged with assault on Antonio Zambonelli.[22]

It is not always clear how much time separated these acts of retaliation. The trial documents record only the month, not the day, and it could be that separate prosecutions, some months apart in time, could in fact relate to a single incident. This seems probable, as in the Budrio case, where the *podestà* proceeded to a supplementary trial on the basis of information received from an accused person. But nor did the law on revenge specify separation in time between offense and response. Revenge could be taken immediately or many years later. The judicial sources at least show that revenge quickly taken was liable to prosecution. And there is some indication that the same was true of delayed revenge. In 1332 one Bessano di Borghesano was held and tried for wounding the son of the man who had killed his father forty years previously (though eventually he was acquitted "as a gift of special grace," because peace had been made).[23] Where prosecutions failed, it was not because anyone invoked the permissive authority of statute-law, but because insufficient testimony could be found to prove the charge. There remains the possibility, of course, that witnesses chose to forget what they had seen, because they considered the offense excused by reason of vendetta. Just as statute law rested its definition of vendetta on public repute, so too prosecutions could fail where public repute adjudged the offense to be a revenge attack. We should, nevertheless, note that at least some prosecutions were completed and that some avengers were convicted and punished.

The trial record also provides another type of evidence in our examination of the relationship between the law on vendetta and the practice of the courts: the technical challenges ("exceptions" or "oppositions") sometimes made to criminal charges by the accused man's attorney (*procurator*).[24] A case from 1388 illustrates this process. In April of that year, one Giovanni da Roncadello, known as *"indivino"* (the "diviner/magician"), was charged with the adultery and abduction of the wife of Giorgio da Mongiorgio, with attempted assassination of her husband and with practicing the craft of "divining" (providing love potions, etc). Giovanni's attorney entered a long list of exceptions to these charges: that the initial complaint had not been made in due time and form, that the witnesses had not been properly summoned nor their depositions correctly recorded, that the witnesses were not creditable because they were Giorgio's servants, that the *podestà* was proceeding improperly by inquisition (which required a clamor against the accused; a single complaint was insufficient), and that Giovanni's confession had been extracted out of fear of torture although, in fact, there was insufficient evidence to subject him to torture.[25] These were exactly the sort of lawyer's quibbles that Italian states attempted, through repeated legislation, to keep out of the criminal process. What is revealing for our purposes is that, despite all the attorney's ingenuity in producing objections, revenge is never deployed as a justification against the most serious charge (that of attempted assassination). And yet it is the attorney who reveals that Giovanni had been the target of armed attack by Giorgio himself. This fact is used only to support the contention that the prosecution witnesses should not be given credence because they were Giovanni's enemies.[26]

This pattern was typical. Exceptions were submitted to the court, arguing that proceedings were invalid for failing to follow statutory procedures and time limits, maintaining that there were defects in the collection of testimony or in the testimony itself, claiming that the crime was not one for which the *podestà* could proceed by denunciation by local officials, or affirming that the victim could be legitimately killed because he was a bandit.[27] No attorney seems to have perceived the relevance to the defense of the statute on vendetta. The conclusion is inescapable: The law on vendetta, though remaining on the statute book, was never used, because judicial practice was to treat revenge as ordinary crime.

This was similar with petitions to the government from those convicted of violent crimes seeking remission, pardon, and rehabilitation. A variety of arguments were deployed by petitioners to catch the compassion of their rulers' youth: poverty, innocence, unjust conviction, accidental wounding, pacification with the victim.[28] Neither revenge nor the provisions of the vendetta law is ever used in this context. Revenge had no legitimacy here: To admit to anger was to reduce the worth of the petition.[29] Thus it seems that, at the point of trial, the legitimate defense of vendetta-killing was not used; nor later, at the moment of petition for remission of sentence, was lawful revenge adduced as a mitigating circumstance. Among all the various considerations pleaded in self-justification, at trial or after, vendetta scarcely ever is recorded.

A rare example of a petition that does mention vendetta arises in 1441, and this allows us to explore further the dark relationship between revenge and the law courts. The case has left two sources, the trial record and a subsequent petition by one of the two sides involved. Let us start with the trial record.[30] In July 1441, the district official for Bibolano made a denunciation of an armed fight between two groups of men, one group of six led by the brothers Simone and Bertoccio di Jacopino, the other group, also of six, consisting of Achille di Giovanni, his two sons, and three of his in-laws, the sons of Fino Panzacchi. Simone's heavily armed band had lain in ambush for Achille and attacked them as they approached, despite the dissuasive efforts of three of Simone's followers, who had not known the purpose of Simone's armed gathering and claimed friendship with Achille. In the resulting battle, multiple wounds were sustained by five men, as a result of which one from Simone's group died, less serious wounds were sustained by two others.

Depositions were taken from four witnesses. All claimed that Achille and his companions had acted in self-defense. They could not flee once one of their number had been wounded, and "almost all [of Simone's] men were much more fierce and robust" than Achille's, "and could have killed them." Most significant was the testimony of the citizen Ludovico Bianchi, who had recently served as Bolognese commissioner in that part of the contado. Aware of the feud (*inimicitia*) between Simone and Achille, and their respective kin (*aptinentes*), he had sought to pacify them, especially because this local enmity posed a threat to the city's security during warfare against a papal army. Bianchi attested that, though Achille and the sons of Fino Panzacchi were prepared to make peace immediately, Simone refused "unless he first conferred with his *aptinentes*," and only if they would accept it. So Bianchi had taken promises from both sides not to attack the other "even if they found them asleep," until Simone brought his reply. Simone did not return. Instead, it was during this interval that the ambush took place. A second witness confirmed this account. Armed with these depositions, the *podestà* in August charged all those involved with armed brawling, but on the following day the case was suspended because of the war. No one could be summoned as access to that part of the contado was cut off. We later learn, however, that Achille and his men were eventually acquitted by the *podestà*.

Four points stand out in the trial record. First, efforts by city officials to pacify rural enmities could simply provide the occasion for them to flare into even greater atrocity. Second, efforts by the common friends of Achille and Simone failed to prevent the ambush.[31] Third, the proximity of armies served as an important backdrop, inciting the vain pacification and perhaps emboldening the attackers. Fourth, the witnesses' claim that Achille and his group acted in necessary self-defense had no effect on the drawing up of the charges: Both sides were indicted.

Achille's petition to the Bolognese *Anziani*,[32] though recounting the central episode in much the same way (suggesting of course that he was the source of the denouncing official's information), makes important additions regarding the origins and outcome of this fight. The origin is stated immediately to lie in an inheritance dispute between four sisters and one Bartolomea di Guidocino. One of the sisters was married to Simone; Bartolomea was married to Achille. The dispute thus arose among women. Marriage spread it into violent male confrontation. There already had been two violent exchanges before Ludovico Bianchi appeared on the scene: the first between Achille and Simone (the two principals, in the eyes of the law on vendetta), the second between Simone's brother, on the one hand, and Achille and one of his Panzacchi in-laws on the other (secondary action). "And so, because of these, capital enmities arose," between Achille, the Panzacchi, their relatives and well-wishers, and Simone and Bertoccio and theirs. Just as he tried to justify the origin of the dispute, so Achille's version of the ambush too tried to suggest that a vendetta cycle had been closed. Simone's companion Scarpello, fatally wounded, ordered before he died that "neither of his death, nor of the wounds he had received should any revenge ever be taken, but of them peace should be made by his brother and his heirs."[33] By creating a history for the dispute (one reminiscent of chivalric violence in defense of women) and by claiming that revenge was not being sought, Achille believed he could more easily obtain the aim of his petition, which was full pardon for all the assaults and injuries and for the murder, the expunging of infamy, rehabilitation, and an assurance of no future prosecution (in direct derogation of the city statutes and despite his lack of pacification with his enemies). After taking information, the *Anziani* granted his requests. This was, of course, an executive decision: The court itself did not take cognizance of the fact that this was a vendetta, nor was the court concerned in the origins of the dispute, but only in the specific woundings and murder, as denounced. Had Achille not had good grounds for excusing his action as self-defense, in other words, had the fight been fair in the eyes of witnesses and participants, both sides probably would have been convicted and we would know of the case only as yet another armed brawl. In any event, it is clear how the action of the court cut across the unfolding of a vendetta, and how one side profited from the court's even-handed intervention to obtain convictions against its enemies. We do not, of course, have to believe Achille's version of the event, constructed as it is around the themes of innocence almost overpowered by cunning, of resistance to the superior force of an enemy, of compliance to the dying wishes of a wounded companion. What is important is to take account of the reasoning of the petition: that the woundings were not done in legitimate vendetta, but in reasonable self-defense. This was the motivation he attributes to himself and his men: They could see no other way to save themselves than by answering force with force. This was allegedly acknowledged by Scarpello in his dying words: Achille and his men had inflicted these wounds "out of necessary self-protection." And this was the concluding request of the petition: that the *Anziani* verify that they had acted in defense and under provocation. Revenge was obviously not an excuse that the *Anziani* would treat sympathetically.

Unlike many accused or convicted criminals, Achille had failed to reach a peace agreement or pacification (*pax*) with his enemies. Deeds or instruments of pacification, when combined with the trial record, can take us further in examining the relationship between vendetta and the law. In 1453 Roberto di Pandolfo of Argellata, along with Giovanni di Cristoforo and one other, made peace with Biagio di Andrea, his brothers and their cousin Giovanni di Giacomo, all of San Giovanni in Persiceto, for their killing three years previously of Pandolfo and Cristoforo (the fathers of Roberto and Giovanni). At the same time and conversely, Biagio, his brothers, and their cousin, made peace with Roberto, Giovanni, and another for Roberto's killing the previous year of Andrea.[34] Here, clearly, we have a vendetta: A father, his sons and nephew kill the fathers of Roberto and Giovanni; Roberto responds by killing the senior of the murderers, the father of Biagio and his brothers. Moreover, we have a vendetta that we might perhaps have expected to be tolerated. The heir of the victim retaliates against the first attacker in direct, primary revenge. But in fact the killings had not been left untouched by the judicial system. Roberto and Giovanni had been prosecuted in June 1452 for their fatal assault on Andrea and had both been banned with a penalty of decapitation and a fine of L.1,000.[35] They did not appear before the court to enter any defense nor when their bans were canceled in 1455 was any mention made of revenge as a reason (the motion to cancel was proposed to the sixteen "out of consideration of Alberto Albergati, commissioner of Cento," a formula that probably concealed a piece of patrician patronage).[36]

A second example confirms this picture. In July 1453, Antonio di Pietro de Fulchi, of San Giovanni in Persiceto, with his sons and his nephew, Alberto di Giovanni, made peace with Antonio di Giovanni de' Prandi, also of San Giovanni, his uncle Giacomo, and Giacomo's other nephew Bartolomeo, for the killing, ten years previously, of Bartolomeo di Antonio de' Fulchi by Giovanni Prandi. Conversely, the Prandi made peace with the Fulchi for the killing in 1451 of Giovanni Prandi by Biagio Fulchi (one of Antonio's sons). Here again we have a vendetta: A father killed the son of his co-villager; eight years later, a brother of the victim killed his brother's murderer. Again, an heir of the victim takes direct revenge. Again the Bolognese local official (as well as the local priest) was involved in the pacification. But this sign of official toleration is belied by the previous prosecution of Biagio Fulchi and of Alberto di Giovanni for the assault on Giovanni Prandi, in which Biagio gave him two blows to the head with a sword, from which he died.[37]

To such cases, further study could doubtless add more. Their significance is this: Historians who claim that vendetta was tolerated both legally and judicially, that late medieval Italy had not achieved a fully penal outlook on conflict but continued to accept a mixed economy of some public and some private justice, have failed to consider in detail the judicial evidence. The evidence shows conversely that statutory tolerance of vendetta (if such there was) was not realized in judicial practice and that judicial prosecution of revenge killings was halted only by political considerations. In other words, local nobles who sat on executive committees or served as governors in the *contado* might be prepared to find ways and means, after prosecution, of excusing or lightly punishing vendetta, but the foreign judges who staffed the civic judiciary were not. They prosecuted crimes regardless of the past relations of conflict between the parties involved.

Acts of pacification, studied individually along with other records, thus advance our enquiry; pacifications studied as a group can take it even further. In the first semester of 1332 nearly a hundred such acts were deposited in the central register office of the commune (the office of the *memoriale*, later the *ufficio del registro*).[38] These covered a broad range of offenses: mostly wounds with bloodshed, death resulting from wounding, arson, and varieties of theft but also rape, kidnapping, perjury, and shaming by pulling a man's hood from his head. Many of these pacifications were issued by the victim to a representative of the offender (a notary or a father on behalf of his son), as the latter was evidently absent from the city, having fled from justice and been convicted in absence. Nearly all of these deeds refer to specific moments of the judicial process: a few to cases in progress, the vast majority to bans (outlawries) issued in the past years. Where judicial process had not yet started, the victim promised not to make or consent to an accusation; where sentence was pending, he expressed a desire for the case to proceed no further; where sentence had been awarded and the absent offender banned, he willed that the conviction be canceled.[39] But the victim no longer had complete control over the trial. Gone were the days when most trials were both initiated and abandoned at the victim's behest.

Now the pacification had a role in the official, penal system of criminal justice: It was legally required before a convicted offender could have his ban canceled and could return to live in his place of residence. Pacifications therefore were aimed overwhelmingly at enabling that process to take place. Far from being part of a parallel, private system of conflict-settlement, they were an adjunct to judicial sentence and ban. They rehabilitated the offender while also attempting to ensure that the victim, satisfied with the public penalty imposed, would not seek revenge when the criminal returned to the community. In requiring formal reconciliation between assailant and victim, the penal system recognized that private rancor might persist after punishment and attempted to deal with this. The requirement for pacification before cancellation of sentence thus worked against private modes of conflict and acted as a support to the public process. This interpretation is supported by the fact that pacifications rarely (if ever) stipulated any amounts of compensation. Their function was not to compensate the victim, but to close off any extrajudicial action.[40]

Comparison of the group of 1332 pacifications with those in the early 1450s can take this analysis further, for it is evident that pacification was not an unchanging practice. The points of significant change between the mid–fourteenth and mid–fifteenth centuries lie in the number of pacifications and the range of crimes they covered, the number and gender of the parties involved, the notarial formulae used, the religious sentiments expressed, the venue of the act of peace itself, and the presence, as witnesses or guarantors, of churchmen, officials, and members of the urban aristocracy. First, the number of pacifications seems substantially reduced. The first six volumes of the new *Ufficio del registro* contain twelve for 1452, twenty-four for 1453, seventeen for 1454, well below the hundred from a half-year in 1332 (and disproportionately below the fall in population since 1348). This is important: Vallerani has argued persuasively that pacification was a structural element of thirteenth-century justice and that it became more frequent with the expansion and strengthening of the judicial system in the latter part of that century, because it was seen as one of a number of legitimate outcomes to trial, other than penalty.[41]

By the fifteenth century, however, pacification, though still a structural element, has changed in its social and judicial character. There was also a slight narrowing of the crimes for which *pax* was made, mainly now homicides and woundings.[42] Further, whereas in 1332 the number of individuals acting on their own was high, in the 1450s the number of group pacifications seems much higher. Thus, a man, his son, brother, and cousin made peace with another father and son for the latter's killing of their cousin, Agnes; one father and his three sons made peace with another father, his three sons, and one grandson for wounds inflicted in fights among only three of them;[43] over two dozen men from the village of Gagio made peace with two brothers from Pistoia for the killing, by four of their number, of a third brother.[44] Such examples could be multiplied (and see above, pp. 7–10).

The formulae used are also now much more inclusive: instead of the traditional (but by no means standard) *pro se et suis heredibus* (for him and his heirs),[45] we now find the broader "pro se suisque coniunctis benivolis et amicis" (for him, his kinsmen, well-wishers and friends),[46] or "nomine omnium et singulorum attinentium benivolorum amicorum et complicium" (in the name of all of his kinsmen, well-wishers, friends and associates),[47] and other such formulations. The pacification now stretched beyond the individual and his immediate family to embrace more distant relatives, and even friends, well-wishers, and adherents. And sometimes the presence (or absence) of kinsmen is specifically noted.[48] But as *pax* was spread through and beyond the family, it also tended to be restricted to males. In 1332, fully one-fifth of the pacifications were made by women, making peace for rapes and other injuries to themselves, or, as heiresses and mothers, making peace with the killers of their husbands or fathers, or with the wounders of their children. Such pacifications disappear altogether by mid-fifteenth century: The first six volumes of the *Ufficio del registro* contain only one made by a woman, when a widow and mother made, for her infant son, a pacification with her husband's killer.[49] Significantly, however, this was merely a confirmation of a *pax* already made by her father-in-law, and it was made with the consent of a paternal kinsman of her son and with the authority of a communally appointed lawyer. In other words, women's former independence to make such acts had been removed, and women now merely confirmed *paix accomplies*, and even then with a controlling male presence.[50] Conversely, what is apparent in the 1450s, but absent in 1332, is pacification for wife-killing.[51] In monopolizing the role of appeasers, had kinsmen become more sensitive to offenses against their womenfolk?

This masculinization was certainly accompanied by the more evident presence of the forces of church, aristocracy, and government. Religious sentiment is more frequently and extensively recorded. The principal parties are said to act not just "out of love of God," or "moved by piety," as in the fourteenth century, but, for example, "knowing that God our redeemer remitted and spared injuries and scandals [*obrobria*], and wishing to follow his commands and example."[52] Sometimes a whole minisermon is recorded: "in the name of our lord Jesus Christ, who, to pacify the human race with God the father took human form from the Virgin and suffered earthly death on the cross . . ." and so on for many lines.[53] These are more likely to be the arguments used to persuade the parties to reconciliation, not the spontaneous thoughts of the persons concerned.[54] Hence the significance of the conclusion of such acts in ecclesiastical space: in the bishop's palace,[55] and the cathedral doorway,[56] in the main civic church of San Petronio,[57] in rural parish churches or their gardens,[58] in convent chapels and monastery buildings.[59] Of course, pacifications did take place in churches in the fourteenth century, but relatively less frequently.[60] And present at such acts we find parish priests, friars, and canons.[61] Whereas pacifications in 1332 tended to be concluded in secular, nonofficial spaces (at the desks or houses of notaries, under porticoes, in the piazza, at or outside the house of the principal or of a third party), a greater number in the 1450s were concluded in the government palace (or other government spaces),[62] in the residences of rural *podestà*,[63] or in the houses of prominent members of the ruling oligarchy (the della Volta, Malvezzi, Sanuti, etc.) or at least in their presence.[64]

Lest it be thought that a comparison of a mere handful of volumes from the communal register office might be misleading—either because the total number of pacifications involved is under 200, or because it might be suspected that not all pacifications were duely deposited there—we can turn to another source of such deeds, the files of papers submitted to the court in connection with ongoing trials (so-called *carte di corredo*). The deeds to be found here relate almost solely to those crimes (wounds with bloodshed) for which prompt submission of pacification brought reduction of sentence, but the limited nature of this category is offset by the fact that such crimes were the most commonly prosecuted.[65] Surviving pacifications in these files confirm the numerical decline between the fourteenth and fifteenth centuries[66] and the gender shift.[67] A comparison between the pacifications from two years' files confirms other features of the picture. Those of 1372 were made predominantly by the individuals involved in violence, assailant and victim. When fathers or husbands are present, it is to act on behalf of sons, wives, daughters, and sons, not as principals to the contract. Only once are the brothers of the assailant and victim drawn in as principals.[68] Pacifications are made in ecclesiastical space (a hospital, a canonry, a cloister)[69] and with the presence of clergymen (priests, friars, chaplains, a monastic prior),[70] but only occasionally in aristocratic houses[71] or official spaces, and then only in siderooms and corridors.[72] By contrast, in 1462, we may note that pacifications more frequently draw in brothers, sons, nephews, and cousins of the principals involved.[73] Frequent is the formula extending the scope of the *pax* even further through the immediate kin, to the affines, the friends and well-wishers,[74] and especially to all male kin and descendants.[75] Even an accidental killing of a boy, run over by an ox-cart, was thought to require pacification by the boy's father and "all his male children, both born and yet to be born . . . and the descendents from his male children in the male line *ad infinitum*."[76] Also evident is the more frequent presence of aristocrats in pacifications concluded in their palaces or following their intercession.[77]

How can we explain these broad developments in the practice of peace between the fourteenth and fifteenth centuries? There would seem to be here an amalgam of social, religious, political, and legal/notarial changes. The greater religiosity may perhaps be attributed to the presence of reforming preachers and churchmen, who are commonly seen as having more real impact on behavior in the fifteenth century than earlier.[78] The greater involvement of the urban aristocracy perhaps reflects their greater power as patrons of clienteles or as masters of neighborhoods,[79] while that of government officials must express a more active desire to pacify social conflicts as a means of reducing levels of violent crime. And it is evidently concern about the effectiveness of pacification that explains the other changes: the more inclusive formula, the involvement of kin as principals, the exclusion of women,[80] the more elaborate promises, and sureties.

Pacification in the fifteenth century was seen as something too important to be left to individuals or women, as both could be corrupted or intimidated easily. More elaborate guarantees of effectiveness were required, both to avoid collusion before pacification and to prevent the taking of revenge by kinsmen afterward. Above all, fifteenth-century pacifications give the appearance of having been organized. In place of the cursory quittance of injury by lone individuals at a notary's desk with a chance gathering of witnesses, we now have officials and aristocratic patrons drawing in the broader kin so as to defuse the potential for revenge that remained. This means that the principal role now assigned to the kinsmen in pacifying the individual's offenses was not evidence of the kin's sense of ownership of all injuries done to or by its members, but of intermediaries' and officials' desire to ensure that the public penalty, however mitigated, was the end of the affair.

NOTES

I wish to thank the Leverhulme Trust for a research grant that enabled me to conduct the archival research on which this chapter is based.

1. See Andrea Zorzi, "Giustizia criminale e criminalità nell'Italia del tardo medioevo: studi e prospettive di ricerca," *Società e storia* 46 (1989): 923–65; idem, "Tradizioni storiografiche e studi recenti sulla giustizia nell'Italia del Rinascimento," *Cheiron* 8 (1991): 27–78; Trevor Dean and Kate Lowe, "Writing the History of Crime in the Renaissance," in *Crime, Society and the Law in Renaissance Italy*, ed. Trevor Dean and K.J.P. Lowe (Cambridge, 1994) and the bibliographies there.

2. Thomas Kuehn, "Arbitration and the Law in Renaissance Florence," *Renaissance and Reformation* 11 (1987): 289–317; idem, "Dispute Processing in the Renaissance: Some Florentine Examples," in idem, *Law, Family and Women: Toward a Legal Anthropology of Renaissance Italy* (Chicago and London, 1991), 75–82; William I. Miller, "Choosing the Avenger: Some Aspects of the Bloodfeud in Medieval Iceland and England," *Law and History Review* 1 (1983): 160–61; O. Raggio, "Etnografia e storia politica: la faida e il caso della Corsica," *Quaderni storici* 75 (1990): 943–44. M. Vallerani, "Pace e processo nel sistema giudiziaria del comune di Perugia," *Quaderni storici* 101 (1999): 316–18. In general, now see T. Dean, "Marriage and Mutilation: Vendetta in Late-Medieval Italy," *Past and Present* 157 (1997): 3–36.

3. For a recent survey: Giorgio Chittolini, "Stati padani, 'Stati del Rinascimento': problemi di ricerca," in *Persistenze feudali e autonomie comunitative in stati padani fra Cinque e Settecento*, ed. G. Tocci (Bologna, 1988).

4. Jacques Heers, *Le clan familial au Moyen Age* (Paris, 1974); Thomas Kuehn, "Honor and Conflict in a Fifteenth-Century Florentine Family," *Ricerche storiche* 10 (1980): 287–310; Furio Bianco, "*Mihi vindictam*: Aristocratic Clans and Rural Communities in a Feud in Friuli in the Late Fifteenth and Early Sixteenth Centuries," in *Crime, Society and the Law*.

5. Cherubino Ghirardacci, *Della historia di Bologna*, ed. Albano Sorbelli, in *Rerum italicarum scriptores*, 2d ed., 33/1 (Città di Castello, 1915–16); Cecilia M. Ady, *The Bentivoglio of Bologna: A Study in Despotism* (London, 1937).

6. On the earlier history of criminal justice in Bologna, see Sarah R. Blanshei, "Criminal Law and Politics in Medieval Bologna," *Criminal Justice History* 2 (1981): 1–30; idem, "Crime and Law Enforcement in Medieval Bologna," *Journal of Social History* 16 (1982–83): 121–38.

7. Blanshei, "Crime and Law Enforcement"; Trevor Dean, "Criminal Justice in Mid-Fifteenth-Century Bologna," in *Crime, Society and the Law*.

8. *Statuti di Bologna dell'anno 1288*, ed. Gina Fasoli and Pietro Sella (Vatican, 1937), 209–10.

9. Dean, "Criminal Justice," 17–21.

10. Archivio di Stato, Bologna, Comune, Statuti, vol. 16, fol. 39v. All further archival references are to the Archivio di Stato, Bologna, unless otherwise stated.

11. Gaspare Nadi, *Diario bolognese*, ed. C. Ricci and A. Bacchi della Lega (Bologna, 1886), 232.

12. For example, Ghirardacci, *Della historia di Bologna*, 176; Archivio di Stato, Bologna, Comune, Curia del podestà, Inquisitiones, 328, fol. 33.

13. O. Mazzoni-Toselli, *Racconti storici estratti dall'archivio criminale di Bologna*, 3 vols. (Bologna, 1866–70), 1:53–54; 2:223–24; Cf. John Larner, "Order and Disorder in Romagna 1450–1500," in *Violence and Civil Disorder in Italian Cities 1200–1500*, ed. Lauro Martines (Berkeley, 1972), 40; Miller, "Choosing the Avenger," 193.

14. For example, Inquisitiones, 238, reg. 7, fol. 107; 240, reg. 4, fol. 145 (boys at play); Carte di corredo, *busta* 165 (1392), petition of Antonio Todiscoli of Castel San Pietro (building site).

15. For example, Inquisitiones, 207, fol. 2; 249, reg. 4, fol. 66.

16. Inquisitiones, 112, reg. 5, fols. 165–69. Cf. for avenging of injuries inflicted by the judicial process, Larner, "Order and Disorder," 56–57; Bianco, *"Mihi vindictam,"* 264.

17. Inquisitiones, 327, fols. 89–90 (Feb. 1327).

18. Vallerani, "Pace e processo," 333.

19. Inquisitiones, 244, fols. 39–43, 42–46 (*sic*).

20. Inquisitiones, 253, reg. 1, fols. 23, 25-v; reg. 3, fols. 83, 113–15.

21. Inquisitiones, 373, fols. 230–1, 246–55.

22. Inquisitiones, 373, fols. 297–300, 364–65, 395–96.

23. Carte di corredo, *busta* 83 (1332), petition of the *massaro* and men of Borgo Panicale.

24. For discussion of tactics used by defense lawyers in gambling cases, see Massimo Vallerani, " 'Giochi di posizione' tra definizioni legali e pratiche sociali nelle fonti giudiziarie bolognesi del XIII secolo," in *Gioco e giustizia nell'Italia di comune*, ed. Gherardo Ortalli (Treviso and Rome, 1993), 17–19.

25. Inquisitiones, 253, reg. 3, fols. 36–45, 82; reg. 5, fols. 16ff, 27vff.

26. Inquisitiones, 253, reg. 4, fols. 15–20.

27. For example: Inquisitiones, 248, reg. 2, fol. 9-v; 249, reg. 1, fols. 47–48, 50v–1, 92v; 250, reg. 1, fols. 35v, 53v; 250, reg. 3, fol. 68; 253, reg. 3, fols. 27, 47; 254, fol. 75.

28. For example: Comune, Signori Pepoli, Suppliche, *busta* 2.

29. Natalie Z. Davis, *Fiction in the Archives: Pardon Tales and Their Tellers in Sixteenth-Century France* (Oxford, 1987), 43–44, 57.

30. Inquisitiones, 1441 (Feb.-Aug.), fols. 229–49v.

31. Cf. Max Gluckman, "The Peace in the Feud," *Past and Present* 8 (1955): 6–9; Steven D. White, "Feuding and Peacemaking in the Touraine around the Year 1100," *Traditio* 42 (1986): 258–59; Miller, "Choosing the Avenger," 163–64.

32. Comune, Signorie Viscontea, ecclesiastica e bentivolesca, Riformagioni e provigioni, *busta* 5 (1440–45), 27 Oct. 1441.

33. "Ordinans quod de morte sue nec de vulneribus sibi illatis non posset nec deberet vendita fieri, sed quod deberet fieri per eius fratrem et eius heredes pax de predictis, quam ex tunc ipse fecit illis qui dictam mortem et vulnera sibi intullerant": ibid. Cf. letters of remission which, following the petitioner's version of events,

limited culpability: M. Bourin and B. Chevalier, "Le comportement criminel dans les pays de la Loire moyenne, d'après les lettres di rémission (vers 1380–vers 1450)," *Annales di Bretagne* 88 (1981): 246–47; Davis, *Fiction in the Archives*, 17.

34. Ufficio del registro, vol. 2, fol. 462.

35. Inquisitiones, 358, reg. June-Nov. 1452, fols. 30–1.

36. Libri partitorum, vol. 2, fol. 7 (27 March 1455); Libri mandatorum, vol. 12, fols. 48v–9 (15 April 1455).

37. Inquisitiones, 357, eg. June-Nov. 1451 (21 Nov.). The following register, which should contain the continuation of this trial, is incomplete.

38. Archivio dell'ufficio dei memoriali, vol. 174.

39. Vallerani, "Pace e processo," 335, 337.

40. Charles Petit-Dutaillis, *Documents nouveaux sur les moeurs populaires et le droit de vengeance dans le Pays-Bas au quinzième siècle* (Paris, 1908), 75–83; Keith M. Brown, *Bloodfeud in Scotland 1573–1625: Violence, Justice and Politics in an Early-Modern Society* (Edinburgh, 1986), 52–56.

41. Vallerani, "Pace e processo," 341–42.

42. Ufficio del registro, vol. 1, fol. 71.

43. Ibid., vol. 1, fol. 188. Cf. the restriction of *lettres de remission* to involuntary homicide: D. Potter, " 'Rigueur de Justice': Crime, Murder and the Law in Picardy, Fifteenth to Sixteenth Centuries," *French History* 11 (1997): 276.

44. Ufficio del registro, vol. 2, fol. 107v.

45. Dean, "Criminal Justice," 37.

46. Ufficio del registro, vol. 3, fol. 235.

47. Ibid., vol. 4, fol. 109.

48. Ibid., vol. 1, fol. 403; vol. 3, fols. 98, 117v, 489; vol. 4, fol. 392.

49. Ibid., vol. 2, fol. 123.

50. Compare the exclusion of women's cases from the Florentine criminal court in the fifteenth century: S. K. Cohn, "Women in the Streets, Women in the Courts, in Early Renaissance Florence," in *Women in the Streets: Essays on Sex and Power in Renaissance Italy* (Baltimore and London, 1996).

51. Ibid., vol. 1, fols. 71, 412; vol. 3, fol. 117.

52. Ibid., vol. 2, fol. 123.

53. Ibid., vol. 1, fol. 43.

54. Cf. the arguments used by a Ferrarese official in persuading a victim to make peace with his attacker: "Dopoi lunga pratica se opero che dicto onfeso vene da mi. Et li feci assai exortatione, quando dipingendoli lo inferno, quando il paradiso, cum aricordarli che quando bene il suo inimico fosse morte lui non seria restorato del suo manchamento" (After a long negotiation, it was arranged for this victim to come to me. And I exhorted him strongly, painting a picture in turn of hell and paradise, reminding him that even if his enemy were dead he would not recover his loss): Filippo Cistarelli to Eleonora d'Aragona, 29 July 1491 (Archivio di Stato, Modena, Archivio segreto estense, Cancelleria, Carteggio di ufficiali camerali, *busta* 1).

55. Ufficio del registro, vol. 4, fol. 317v.

56. Ibid., vol. 1, fol. 403.

57. Ibid., vol. 2, fols. 123, 506; vol. 4, fols. 238, 311v; vol. 6, fol. 28.

58. Ibid., vol. 1, fol. 412; vol. 2, fol. 510v; vol. 3, fol. 107v; vol. 4, fols. 366v, 405v.

59. Ibid., vol. 1, fol. 257; vol. 3, fol. 495.

60. Memoriale, vol. 174, fols. 74, 123, 223v, 286, 430, 569v.

61. Ufficio del registro, vol. 1, fols. 482v, 510v; vol. 3, fols. 98v, 495; vol. 4, fols. 32, 317v, 364, 405.

62. Ibid., vol. 1, fol. 285v; vol. 2, fols. 22v, 283v; vol. 6, fol. 28.

63. Ibid., vol. 1, fol. 331; vol. 2, fols. 188, 462; vol. 3, fol. 242v; vol. 4, fols. 32, 230, 451; vol. 5, fol. 99; vol. 6, fol. 215v.

64. Ibid., vol. 1, fols. 104v, 257, 403, 482v; vol. 2, fols. 99, 283v, 506; vol. 3, fol. 324v; vol 4, fols. 60, 109v, 415; vol. 5, fol. 64; vol 6, fol. 28.

65. Dean, "Criminal Justice," 18.

66. Numbers generally oscillate between twenty to forty in the fourteenth century (e.g., 1332, 1342, 1372, 1382, 1392), and between five to twenty in the fifteenth century (e.g., 1402, 1403, 1412, 1442, 1452, 1462): Curia del podesta, Carte di corredo, *sub annis*.

67. Surviving pacifications by women: two in 1342, eighteen in 1352, four in 1392, one in 1402, one in 1412, none in 1462 (ibid., *sub annis*).

68. Carte di corredo, *busta* 129 (8 July 1372).

69. Ibid., 4, 6 June, 13 July, 5 Aug., 2 Sept., 12 Nov.

70. Ibid., 13 Feb., 21 May, 5 Aug., 27 Sept., 10 Nov., 2 Dec.

71. Ibid., 24 June, in the courtyard of the Galluzzi family.

72. Ibid., 27 Sept., 5 Nov., 17 Nov.

73. Carte di corredo, *busta* 294 (4 Feb., 4 March, 22 May, 12 Sept., 24 Dec. 1462).

74. Ibid., 4 Feb., 11 May, 22 May, 3 July, 12 Sept., 24 Dec.

75. Ibid., 4 March, 24 Dec.: "nomine omnium et singulorum filiorum et ascendentium et descendentium ex linea masculina."

76. Ibid., 12 July.

77. Ibid., 29 Jan., 4 Feb., 12 Sept.

78. Alessandra Rizzi, "Il gioco fra norma laica e proibizione religiosa: l'azione die predicatori fra Tre e Quattrocentro," in *Gioco e giustizia*, 165–66. However, see Vallerani, "Pace e processo," 316–17, 345, 353.

79. A. De Benedictis, "Quale 'corte' per quale 'signore'? A proposito di organizzazione e immagine del potere durante la preminenza di Giovanni II Bentivoglio," in *Bentivolorum magnificentia: principe e cultura a Bologna nel Rinascimento*, ed. B. Basile (Bologna, 1984), 17–23.

80. Cf. the "Strengthening of a Masculine, Patrilineal Ethos" in fifteenth-century Florentine funerary practices, Sharon T. Strocchia, *Death and Ritual in Renaissance Florence* (Baltimore, 1992), 125–26, 213–14.

Female Criminality and Subversion in Early Modern Ireland

Andrea Knox

Female criminality and subversion in the early modern period has been the focus of several recent studies.[1] The work of Laura Gowing and Sharon L. Jansen on female crime in early modern England has highlighted both treasonous words and the language of insult as areas of particular focus for early modern authorities.[2] This kind of scholarship is a departure from early studies of English crime, which often conflated areas such as theft and moral crimes (such as adultery) and was often governed by modern conceptions of "serious crime" such as burglary, robbery, rape, and murder.[3] Studies that focus on specifically female crimes have moved recently from these "serious" areas where women were more often the victims or accomplices to crimes that women perpetrated. Female crime in the early modern period came to be defined increasingly as verbal and disruptive. From litigation over sexual insults to the relatively small number of English women tried for treasonous words, oral political resistance became a focus for English authorities. The background of specific tensions of the period offers an explanation for the concentrated focus upon female disorder. The growing influence of the reformation and the accompanying ideas of familial control helped to shape the ways in which society came to be organized.[4] The growing power structures in early modern England sought to regulate and order the lives of the population at every level of society. English courts began to deal more commonly with the unruly words of women, from the scolds and gossips through to the seditious and treasonous words of women. Scholars who have argued for the use of litigation together with women's testimonies have shown women's use of legal agency.[5]

While these studies have broadened the focus of the history of female criminality in the early modern period, both American and European scholarship have tended to center on the experience of English and continental women. Irish female criminality and subversion has been omitted from the European context of female experience.[6] One of the reasons for this is the nature of sources relating to female criminality. The limited number of convictions of Irish women in contrast to men, and in contrast to English women, has meant that Irish female subversion has not been regarded as being of historic interest. Moreover, with English presence in Ireland expanding from the sixteenth century onward, official records represent a history based on external observations of Irish women.

This chapter will address aspects of female criminality and subversion throughout the early modern period. While historians of early modern Ireland have emphasized the lack of shared Irish identity before the seventeenth century, female networks appear throughout the sixteenth and seventeenth centuries. There is a considerable array of sources that reveal the widespread involvement of women in antisocial behavior that came to be defined as criminal and women's active political roles in the numerous periods of rebellion against the English.

By the sixteenth century, the English presence in Ireland was expanding, with English and Scottish Presbyterian lawgivers operating as magistrates and court recorders.[7] English attitudes toward Irish women contrasted starkly with those toward English women. English views of Irish women concentrated on racial and gender prejudices and specifically defined Irish women as rebellious and disorderly, with a particular talent for corrupting Irish men to rebellion.[8] Working against this was an internal environment within Ireland where women were not perceived as a threat to existing social order. At a time when English men criminalized and indeed demonized women, the Irish did not follow; nor, more important, did Irish women become victims of anglocentric views of female criminality and antisocial behavior.

This is not an empirical study of conviction rates, but rather an examination of the preoccupations and motivations of women and how these were expressed in female testimony. Women's testimonies reveal women's voices and how women were the knowing subjects of their own crimes. Furthermore, I will examine whether female testimony manipulated official responses to their crimes. In focusing upon Irish female experience, it is necessary to place Irish women in their European context while also highlighting the distinctiveness of the Irish female experience.[9]

Ireland had a distinct culture, and factors such as region, status, and clan membership cut across gender experience. Early modern notions of female aggression and criminal and antisocial behavior were explained by contemporaries through biological and cultural models. Biological explanations centered on women's inherent weakness: Women were imperfect creatures, more prone to temptation than men. Cultural explanations acknowledged women's active involvement in criminality and wider antisocial behavior. Across Europe male expressions focused upon the female sex as the disorderly sex.[10] However, these were not straightforward models and were often applied together.

Legal source material from this period derives from indictments against women that specify charges and also provide comments made by a magistrate or recorder as to the nature of the crime and, in the case of English magistrates, their views of Irish women. The Irish legal records that exist include a wide variety of legal deposition collections from Antrim and Armagh, both of which are in the north of Ireland.[11] I have used the quarter session books of the Templepatrick Presbyterian Church court covering the years of 1646 and 1647. Both of these collections cover indictments, depositions, and the testimonies of witnesses and the accused.[12] The corporation records for Carrickfergus and Belfast deal with local regulations but do not highlight female criminal activities. The Clonmel Assizes in Tipperary, in the south of Ireland, deal with female criminality from 1663 to 1685.[13] These records deal with female theft and female aggression. They also detail convictions of women who traded ale without a license, many of these women being serial offenders working on the economic margins and often suspected of selling ale and stolen goods in order to raise funds for the purpose of rebellion. This suspicion is stressed by English judges and magistrates in the Dublin Corporation records that cover the period 1573 to 1634.[14] Depositions and indictments focus upon women tavern keepers as conduits, receiving stolen goods and trading them from taverns. These records are overlaid with a moral view of the sexual activity of the "evil disposed whores and concubines" of the taverns of the city.[15] The link between women, crime, and rebellion is made in the few witchcraft depositions recorded in Armagh in 1672.[16] Attitudes toward women and priests as figures of subversion are recorded in the depositions of Kildare and Westmeath from 1641 to 1682.[17] Records that deal specifically with women rebels include the Calendar of State Papers relating to Ireland.[18] The Carew manuscripts also record the activities of specific women involved in rebellion against the English.[19]

The employment of court depositions and accusations alone in a study of female criminality would offer a one-sided view of female criminality and subversion. The employment of female testimonies, wherein women offered their own explanations and pleas of mitigation, allows us to move from a model of victimology to one of proactive female behavior.[20] Focusing upon female testimony, as well as official accounts, also offers the opportunity to uncover the ways in which women stretched the boundaries of social conventions within which they were confined, empowering themselves and acting in defense of what they perceived as their own interests.

During the sixteenth and seventeenth centuries, prosecutions of women in manor courts and quarter sessions for antisocial activities such as scolding, slander, cursing, swearing, and inciting men to drunkenness increased significantly in England. The focus of greatest popular concern, certainly until the mid–seventeenth century, was not the abusive husband, but the violent disorderly wife.[21] A disorderly wife meant a gender imbalance within the marriage and resulted in a woman who was not under the control of her husband. Testimony and popular literature of the period supports this idea, with the frequent intervention of neighbors, who would often comment upon the power witnessed in female behavior that was deemed excessive or inappropriate in a wife.[22] Female scolds formed the center of female aggression, albeit verbal. Female aggression in all its forms was of interest to the wider society. Dolan maintains that popular literature revealed contemporary concerns, with pamphlets and ballads about actual crimes being printed soon after the woman was sentenced and sometimes after the woman's apprehension, before judgment and sentencing took place.[23] The English exported these views to Ireland and voiced them within their responsibilities as ministers, magistrates, and recorders.

In the County of Antrim, the quarter session books of 1646 and 1647 show a concentration of crimes against the peace, moral crimes in which women participated to a high degree.[24] A thematic breakdown shows eight major areas of female criminality: women inciting men to drunkenness and women drinking on a Sunday while preaching was taking place, women scolds, women slanderers, women involved in witchcraft, women cursing and swearing, women profaning the Sabbath, women fornicators, and women adulterers. What is interesting is the testimonies and treatment of those indicted for these crimes.

First, it is worthwhile to make a comparative point about the treatment of witches, scolds, and slanderers. At this time in England and reformed Europe, witches would have found it very difficult to deny and escape a charge of witchcraft. But in Ireland in the only case of witchcraft noted at Templepatrick, the woman denied the case and does not appear to have been sentenced. She was simply questioned at the Presbytery.[25] Templepatrick and most of Antrim was still a largely rural area in the mid–seventeenth century. Dublin, which was much more urbanized, also had few cases of witchcraft. In a case that came to the attention of the civic authorities in 1630, John Cave died of dehydration after being bewitched by a woman leaving him in a state of strange melancholy that prevented him from drinking anything.[26] Cave had informed his friends of the reason for his debilitation, and they had informed the authorities after Cave's death. No woman was named, and the record of these events focuses on an explanation of Cave's death, which appears to be closer to the hearing of a coroner's court rather than a trial of female criminality.

Ireland was a country that remained largely untouched by the European witch craze, citing witches and wizards as characters in stories for entertainment. However, the incoming English and Scottish lawgivers arrived with their own preconceived views of witchcraft. These are clearly expressed in the records made by Henry Pyerce, the recorder at Westmeath,

in 1682.[27] Pyerce's concerns relating to witchcraft were twofold. He noted
that witches were rarely heard of, rarely detected, and rarely convicted.
When they were observed in action, the "ignorant priests" used exorcisms,
holy water, consecrated relics, and amulets that they hung around children's necks.[28] Pyerce does not confine himself to recording the actions of
Westmeath manor court, but he records his surprise at the persistence of
traditional customs of the area. This reveals two important features. The
Irish did not recall the legislation, courts, and brutal punishments of England and much of Europe. Further, the power of the English to prevail
upon Irish society does not appear to have overturned every indigenous
custom. Rather than recourse to direct confrontation, many English and
Scottish administrators introduced laws that gradually shaped the government of the country.

The apparent liberality of imported judges and courts reflects the ambivalence that these foreign authorities felt toward the Irish and their awareness of the problems that direct confrontation brought about. This
ambivalence is clearly seen in the treatment of authorities in the case of
Stephen Browne, a Carmelite friar who was accused of bewitching an unnamed girl in Dublin in 1631.[29] The record states that the girl pretended
to be possessed by the devil, on whom Stephen had used exorcisms. Both
Browne and the girl were jailed, and the girl was questioned further. The
authorities were unsure whom to believe. They wanted to control priests
but recorded that the girl "pretends" to be possessed.[30] The authorities did
not shake off their distrust of the girl's testimony, but punished the priest
by a fine, the pillory, and a prison sentence. This treatment was mild by
European standards. The fear authorities had of Catholic recusants was
balanced by their suspicion and distrust of the testimony of young women.
The articulations of authorities also reveal the slippage between their belief
in women as witches and the idea of a person being possessed.

The crimes of scolding and slander were becoming more of a focus
throughout the early modern period. Gradually, this behavior changed
from being defined and treated as antisocial to being criminalized. Historians have noted that the criminalization of women intensified during periods of conflict and unrest.[31] Lynda Boose has used the literature of the
period to show how gender concerns were reflected not just in the lives of
the elite but throughout all of English society.[32] The Tudor and Stuart
English distilled their concern over the unruly woman who exercized her
sexuality or her tongue. The crimes of being a scold or a whore were often
conflated into the accusation of being a "whore of the tongue."[33] Punishment was often severe and usually public, forming a considerable draw for
the local population. The ducking stool and the branks, a device that im-
mobilized the tongue, were used on women in England and Scotland but
not in Ireland. The reasons for this are again bound up with the nature of
Irish society and the widespread reluctance to demonize women. The Tem-

plepatrick records cite two cases of scolding and two of slander. In each case the punishment was to make a public apology and then to stand in a public place for a time.[34] Although one of the slanders had been an accusation of witchcraft against a local man's mother, the accuser received the kind of sentence befitting a breach of the peace. In another case between two local women who had scolded each other, they explained their behavior away as a minor dispute. In this way, women appear to have reduced their punishment.

The women who were convicted for drinking, inciting men to drink, and cursing and swearing were similarly punished by being sharply rebuked and made to promise to behave in a more Christian fashion. This type of punishment differs from that meted out in other European states at this time. There is, however, a similar concentration of regulations concerning personal conduct. Antrim, in the north, had manor courts controlled by English and Scottish Elders. Even the word Elder had been transported from Scotland.[35] Some ministers and recorders were salaried, while others relied upon local payment, which allowed the possibility of bribes from criminals attempting to avoid punishment or those who wished to avoid court altogether. This perhaps partially explains why many punishments were so mild and why many women were let off with a warning. In Ireland, women did have access to their own money and property and had limited rights of inheritance. Henry Pyerce, the recorder for Westmeath, commented upon inheritance law and the practice of dividing estates and property between male and female offspring, whether they were legitimate or not.[36] Poorer women who were charged with drinking or profaning on the Sabbath were usually bound over to keep the peace. Their testimonies offer confession of the misdemeanor, an excuse for the behavior, and words of contrition. A confession and an apology appear to have been the chosen method of negotiation rather than a confrontation.

The crime of fornication appears regularly in the Antrim quarter sessions. Fornication was defined as sex between unmarried people. Most of those charged with fornication were not fined but had to stand in a public place on the next Lord's day. The fornicators often appear as serial offenders and go through a series of public punishments, including being whipped at the next market day, and having to stand in a public place of repentance on the next Lord's day and offer a public confession of their faults. Given that the regulations were meant to control personal conduct, they do not appear to have shamed sufficiently the inhabitants of County Antrim.[37] The very serious crime of adultery, which brought with it great shame in English society, does not appear to have had the same impact in Ireland. In one Antrim case both parties had the opportunity to testify, and both claimed to have slept in the same bed, naked, for three nights out of necessity because they needed to monitor the health of a sick child.[38] The Presbytery found the case unclear and were reluctant to act upon it. The leniency of these judgments appears to rest upon the confession and contrition of the accused, or the ability to provide a plausible excuse.

Another reason for fornication appears to have been offered by women who maintained that they believed that they were married. This did have some plausibility, given that the Irish had several different forms of marriage that appear to have confused English and Scottish settlers.[39] While these moral and antisocial crimes occupy the best part of the Presbytery's dealings, the punishments, a sharp rebuke and standing in a public place on the Sabbath, do not seem to have deterred many women from these types of behavior. Both Irish women and men appear to have worked together in order to subvert outside authority. Outright confrontation seems to have been avoided on many occasions during a period of conquest and settlement. Commentators like Henry Pyerce, writing to the Bishop of Meath in 1682, expressed the view that the Irish "were in the past rude and barbarous, but by long converse and domination by our English, and by statutes and laws to abolish the worst and most rude of their usages, the people have become more polite, civil and accommodating."[40] This accommodation may have suited indigenous women and men who chose which English customs to adopt and adapt and which of their own customs to maintain.

In the area of crimes against property, there was often a crossover with crimes against the state. Irish women were involved as fences, selling the goods gained from robberies. Depositions from County Westmeath in the 1640s detail convictions of women for receiving and dealing in stolen goods.[41] The recorder cites the women who disposed of the stolen goods as active rebels, plotting against the English. This has a twofold significance. Women were accorded the status of rebels in their own right, and their criminality is doubly significant in that it spans crime against property and crime against the state. Concerns about the state, and about social order, are also clearly addressed in depositions from Armagh in 1641 that concern local risings against the English.[42] Armagh is a northern, inland county, and in these depositions both sides made accusations against each other. The Armagh locals accused the Protestant settlers of being in league with the devil, and the settlers accused the Pope and the Catholics of following Satan.

In Dublin, the town corporation was most concerned with "the evil disposed women who are at this present keeping of Taverns in this city where apprentices and others are enticed to whoredom and consummation of their masters goods, embezzling and stealing goods which are received by their concubines."[43] The English recorders note this activity as early as 1582 and record instances of women acting as receivers. Women were acting as conduits, using taverns to fence from, and the civic authorities turned their attention to this. The city of Dublin was concerned about the moral lives of its inhabitants and moved to regulate the suburbs. The rural areas of

Westmeath and Antrim were much slower to regulate. The Easter Assembly of the Dublin corporation acted to expel "bad livers" in 1573.[44] These bad livers were unmarried fornicators who were expelled from the city unless they married an honest man. This was very different from the rural experience of female and male fornicators who were given a warning.

Regulations in urban areas reveal a distillation of English fears over moral and social crimes and antisocial behavior. The fear of rebellion was always present. English views on this even extended as far as the clothing that Irish women wore. Irish women who wore the mantle were invoked as figures of disorder, hiding illegitimate pregnancies and hiding and feeding the bastard once it was born. (The mantle is a large oblong piece of handwoven fabric that could be used to wrap around the body as an external garment.) The mantle was also a garment that transgressed family, class, and political categories. All classes in Ireland wore the mantle, thus frustrating English ideas about social hierarchy through dress. However, this was not simply a view of racist misogyny that reinforced hostility toward cultural difference. Irish women across the social spectrum were also involved in rebellion against the English.

William Palmer has detailed the women who were at the heart of the rebellions and women who assumed diplomatic tasks normally considered more appropriate for men.[45] English observers openly acknowledged female participation in seditious and disorderly behavior of their own volition, not directed by men. This was not simply anti-Irish feeling or paranoia but the reflection of real activity against the English and, more significantly, female networks. Many women did play an active political role in early modern Ireland. Lady Agnes Campbell, sister of the Scottish Earl of Argyle, married Turlough Luineach O'Neill after the death of her first husband, James MacDonnell, Lord of the Isles of Scotland, who died in 1565. When Agnes entered Ireland, she was reputed to have brought with her a dowry of 1,200 Scottish mercenary troops.[46] Agnes was also reputed to have dominated her chieftain husband and to have made herself strong in Ireland.[47] Whatever her reputation, Agnes did network with other women, including those outside of Ireland. Agnes' daughter, Finola O'Neill, married Hugh O'Donnell in the mid–sixteenth century, and the two worked together to bring Scottish forces into Ireland to maintain Ulster's independence from Dublin, which was controlled by English administrators. In 1588, Inion Dubh, the wife of James McDonnell, was reported to the Lord Deputy of Ireland for publicly stating that she would hire the Spaniards to stir up wars against the English.[48] On a few occasions the Spanish and the French did join forces against the English in Ireland, although ultimately this did not undermine English authority.

Women did play a very real role in subversion, often at risk to their own lives and those of their families. The punishment of women rebels when captured was as severe as that meted out to men, with wives of Irish chieftains being executed.[49] Since this is a period that David Underdown depicts as a time of breakdown in social order, which emerged from a period of strained gender relations, the attitudes of the English toward Irish women can be seen in this context.[50] Irish women were not just scapegoated, but actually were seen to be motivators and at the heart of rebellion. Their own words support this, and under pain of torture and death none of them deny it. References to women in public records are limited, but where they do occur women are given full credit for taking independent action. Lady Janet Eustace, the wife of Sir Walter Delahide was cited by Cromwell's advisors as the instigator of the O'Connor rebellion.[51] This was corroborated by everyone who came into contact with Lady Eustace. Although the political influence of elite women may have been limited ultimately by deference to their husbands, nonetheless they expected to play a full part in rebellions, going as far as instigating them.

Finally, an examination of the meanings and motivations women expressed in their actions and testimonies offers a very different view than that given by official records. Merry Wiesner has noted that throughout Europe women charged with criminal acts often wrote their life histories, which were then sold as small pamphlets, the more sensational examples often becoming bestsellers.[52] These women were motivated by the hope of vindicating their behavior and by the need to support themselves financially while in prison. Within these pamphlets, they manipulated female stereotypes in order to appear less culpable. Irish women left records that told of their experiences.

Katharine Simms has focused upon the literature that Irish women and men left, which was part of the Irish bardic tradition.[53] This was a different literary tradition to those in Europe, with elements of storytelling, but many included the accounts of real women. There is another factor that sets some of these elite Gaelic women apart. Women from the Gaelic-speaking aristocracy had a superior standard of education in comparison to many of their European sisters. Many of the women connected to the Scottish court were not only literate, but were talented linguists also. For some elite women, speaking Irish and English was not enough, and they were proficient in Latin and often in French and Italian.[54] Women of the lower orders were often fluent in Irish and English, certainly by the onset of the seventeenth century. One of the reasons for the accommodation that Pyerce cites in respect to the Irish is their gradual use of the English language. For the Irish, this offered an opportunity to adopt a language that would allow them to understand the English while maintaining Irish for their own purposes.

Confession or denial? Women still had to make that choice in court. When they confessed and expressed contrition, there was a possibility that magistrates and judges might respond more sympathetically to this. The courts appear to have been less angered by social and sexual transgressions than by anything connected with rebellion. This was borne out in their sentencing policies. It was rebellion that added a different dimension to the criminality of Irish women and their Scottish allies. These women were not perceived simply as the enemy within, but as instigators of conflict. Women like Agnes Campbell were proud to be known as allies, or part of the struggles of the Irish against the English. Where denials emerge in court, they were sometimes upheld, even in witchcraft cases. Irish men do not appear to have demonized their women in the same way the English did, and women appear to have had more opportunity to defend their own reputations.

A certain level of belief in women's testimonies appears, at least in some cases of social transgressions. In cases of adultery and fornication, women's testimony often centered on the explanation that she had been deceived, promised marriage, or believed herself to be married. In April 1647, Jenet Leich was brought before the session of Templepatrick on a charge of fornication. She maintained in her testimony that she "had her name buiked for marriage and their bands gave to ye treasurer."[55] There was no further evidence to the contrary of a public or private undertaking to marry, and no further action was taken by the court. At the December assizes in 1646, Marion Begs confessed her fornication with a neighbor and offered both "mine confession and mine sickness" as reason for her previous nonattendance at the assizes for the hearing of her case.[56] The testimonies of three of the scolds heard in Antrim—Jean Cunningham, Agnes Schirila, and Agnes Dazell—reveal how they confessed to minimize their punishment. Schirila told the magistrates that she had threatened Cunningham with "a warning from God," and Dazell had called her "an hell sow, and she would cut her keil and stow her peits" (steal her fuel).[57] Confession minimized the punishment, and women's words appear to have been accepted without further questioning. This belief in women's testimony was not due to any inherent leniency on the part of magistrates but has more to do with the constructive testimonies of women. The English and Scottish magistrates in Ireland did not apply the same sentencing as they did in their own countries. Their decisions reflect the lack of accusations of the indigenous population against women and the broader perceptions about women in Ireland.

The testimonies of women form active strategies deployed against patriarchy. Sometimes in Ireland men worked with women against the English; sometimes they did not. Irish solidarity could not always be relied upon. Consequently, women had to rely upon their own resources. The English concern with unruly women was always present. Concern over Irish women had an added dimension. It was women's oppositional voices and actions that were most feared and suspected. The public statements men made, whether accusers or magistrates, were often about masculinity, power, and class. The public statements women made were often about reputation, honesty, and morality. In the court statements of those women accused of social transgressions, they made full and often ironical use of the common explanations of their behavior: their age, their dependents, their poverty, their grief, their melancholia, their need to defend themselves, the fact of being a woman and therefore predisposed to weakness, or lacking full knowledge of the situation. Not all women had internalized these views of themselves. Women deployed these strategies in order to mitigate on their own behalf and, therefore, actively circumvented male power.

NOTES

1. See Laura Gowing, *Domestic Dangers: Women, Words and Sex in Early Modern London* (Oxford, 1996); Sharon L. Jansen, *Dangerous Talk and Strange Behavior: Women and Popular Resistance to the Reforms of Henry VIII* (New York, 1996).

2. Ibid.

3. See Jim Sharpe, *Crime in Early Modern England 1550–1750* (London, 1984), 5, for a critique of early crime studies.

4. For family order, see Jim Sharpe, "Domestic Violence in Early Modern England," *Historical Journal* 24:1 (1981): 29–48.

5. Jansen, *Dangerous Talk*; Jim Sharpe, "Women, Witchcraft and the Legal Process," in *Women, Crime and the Courts in Early Modern England*, ed. Jenny Kermode and Garthine Walker (London, 1994), 106–24.

6. Few studies have addressed Irish female criminality, and they have tended to be biographical accounts of individual women. These include Anne Chambers' *Granuaile: The Life and Times of Grace O'Malley c. 1530–1603* (Dublin, 1979) and her *As Wicked a Woman: Eleanor Countess of Desmond c. 1545–1638* (Dublin, 1986).

7. Jon G. Crawford, *Anglicizing the Government in Ireland: The Irish Privy Council and the Expansion of Tudor Rule, 1556–1578* (Dublin, 1993); Liam Irwin, "The Irish Presidency Courts, 1569–1672," *The Irish Jurist* 12 (1977): 106–14.

8. The records relating to disorderly women include: Gilbert MSS, Dublin; MSS 817, 836, 883, Trinity College, Dublin; and the Calendar of State Papers relating to Ireland, 24 vols., Public Record Office, London, herein referred to as CSP Ireland.

9. A recent collection that has attempted to address the position of Irish women in the Middle Ages within a European context is Christine Meek and Katharine Simms, eds., *The Fragility of her Sex? Medieval Irish Women in their European Context* (Dublin, 1996).

10. This point has been made by Natalie Zemon Davis, *Society and Culture in Early Modern France* (Cambridge, 1987), 124.

11. These are held in the Public Record Office of Northern Ireland, herein referred to as PRONI.

12. In PRONI, MS 475. They are reproduced in W. T. Latimer, ed., "The Old Session Book of Templepatrick Presbyterian Church," *Royal Society of Antiquaries of Ireland Journal* 31 (1901): 162–75, 259–72.

13. Clonmel Assizes MSS 4809 and 4909, National Library of Ireland.

14. Dublin Corporation Records, Gilbert MS 42, fol. 169, Dublin City Library, herein referred to as DCL.

15. Gilbert MS 42, fol. 16, DCL.

16. Armagh Depositions 1672, MS 836, fols. 446–47, Trinity College, Dublin, herein referred to as TCD.

17. Westmeath Depositions 1641–1682, MSS 817, 836, 883/1, TCD.

18. CSP Ireland, 1509–1608.

19. Sir George Carew MSS, Lambeth Palace library, London.

20. Women's testimonies are drawn from both secular and religious courts.

21. Sharpe, "Domestic Violence," 44.

22. Ibid.; see also Lynda E. Boose, "Scolding Brides and Bridling Scolds: Taming the Woman's Unruly Member," *Shakespeare Quarterly* 42 (1991): 195.

23. Frances E. Dolan, *Dangerous Familiars: Representations of Domestic Crime in England, 1550–1700* (Ithaca, NY and London, 1994), 6.

24. Latimer, "Old Session Book," 162–75, 259–72.

25. Ibid., 269—the case of Janet Watson.

26. Gilbert MS 169, fol. 204, DCL—the case of John Cave.

27. MS 883/1, fols. 296–98, TCD—witchcraft depositions.

28. Ibid., 297, TCD—comments of Henry Pyerce on Catholic priests.

29. Gilbert MS 169, fol. 200, DCL—the case of Stephen Browne.

30. Ibid., MS 169, fols. 200–205.

31. This point is made by Jim Sharpe, "Defamation and Sexual Slander in Early Modern England: The Church Courts at York" (York: Borthwick Institute, 1980), 3.

32. Boose, "Scolding Brides and Bridling Scolds," 179–213.

33. Ibid., 195.

34. Latimer, "Old Session Book," 268–69.

35. In the Church of Scotland, "elder" usually meant a senior member who had official law responsibilities.

36. MS 883/1, fol. 296, TCD.

37. Latimer, "Old Session Book," 261.

38. Ibid., 261.

39. For varied marriage arrangements, see Liza M. Bitel, *Land of Women: Tales of Sex and Gender from Early Ireland* (Ithaca, NY, 1996), 39–65.

40. MS 83/1, fol. 336, TCD.

41. MS 817, fol. 8, TCD.

42. MS 836, fol. 49, TCD.

43. Gilbert MS 42, fol. 16, DCL.

44. Ibid., 17.

45. William Palmer, "Gender, Violence and Rebellion in Tudor and Early Stuart Ireland," *Sixteenth Century Journal* 23:4 (1992): 669–712.

46. See Katharine Simms, "Women in Gaelic Society during the Age of Transition," *Women in Early Modern Ireland*, ed. Margaret MacCurtain and Mary O'Dowd (Edinburgh, 1991), 35.

47. Cited in Palmer, "Gender, Violence and Rebellion," 701.

48. Ibid.

49. Ibid., 710.

50. David Underdown, "The Taming of the Scold: The Enforcement of Patri-

archal Authority in Early Modern England," *Order and Disorder in Early Modern England*, ed. A. Fletcher and J. Stevenson (Cambridge, 1985), 116–36.

51. Calendar of State Papers relating to Henry VIII, II, pt. iii, 228.

52. Merry E. Wiesner, *Women and Gender in Early Modern Europe* (Cambridge, 1993), 166.

53. Katharine Simms, "The Poet as Chieftain's Widow: Bardic Elegies," in *Sages, Saints and Storytellers*, ed. D. O'Corrain et al. (Maynooth, 1989), 400–411.

54. See Simms, "Women in Gaelic Society," 32–42.

55. Latimer, "Old Session Book," 261.

56. Templepatrick Assizes, 8 Dec. 1646, MS 475, PRONI.

57. Latimer, "Old Session Book," 268.

Foucault *Redux*?: The Roles of Humanism, Protestantism, and an Urban Elite in Creating the London Bridewell, 1500–1560

Lee Beier

George Taylor, a vagabond brought into this house the 22 of April 1560, for that as a varlot he feigned himself mad and had pulled down the (Lord) Mayor's proclamations, and did here break a door and lock, and being well whipped became very quiet and tame, and so was committed to the labour of the mill.[1]

Ellen Pope, a straggler and common harlot, brought into this house the 21 of May 1560, for that she was found in (*sic*) streets as a filthy harlot, and therefore committed to the labour of this house.[2]

The house in which Taylor and Pope were imprisoned and put to hard labor was Bridewell, a prison workhouse founded in London in 1553. Taylor and Pope typify the kind of people incarcerated in Bridewell in the Elizabethan period—the vagrant and the prostitute. Although often described as a "hospital," a title the institution bears to this day, Bridewell was nothing of the kind. It was not a medieval hospital, which provided refuge for the poor and sick who entered voluntarily; nor, obviously, was it a modern medical facility. Bridewell was a new kind of prison, whose regime of incarceration and hard labor constituted a revolution in penal practice. It attempted to reform criminals and to change their character as well as their behavior, whereas medieval prisons were for pretrial detention or short-term coercive purposes such as payment of debts.[3]

Bridewell was the prototype for bridewells established in English towns from the 1560s and for the "houses of correction" required by statutes in 1576, 1598, and 1610. The institutions proliferated in the seventeenth and eighteenth centuries and formed part of the English penal system up to the mid–nineteenth century.[4] The concept of correction and its institutional embodiments spread to Scotland, Ireland, and the New World. In 1632, the city of Edinburgh established a bridewell, hiring as its first master an English "stranger expert therein"; Dublin later instituted one, as did Canadian provinces.[5] The term *correction* passed into U.S. law, where states still have departments of that name responsible for prisons. The word *bridewell* was still being employed by Chicago's juvenile delinquents in the 1920s. London's Bridewell survived in various guises and locales up to 1855, when it was merged with the new Holloway prison.[6]

This chapter poses the question, why Bridewell? Some political and economic explanations are examined in the first section. The second part discusses Michel Foucault's work on madness, which was among the first to argue that the foundation of prison workhouses or bridewells in early-modern Europe was part of a larger movement of incarceration, followed by cultural, institutional, humanist, and Protestant factors and influences. Foucault's hypothesis has been criticized for reducing "all social relationships to issues of power."[7] But it has also received implicit support from historians who see imprisonment as predominantly secular in origin and political in objective, as part of a process that "substituted a repressive and public order-oriented view of the poor for the image of holy poverty."[8]

Judging by Bridewell's origins, what lay behind the new thinking and policies? The third and fourth sections of the chapter assess the impact of these variables: humanistic calls for the reform of charitable institutions and penal practices, the actions and attitudes of London leaders, and the role of Protestant feeling in the creation of Bridewell. Through this case study the chapter reexamines recent interpretations, which have argued that humanism and magistrates' policies were the key elements in shaping sixteenth-century social policies and which have played down the influence of Protestantism. In Bridewell's case, however, it seems that humanistic influences were surpassed in importance both by London's governing elites and by Protestant zeal for social reform. In the conclusion, the chapter assesses Foucault's contention that the new policy of incarceration had political and social significance beyond the history of punishment.[9]

POLITICAL AND ECONOMIC FACTORS

Early studies of Bridewell examined it in political terms. Emily Leonard and Beatrice and Sidney Webb considered it as the part of the Old Poor Law that first sought to put the unemployed to work.[10] They also discussed Bridewell in the context of the re-organization of London hospitals between 1547 and 1553, when five municipal hospitals, including Bridewell, were founded or refounded under the authority of the City of London. St. Bartholomew's was refounded in 1546 to care for the sick poor and Bethlehem for the mad. St. Thomas's in Southwark was reestablished in 1552 to treat the ill, especially syphilitics, and Christ's Hospital, a new foundation, was created for orphans. To Leonard, Bridewell "was the greatest innovation and the most characteristic institution of the new system," because it attacked the universally condemned nuisance of vagabondage.[11] Neither Leonard nor the Webbs gave much attention to the genesis of Bridewell, nor to its penal aspect. Writing from a perspective of early twentieth-century optimism about state intervention, they assumed it was a natural historical development.

There are four economic explanations of bridewells, none of which is wholly satisfactory. The first claimed that the profit motive lay behind imprisonment, the aim being to increase the productivity of labor by creating a disciplined work force.[12] This argument has come under fire.[13] Bridewell's early documentation shows that the suppression of vice was the first priority, while efficiency took second place. Rules of 1557 said that "this house is specially erected to the condemnation of idleness" and that employing mill workers there would be "commendable for the excluding of that hateful enemy idleness, and also profitable to the house."[14] On the continent, prison workhouses cost more than they produced. When production was marketed, there was difficulty selling the goods, which were of poor quality and priced too low to cover costs. Going into the red, towns resorted to taxation and lotteries; in England's shires bridewells had to be bailed out by special taxes.[15]

A second economic explanation is that bridewells were developed to police labor in transition from unfree to free status. Before the fourteenth century, labor relations were adjudicated in manorial courts, but with increased numbers of free laborers after the Black Death, new institutions took over. Bridewells smoothed the transition by controlling free labor, it was thought.[16] These arguments need to be qualified. The bridewells did not regulate free labor per se, but enforced the vagrancy laws, which governed a system of dependent labor. Bridewells policed servants and apprentices, who formed a large, volatile element in the early modern labor force[17]—among vagrants in Bridewell with occupations listed between 1597 and 1608, three-quarters were either servants or apprentices[18]—and bridewells continued to be used to regulate these groups into the early nineteenth century.[19]

A third economic explanation is geographical, because the first bridewells were established in early centers of capitalism, above all port and manufacturing towns.[20] But if capitalism were important, why were no bridewells created in Italian cities, which were the most urbanized and capitalistic in Europe? One reason is that galley service was used to punish criminals in Italian and other Mediterranean states.[21] A second is that Italian states pursued alternative strategies for "correcting" people, which rarely included incarceration. From the late fourteenth century, reforms were instituted in hospitals for the sick and poor, including greater lay control, centralization, isolation during epidemics, and education. But when "enclosure" policies were pursued, they were temporary measures in times of famine or epidemic.[22] Third, the religious culture of Catholic societies was slow to reject mendicancy, which was still considered a "natural right" in the late seventeenth century. To lock up someone for begging could be interpreted as criminalizing it, a Jesuit warned.[23]

A fourth economic explanation of bridewells connects them to medium- and short-term crises. One authority stated that imprisonment in the six-teenth century was a response to increased vagrancy and poverty. These conditions resulted from increased hardship among the poor, who lost ground because of population growth, the inflation of prices, and depres-sions in manufacturing.[24] In the countryside, new social and penal policies are linked to these conditions.[25] In towns, fear of "the dangerous classes" increased during economic downturns. The result was institutional inno-vation, including poor law reforms and bridewells. Such conjunctures of economic setbacks and state action occurred from the early sixteenth to the mid–nineteenth centuries.[26]

A good case can be made for the impact of short-term crises in the period when Bridewell was founded. Price inflation was marked, caused by poor harvests in 1549, 1550, and 1551 and by the debasement of the coinage.[27] There were other irritants as well. Woolen cloth exports suffered a sharp reversal between 1551 and 1553, and London clothworkers were probably thrown out of work.[28] Wars against France and Scotland reached stalemate in 1549, and the ensuing demobilizations must have flooded the labor mar-ket, considering that 48,000 men—the largest host England had ever sent to foreign parts—were mustered for the conflicts.[29] Historians are begin-ning to document how these upheavals affected London,[30] and it is certainly conceivable that they might have triggered a rethinking of social policies. But there are limits to how much these conditions influenced the founding of Bridewell. By themselves, they do not explain why one correctional strat-egy, that involving incarceration and hard labor, was adopted, while others, such as those based on Italian models, were not. At some point, normative considerations must have supervened over material ones.

CULTURAL FACTORS

Cultural explanations of early modern incarceration were stimulated by Michel Foucault's *Folie et déraison*, published in Paris in 1961. While fo-cused on the treatment of the insane, the book actually concerned the broader subject of imprisonment. Foucault, describing the locking-up of the mad in the eighteenth and early nineteenth centuries, argued that the seventeenth-century "grand renfermement" of the poor was an important phase in the process. He cited English bridewells among the earliest ex-amples of such institutions. The change came about, he contended, because of new attitudes toward the poor. Whereas in the Middle Ages they enjoyed a positive status, in the Renaissance and Reformation they were linked with sinfulness and disorder.[31]

Foucault's work on the treatment of the mad has provoked criticism.[32] One objection is that in searching for "the essence of an age, its *episteme*," he employed simplistic generalizations that were contradicted by empirical evidence.[33] His model, another scholar protested, was of "dominance and control," which reduced history to a story of "controllers" and "controlled." He ignored the plurality of interest groups in many societies, the distinction between socialization and social control, the likelihood that all the assumed controllers did not necessarily agree, the hiatus between their aims and achievements, since history often involves unrealized ambitions and unintended consequences, and that the regulation of social life, whether past or present, includes complex moral issues.[34]

There are several specific difficulties with Foucault's account of early modern incarceration. He exaggerated its importance, implying that locking up the poor became the norm. This was not the case in England, which provided "outdoor" relief in their homes to the vast majority up to the time of New Poor Law of 1834.[35] Foucault was also mistaken about who was incarcerated in bridewells. Most inmates were petty offenders like Taylor and Pope—vagrants, prostitutes, runaway servants and apprentices, thieves—and their numbers were small compared to the global population of poor. Moreover, most of them were adolescent males, whereas the poor were mostly females.[36] Foucault also ignored the principal actors—those who designed and administered bridewells and those who experienced them as prisoners.

Foucault's account is weak on the conditions leading to the creation of bridewells. Instead of attempting to pinpoint these circumstances, he provided a laundry list of early modern history, which is so long that it is almost worthless.[37] His chronology was faulty. He described imprisonment in a "classic age," which he did not define but which, based upon the sources he cited, centered on the seventeenth and eighteenth centuries. But most of the developments he described originated in earlier periods.[38] Bridewells were first created in the second half of the sixteenth century. He misunderstood the Middle Ages, which he thought viewed the pauper with a "positive mystique" that the Renaissance removed. But the late medieval period saw a demystification and criminalization of the able-bodied poor, which was reflected in change toward "a pronounced punitive and corrective side" in hospitals.[39] Foucault's suspect chronology was partly the result of poor geographical coverage. His chapter on the "grand renfermement" focused on France and the enclosure of Paris paupers in a new hospital in 1656.[40] This meant that he missed earlier developments elsewhere, including London's Bridewell and the Amsterdam *tuchthuis* (house of correction) founded in 1596, even though secondary accounts existed.[41] Foucault's analysis was also flawed by teleology. His unwillingness to examine the genesis and administration of institutions arose from his overriding interest in their presumed outcomes, above all the creation of a "political technology" for the production of behavior.[42] Foucault was not interested in studying the past for its own sake. He wanted to deploy historical knowledge to change the present. To him history was a "curative science," a way "not to discover the roots of our identity but to commit ourselves to its dissipation."[43]

Despite its faults, *Folie et déraison* broke new ground. In the early 1960s, social historians were focusing on three areas: long-run economic and demographic changes, social explanations of politics, especially revolutions, and the struggles of the oppressed against the dominant classes. All three approaches, though less so in the third case, employed quantification and collective biography.[44] Foucault stood outside these schools and methodologies. The history of social institutions was a subject that was out of fashion.[45] His methods were heterodox, eschewing prosopography and quantification. He ignored chronology and archival sources, two of the historian's most sacred methods.[46]

Yet Foucault's contribution was not negligible. First, he put the history of social institutions on the map by maintaining that they were expressions of important power relationships in society. By studying the marginalized and criminalized, he implied that one could discover the political norms and processes of a society. Second, Foucault raised questions about the nature of power as expressed in social institutions. For instance, he contended that institutional reforms of the Enlightenment resulted in more effective forms of repression, thus attacking the long-cherished liberal belief that the period was a progressive one in European history.[47] Third, Foucault stimulated research on many subjects—the poor and the insane, attitudes toward them, and their treatment in the law and institutions, as well as the history of crime, criminals, and judicial systems. Fourth, Foucault's work fostered cultural and literary approaches to these subjects, because he rejected the traditional "history-of-ideas" approach, which studied them with reference to their intellectual preconditions. He examined ideas in order to understand "the way we live social relations through the grid of meaning and language."[48]

Stimulated by Foucault's controversial work, social and cultural historians have reexamined the subject of early modern incarceration. To describe the process of reforming the poor, they have borrowed from anthropologists the concept of acculturation and from the sociologist Norbert Elias the notion of a "civilizing process." Tougher law codes and policing, including the incarceration of beggars, are considered part of a movement aimed at reforming morals, which advanced most rapidly in cities.[49] Pieter Spierenburg applied the Elias model to the foundation of bridewells in northwestern Europe. Imprisonment, he argued, was part of a campaign of moral reform, which locked up people to alter their behavior, to make them upright and industrious citizens, and to create an orderly society.[50]

These explanations of imprisonment stress the role of humanism. Whereas early Protestants were once assigned the leading ideological role because they allegedly favored a "work ethic," the new consensus favors humanism, which inspired magistrates from both sides of the confessional divide.[51] It is argued that Erasmus and Vives created "a new social type: a pious, self-controlled, industrious lay person, active in civic and ecclesiastical affairs, seeking always the common good." This person was the product of biblical and classical education, that resulted in moral improvement. For backsliders, punishment was appropriate, but it should reform their character rather than just chastising them. So pervasive was the humanist social paradigm that the early Protestants adopted it and, contrary to the old views, added little to it.[52] In fact, Luther and the English "commonwealthsmen" were backward-looking, it is asserted. Unlike the humanists, they did not seek to restructure society; they were urbanophobic and critical of the wealthy.[53]

Humanism is also cited as the critical ideological variable in recent work on Bridewell. A study of mid-Tudor social policies argued that, while Edwardian Protestantism stimulated expectations for social reform, it was not "a sufficient explanation for new trends in poor relief." Instead the main influences were "civic and Erasmian humanism."[54] A recent monograph on prison workhouses in northern Europe similarly downplays Protestantism in Bridewell's genesis, citing the institution's continuity in the reign of Mary I,[55] while a book on Elizabethan London, although crediting the influence of Edwardian reformers, thinks that Protestants derived their views on poverty from humanism.[56]

Who created Bridewell is also debated. The traditional view assigned responsibility to a coalition of the Protestant divine Nicholas Ridley, bishop of London, and city magistrates, who pressurized the crown to grant the disused royal palace.[57] But some later accounts tip the balance in the magistrates' direction. One states that the key figure in London's hospital reforms was Sir Martin Bowes, a goldsmith and political figure, with Ridley playing a supporting role.[58] A second questions Ridley's role and highlights the magistrates' initiative.[59] Only recently have some scholars revived the Protestant factor, crediting clerics with the spiritual impetus behind magisterial action and citing two Protestant lord mayors.[60] Was Protestantism important in the creation of Bridewell, or not? Was there one *"episteme,"* which was humanistic, or possibly more?

INSTITUTIONAL MODELS

Bridewell had no obvious institutional antecedents. F. R. Salter's statement that a house of correction was established in the mid-1520s in a dissolved nunnery near Zurich resulted from the misreading of a document, which stated that a pesthouse was created.[61] Another possible forerunner was the Aûmone-Générale of Lyon, founded in 1534 to reform charitable institutions, which put able-bodied beggars to hard labor on public works and also imprisoned vagrants. Here were two germs of Bridewell—forced labor and imprisonment—but there is no evidence the Aûmone forced to work and locked up the same persons, nor that the aim was character reform.[62] A stronger case for precursors are the "bettering-houses" established in the Netherlands and western Germany from the 1480s to the 1530s, which sought to reform delinquent youth through imprisonment. Some of the houses were located in monasteries, while others were established by secular authorities in Amsterdam (1496), Rotterdam (1507), and Gouda (1530). The concept of character reform anticipates a basic principle of Bridewell, but the similarity should not be pressed too hard. The bettering-houses did not lock up a wide range of offenders and force them to work, as Bridewell was to do. Nor is there much evidence that they had continuous existences.[63] Another possible prototype for Bridewell appears in the writings of the Polish humanist Modrzewski, who wrote in 1551 that able-bodied beggars should be forced to work. But he did not propose forced labor in special institutions, and his work was not published until five years after Bridewell was founded.[64]

Lacking institutional models, one must look elsewhere for the Bridewell idea, and humanism is the most commonly cited source. Humanists, with their interest in moral philosophy, led the movement to reform manners, initially focusing upon the nobility but eventually encompassing the poor and criminal classes. The campaign included elements that set the scene for Bridewell: A belief in the utility of punishment for both convicts and society, a willingness to alter the criminal law so that penalties were appropriate to offenses, commitment to a well-ordered state and a hatred of political disorder, whether sedition and riots or simply crime and disease in the streets, suspicion and dislike of beggars, whom they considered able-bodied frauds, and hospital reform to root out corruption but also to make the institutions capable of improving their inmates.[65] The notion of reform through incarceration dated from Plato, a darling of the humanists. In *The Laws*, he proposed prisons called "reform centers" for crimes of impiety. Inmates would receive visits from members of a special council, which would "admonish them and ensure their spiritual salvation."[66]

Humanists' proposals resembled the Platonist model of correction. A leading text on the poor was *De subventione pauperum* by the Spaniard Juan Luis Vives, published in Bruges in 1526. Vives is no longer credited with inventing poor law reforms, because numerous communities, including the city of Bruges to whom his pamphlet was directed, were implementing them before his tract was published.[67] Nevertheless, many scholars—despite failing to examine the coercive elements of his program—

still consider Vives to represent the humanist social agenda, and so his text is analyzed here for its relevance to Bridewell.[68] Vives' reforms were sweeping and granted extensive powers to secular authorities: the supervision of hospitals, although they could not change the founders' wishes; the surveying of pauper households to determine their needs, if necessary by consulting neighbors; the banishing of immigrant beggars; the creation of special workshops to employ those who could work, including the old, infirm, even the blind; the founding of new hospitals if the poor proved to be too numerous; and special schools for orphans and young girls.[69]

To enforce these policies, Vives proposed penal methods, including incarceration. The city's senators were empowered "to coerce and compel obedience, even to the point of imprisonment."[70] Even the dissolute must be fed, but they were to receive shorter rations and harder work. Then they might "repent of their prior life and not relapse as easily into the same vices."[71] He assumed the poor would resist: "captivated as they are by a certain sweetness of inertia and idleness, they think activity, labour, industry, and frugality more painful then death"; "these poor, buried in squalor, filth, shame, idleness, and crime, think they are being dragged into slavery if their condition is ameliorated." The authorities should ignore their resistance and treat them as fractious children. They should also disregard protests against extraordinary uses of the law, "for laws are of benefit even to the law-breakers themselves by correcting and checking them in their wrongdoing."[72]

There were five main themes in Vives' manifesto which found resonance in the London magisterial elite: sedition, disease, crime, citizenship, and piety. He cited the threat of revolution as justification for taking action. He observed that the "poor envy the rich, and are angered and resentful that the wealthy have so much money." Their children starve while the rich "insolently flaunt their wealth, which has been wrung from these destitute and others like them." He cited civil wars in which the mobs attacked the wealthy—ancient Greek and Roman rebellions, but also "riots in our own times and regions." In his conclusions, Vives maintained that by implementing reforms of the poor "the state will gain enormously" because the poor would not participate in sedition and revolutions.[73]

Vives' second rationale for disciplining beggars was to stop them spreading infectious diseases. "A mutual danger imperils the commonwealth from the contagion of disease," he stated. He described how parishioners were besieged as they entered church by "squadrons of the sick, the vomiting, the ulcerous, the diseased with ills whose very names cannot be mentioned." The open sores of mendicants were forced upon the eyes, mouths and noses of the citizens, "and almost on the hands and body as they pass through." "How shameless such begging!" Some mendicants mingled with the congregation after leaving someone dead of the plague. Isolating the sick poor would eliminate "a spectacle revolting to nature and even to the most humane and compassionate mind."[74]

The crimes of the poor were a third concern. Vives described how "those without means of subsistence are driven to robbery in the city and on the highways." Adolescent females "put modesty aside and, no longer holding to chastity, put it on sale for a bagatelle." Once prostitutes, they could "never be persuaded to abandon this detestable practice." Old women "take up regular pandering and then sorcery, which promotes procuring." To check such crimes, he proposed reestablishing the ancient Roman office of censor, who would inquire into the lives and morals of the poor and "study whether all of these persons lead a frugal and sober life." The censors would police people's employment and suppress prostitution, gambling, and drinking.[75]

By reforming the poor, Vives maintained, civic life would improve. Peace and concord would prevail; crime, class hostility, infectious disease, and the threat of revolution would be checked: "it will be safer, healthier, and pleasanter to attend churches and to dwell in the city." The poor would become useful citizens. This was not an active form of citizenship, of voting and participation in government. Rather, the emphasis was upon behaving oneself. As in Thomas More's *Utopia* (1516), Vives shifted policy from penal measures to character reform and prevention: "it is much more important for magistrates to work on ways of producing good citizens than on punishing or restraining evil-doers. How much less need there would be of punishment if these matters were attended to in the first place!" Vives' vision would be realized by teaching boys and girls "letters, religion, temperance, and self-support, all of which form the basis of an upright, honest, pious life." As a result, they would become "more virtuous, more law-abiding, and more useful to the nation." By improving their judgment and piety, they would "live among men as educated and disciplined persons, observing human laws"; they would even "hold back their hands from violence."[76]

The final component in reforming the poor was Christian piety, which Vives argued was imperiled by unregulated begging. Because beggars wandered about cadging a living, they "do not receive the sacraments and they hear no sermons." In fact, as far as anyone knew, they lived outside the church because "we do not know by what law they live, nor what their practices or beliefs [are]." The negligent bishop did not consider "such shorn sheep as belonging to his fold and pasture," so they went without instruction and without confessing sins and led "most disorderly lives." The fault was not with the poor but with officials "who do not provide adequate regulations for the good government of the people."[77] Training needy children in institutions would "form the basis of an upright, honest, pious life." Piety and honesty would result: "they will be . . . Christians." The overall result meant "restoring many thousands of men to themselves and winning them for Christ! That is heaven's profit, for innumerable souls will be liberated through religion."[78]

Such ideas resonated in Henry VIII's England and in the city of London. A decade before Vives' publication, *Utopia* had decried capital punishment for thieves and vagabonds, arguing that they should be reformed through forced labor. Hard labor as slaves was the standard utopian punishment, and genuine reform was required for remission. Prisoners had to show "they are more sorry for their sin than their punishment" before they were released. More's argument included notions of state power, profit, and deterrence. It was "more advantageous to the state" to enslave criminals than to execute them, because "their labor is more profitable than their death, and their example lasts longer to deter others from like crimes."[79]

In the 1530s, statements favoring coercion and compulsory labor became quite common. As remedies for idleness, the humanist Thomas Starkey proposed government intervention to require education or craft training for children beginning at age 7 and obligatory military service for young men. Anyone who would not work "as a drone bee does in a hive" should be banished. To police morals he adopted Vives' system of censors.[80] Forced labor appears in draft poor laws of the mid-1530s. For vagabonds they proposed ambitious schemes of compulsory labor on public works. Altering prisoners' behavior was central to the plans, which designated as "correctors of idleness" the officials in charge.[81] These sweeping proposals did not reach the statute book, but provision for compulsory labor increased in the poor laws. An act of 1531 unrealistically provided that vagrants put themselves to work after being punished and returned to their parishes; a 1536 statute ordered local authorities to employ them without specifying any mechanism, while that of 1547 created a system of enforced slavery for convicts. Even the relatively benign Act of 1549–50, which repealed that of 1547, retained the principle of forced labor.[82] Apparently, none of these laws was enforced, but they show the way thinking was developing.

There were clear points of convergence in Vives' and London magistrates' positions on the poor. In fact, city officials were articulating views similar to the humanist's *before* he published his tract. It would be surprising, of course, if there were no concordance in the humanist's and the magistrates' agendas. Vives was living in England when his tract was published, and in all probability he wrote it there, having spent four years in Oxford and London from 1523 to 1527. The idea for the pamphlet, he reported, originated with a member of the urban elite, a Flemish friend in Oxford who was mayor of Bruges when it was published. The focus of the tract was urban. It was addressed to the councilors and senate of Bruges, upon whom it called to take action.[83] But we might also expect differences between a humanist scholar and urban rulers. Their views certainly diverged on the question of voluntary poverty. Both Vives and the London elites criticized begging by the able-bodied, but the humanist writing in the mid-1520s presented his views obliquely, without proposing a wholesale ban.[84] In contrast, as is shown below, London officials virulently attacked monasteries and the mendicant orders.

Yet there were also many similarities between the humanist's views on beggars and those of London magistrates. Like Vives, they were concerned about public order and sedition. "Suspect persons" were targeted by the Court of Aldermen, whom they often defined as "vagabonds and idle persons." On 13 November 1514, for example, a search was ordered of "all hostels and all other suspicious places" for "idle or suspicious persons and vagabonds." Many such orders were issued in early Tudor London.[85] Sedition was linked to the poor in London, just as in Vives. In January 1518, the Privy Council ordered London to "make enquiry of all such persons as have held any seditious words." The city's response was a thorough survey of the poor lasting several weeks. In the manner of Vives' censors, but eight years before his pamphlet, aldermen appointed parish officials to list "all the impotent, poor sick or sore persons living only upon the alms of the people" and the names of "all mighty valiant and strong beggars, vagabonds and suspect persons abiding or resorting to within their said parish." Further orders followed the January ones; in July a vagrant actually confessed to writing a seditious bill and was sent to Newgate "for his bold presumptuous words."[86]

The London elites linked vagrants with infectious diseases. As early as Henry VI's reign, the connection was suggested in an order banishing vagrants and lepers. In 1498, syphilis was targeted in orders that "all vagabonds and other[s] infected with the great pox avoid the City."[87] From the 1530s, curbing disease was a prominent theme in the city's case for securing grants of hospitals. A petition of 1538 cited the threat of infection if the sick poor were not institutionalized. In words recalling Vives', it reported "miserable people lying in the street, offending every clear person passing by the way with their filthy and nasty savours." Also reminiscent of the humanist was the document's description of "the great multitude of people, some sick and some whole, which daily resort to the parish churches within your said city, to the great nuisance of the parishioners and inhabitants." The mendicant orders were alleged to have large churches that were closed to the public, while the parishes had smaller ones where the "severing of sick and infected persons from the whole" was impossible. As a result, "great infection and other inconveniences" were likely to occur.[88]

As for Vives, the crimes of the poor were a source of anxiety to city magistrates. Vagrancy had long been an offense and was the subject of numerous orders and searches. It was viewed as the opening of Pandora's box.[89] In 1520 and 1521, vagabonds were described as "privy bribers and pikers," that is to say, thieves.[90] City officials also connected vagabondage with robbery, prostitution, fraud, and slander. In 1522, they ordered searches in the city and suburbs in Middlesex for vagrants commiting highway robberies.[91] In 1534, five prostitutes described as "mighty vagabonds and miswomen [sic] of their bodies" were imprisoned and carted to Smithfield "to sit upon the cucking stool and to be washed over the ears." After Bridewell was established, a separate ward was created for prostitutes; up to the 1590s, sexual offenses accounted for roughly half of the cases heard by governors.[92] Mendicancy could even lead to defamation. When four beggars were ordered whipped behind a cart in 1548, one had the audacity to slander Sir Martin Bowes and Sir George Barne.[93]

Like the humanists, London envisaged making of the poor better Christians and citizens. The city's petition of 1552, requesting the grant of Bridewell palace, which was written in the name of the poor, said that by giving them work there they would have "occupations for the continuing of us and ours in godly exercise." They would escape the snares of sin: "we shall no more fall into that puddle of idleness which was the mother and leader of us into beggary and all mischief." The grant of the palace would fulfill "our hope of deliverance from that wretched and vile state" and heal "our old sore of idleness." They would become virtuous members of society: "from henceforth [we] shall walk in that fresh field of exercise which is the guider and begetter of all wealth, virtue, and honesty."[94]

Similar to Vives, Londoners focused upon youth as the crucial period for developing virtuous and productive citizens. By employing the young in Bridewell, "neither the child in his infancy shall want virtuous education and bringing up, neither when the same shall grow unto full age shall lack matter whereon the same may virtuously employ himself in good occupation or science profitable to the common weal." But Londoners gave greater attention than Vives to issues of profit and loss. Their suit to the Privy Council in 1552 said that Bridewell would ensure that "the forward, strong, and sturdy vagabond may be compelled to live profitably to the commonwealth."[95] Here the stress was upon canceling a debit, ensuring the vagrant was no longer a charge. So while employing the language of the humanist, stressing "virtue," "wholesome exercise," and education, magistrates had more practical aims as well. They were interested in restoring people to "wealth," in making them "profitable members," in benefitting the common weal. Their attention to profit and loss provides some limited evidence that values one associates with a later age of "political economy" showed up in the mid–sixteenth century.[96] All told, although both humanists and magistrates cited matters of the faith in their critiques of vagrancy, the latter group gave greater emphasis to secular values of power and profit.

HUMANIST AND PROTESTANT INFLUENCES

Humanists were not alone in calling for new regimes of hard labor. Protestant clerics, too, favored punishment and compulsory work for able-bodied vagrants, although none went as far as espousing incarceration. For their part, London's Protestant magistrates developed thorough-going critiques of voluntary poverty. Both lay and clerical Protestants, moreover, were inspired by their faith, as well as by secular concerns, to take action and, in doing so, were far more effective than the humanists. A common Protestant view quoted St. Paul—"he that does not labour, let him not eat"—but some reformers went further.[97] In a sermon before the king and Privy Council in 1550, Thomas Lever denounced the idle vagabond, whom he said should receive "due correction to punish his fault."[98] In his poem "Of Beggars" (1550), Robert Crowley proposed forced labor and corporal punishment for the able-bodied: "such as do counterfeit, having their strength, ought to be constrained to work what they can, and live on their labours, as beseemeth a Christian." If they refused, they should be refused food and "perhaps sometime with scourges be beat."[99] Like Crowley, the Strasbourg reformer Martin Bucer addressed the issue of forced labor in a tract published in English after his death in 1551. As Lever had, he called upon "good magistrates" to ensure that no one begged, but added that "those able to labour, should be forced to labour."[100]

There were other similarities between humanist and Protestant positions on social questions. Like More and Vives, Protestants were critical of the legal system when it hanged the needy or imprisoned them in old-style jails.[101] Both groups decried popular rebellions[102] attacked monastics and mendicants for their wealth and immorality,[103] called upon the secular authorities to deal with poverty and vagrancy,[104] nourished high hopes for the results,[105] and were disappointed by the crown's failure to use monastic lands for social and educational purposes.[106] But the reformers' views were not carbon copies of the humanists' views. From the 1530s through the early 1550s, Protestants analyzed economic changes, which the humanists misunderstood or ignored. As moral philosophers, the humanists concentrated on the evils of idleness and institutional remedies through education and "correction."[107] In contrast, Protestant laymen and clerics discussed the economic origins of hardship, which they traced to the wool trade, conversion of land from arable to pasture, debasement of the coinage, and rent inflation. Whether factually correct or not, forward or backward looking, these writers should not be dismissed as nostalgic and moralistic dreamers. That they did not take a cool, secular stance on these issues, as did Sir Thomas Smith, highlights Smith's eccentricity in an age when Christian ethics were widely assumed to be the basis of social norms.[108]

Protestants also differed from the humanists in actively and effectively pursuing institutional changes. By comparison, the humanists had little to show for their efforts in institutional terms. Vives and More got on the wrong side of Henry VIII's first divorce; Thomas Starkey whinged about the sale of monastic lands but was politically ineffective; Richard Morison was a clever propagandist but was mainly interested in advancing his own fortunes.[109] In contrast, Protestant clerics pressurized the city and the crown to reform London's hospitals, which led eventually to the founding of Bridewell.

The reformers' effectiveness in pushing institutional initiatives included several elements. The first was their willingness, which many Catholic humanists did not share, to countenance the destruction of religious orders and their properties. Criticisms of monastics, friars, and their wealth were centuries old, but from the late 1520s there was a chorus of reformist opinion calling for their dissolution. Beginning with Simon Fish's vituperative assault of 1529, attacks mounted on the monks' morals, doctrines, and their very existence. By 1542, the offensive included all church wealth from chantries to the bishops.[110] Second, reformers were prepared to pressurize the city to take action on the poor and the dissolutions. From 1542 to 1550, reformist publications shamed and hounded Londoners to do something about the poor and former church properties. Brinklow, in 1542, accused London of making "no honest provision for the poor." Latimer preached at St. Paul's in 1549 that "London was never so ill as it is now," because "in London their brother shall die in the streets for cold, he shall lie sick at the door, and perish there for hunger." Lever described in sermons at St. Paul's and before the king in 1550 how the poor begged in the streets while the rich despoiled chantries, schools, and universities.[111] Third, the evangelicals had the means and the opportunity to propagate their views. Under Protector Somerset they enjoyed freedom of the press and pulpit, and they used that liberty to make themselves heard. Fourth, the reformers were zealots whose passion for prosletyzing the faith, condemning sin, and promoting good causes made them effective. They were probably annoying—Latimer publicly harangued against "proud men of London, malicious men of London, merciless men of London," and told them, "Repent, O London! repent, repent"—but given the progress of the land sales, they had a point.[112] Fifth, Latimer and his supporters found sympathetic support among the London elites.

Both humanist and Protestant influences played parts in the foundation of Bridewell. In providing intellectual justifications for correction, the humanists were important, but the evangelicals ultimately played a greater role through their zeal and activism. The critical group, however, were London elites who created Bridewell. There are two important pieces of evidence about this group. First, it seems they shared the evangelical bent of the Protestant clerics. Second, they were the main agents in devising a regime of hard labor and imprisonment. If we take as the key actors the twelve men who signed the supplication of 1552 requesting the grant of Bridewell, there is little sign that humanistic ideas directly influenced them but considerable evidence that Protestant ones did. Two of the signatories, Thomas Berthelet and Richard Grafton, were London printers and directly involved in the world of ideas. Berthelet was the royal printer and published humanistic works, while Grafton printed the "Great Bible."[113] But although both men were well placed to know about humanistic ideas on poor relief, we have no evidence that they or the other ten actually did.

There is evidence, however, that Protestant clerics and laymen made their mark upon Bridewell. The standard account by the Elizabethan John Howes assigned the greater influence to London preachers and Bishop Ridley, who in a sermon before Edward VI entreated the king "to have a care for the the relief of the poor." Edward reportedly asked letters to be written to the lord mayor calling for action. There is some independent corroboration of this account in a sermon by Lever in 1550 in which he expressed confidence that a "good bishop" was about to act.[114] Another version, which is better supported by evidence, is that the lord mayor in 1551–52, Sir Richard Dobbes and the authors of the supplication of 1552 were instrumental. This version also receives support from Ridley's own accounts of events, which gave responsibility to Londoners and specifically to Sir George Barne.[115]

Ridley's well-known initiative was a letter of 1552 to William Cecil, a secretary and important figure in Northumberland's Privy Council, in which the bishop begged in reformist, Christo-centric language for the grant of Bridewell "to lodge Christ in" those who "hath lain too long abroad . . . without lodging[,] in the streets of London, both hungry, naked and cold."[116] But clerics were not the only ones to use evangelical vocabulary. A two-part petition of 1538 from the lord mayor, aldermen, and Common Council to Henry VIII requesting the grant of three hospitals and four London monasteries contained a full-blown critique of voluntary poverty, monasteries, and the mendicant orders. In the name of the poor—"for the relief of Christ's very images, created to his own similitude"—it attacked canons, priests, and monks for "carnally living as they of late have done . . . for their own singular profit, lucre and commodity only."[117] Its attacks upon the friars were vitriolic and antipapal, asserting they were "founded by the Bishop of *Rome*, his usurped authority and not of God's word, under color of simplicity and wilful poverty," and under such pretense had "procured themselves houses, churches, and other places within this your said city." They praised Henry VIII as "the elect and chosen vessel of God" and for destroying the friars "to the great exaltation of Christ's doctrine and the abolition of Anti-Christ, their first founder and beginner."[118] It would be hard to find a closer resonance of Fish's attacks of 1529.

Similar evangelical, Christo-centric rhetoric appeared in the city's supplication of 1552 for the grant of Bridewell palace. It beseeched the king to "hear us speaking in Christ's name, and for Christ's sake have compassion on us." Echoing St. Paul's vision of Christian society, it described the poor "as the poor members of our Saviour Jesu Christ." It cited Christ's sacrifice as the key event in the faith, requesting Bridewell palace "in our said master's name, Jesu Christ, that we, for his sake, and for the service that he hath done to your grace, and all the faithful commons of your realm, in spending his most dear and precious blood for you and us."[119]

The supplication was not, it seems, mere rhetoric. The preambles to the wills of its signatories and their biographies show that they were in the Protestant camp almost to a man and that many, by the standards of the mid-sixteenth century, were radicals. The twelve included leading figures in London government, the professions, and publishing: John Ayliffe, Barne, Berthelet, John Blundell, Bowes, William Chester, Grafton, John Gresham, Rowland Hill, Andrew Judde, Thomas Lodge, and John Marshe.[120] Of the twelve, wills survive for nine—all but Berthelet, Chester, and Grafton. Of course, this evidence is not absolutely contemporary with Bridewell's founding in 1552–53, and the much later wills of Bowes (1565) and Lodge (1583) should probably be ignored. Nevertheless, there are good reasons to take seriously the probate evidence. First, most of the wills were not made in periods remote in time from Bridewell's foundation: seven of the nine were drawn up between 1554 and 1560. Second, we have other evidence of the evangelical feelings of the testators, including the supplication of 1552, to which they put their names.[121] Third, we know from other sources that some signatories whose wills were not found were sympathetic to the Protestant cause. Chester was praised by Foxe for his humanity toward condemned heretics when he was sheriff in 1554–55; Thomas Becon preached the sermon for Chester's wife's obsequies in 1560. Grafton we have already met as the printer of the first official Protestant Bible.[122]

Preambles to wills could be written by clergy and scriveners, but it is unlikely they would diverge greatly from the wishes of the testator and his family. If reference to the Virgin Mary and the saints as intercessors typified Catholic beliefs, only one will of the nine evinced any loyalty to the old faith.[123] Judde, whose will was probated in September 1558, commended his soul to God the father, Christ, the Holy Ghost, the Virgin Mary, and "all the holy and blessed company of heaven." Despite this mixed bag of old and new doctrines of intercession, Judde's preamble, like most of the others, was Christo-centric. It specified that salvation was through Christ's sacrifice—"verily trusting and believing that by and through the merits and passion of my saviour and redeemer, Jesus Christ, and true belief in him to have foregiveness and remission of my sins and to be partaken of his glorious resurrection"—which by mid–sixteenth century standards put Judde on the radical side of the faith. In fact, six of the seven dating from the years 1554–60 stressed the intercession of Christ. Gresham's preamble in 1554 waxed eloquent, commending his soul to God "and to my saviour and redeemer Jesus Christ his only begotten son, by and through the merits of whose bitter passion I trust to have remission of my sins."[124] The only testator not to mention Christ's mediation was Hill, cited as the first Protestant lord mayor and a severe moral disciplinarian. On his deathbed in

1560, he occupied a moderate position vis-à-vis his fellow Bridewell foun-ders.[125] Overall, based upon their preambles and the evangelical language of their official documents, there is good reason to think that the London elites who founded Bridewell shared the zeal of the Protestant clerics.

It was this elite group that played the leading role in making Bridewell a prison. At the outset, they and Ridley apparently envisioned an omnibus-type institution in which the penal element was limited. The city's suit to the Privy Council for the palace said it would cater for the unemployed as well as convicts. It promised to employ people who fell on hard times because they were out of service, sick, the cast-offs of war, "or other ad-verse fortune." "[B]y making some general provision of work," it would employ the "*willing* poor." Children who were "unapt to learning" and could find no service would "there be exercised and occupied." The sick who were cured—presumably in St. Bartholomew's and St. Thomas's hos-pitals—would be put to work in Bridewell so they would not wander and beg. Persons acquitted at quarter sessions who needed work would also be accepted.[126] Ridley described a similarly varied group of inmates in his farewell letter in 1555. He referred to no penal elements at all and described Bridewell as a "house of occupations" for those needing work.[127]

But Bridewell's founders did not create a voluntary workhouse, and there seems little doubt that they were responsible for making it a prison. In their suit they clearly intended to use coercion on the vagabond, who, it was stated, "may be compelled to live profitably to the commonwealth" by being "brought" to Bridewell. The terms "compel" and "bring" strongly suggest a trip there would not be voluntary, and the document said nothing about the freedom to leave.[128] The involuntary nature of stays in Bridewell was spelled out in later documentation. The documents of June 1553 grant-ing Bridewell to London gave city officials the authority to search for and apprehend vagabonds in London and Middlesex, to commit them to the institution, and to punish them.[129] As regards sentences, Bridewell's ordi-nances of 1557 specified indefinite ones. The first paragraph called it a "house of continuance," which suggests a place for long-term stays rather than adjournments. This interpretation is backed up by the detailed pro-visions for sentencing. The "idle strumpet and vagabond," the document stated, were to "remain in Bridewell to labour so long as they were whole," that is, able-bodied. If they were ill, they would be sent elsewhere for treat-ment, but they were to be returned to Bridewell when they recovered "and not set at liberty into the highways, as it hath been accustomed, by means whereof was made of a sick beggar an whole thief."[130] In sum, commitment to Bridewell would be involuntary, and sentences would be open-ended.

CONCLUSIONS

Bridewell's beginnings suggest that there was something resembling a single "*episteme*" favoring compulsory work for the able-bodied poor and that few, if any, moral dilemmas existed over the question. The position was not, however, a uniquely humanist one, because it was shared by Protestants. There were varying degrees of interest in imprisonment. Humanists raised the possibility, while Protestant clerics did not. It was members of London's Protestant elites who actually took action to create Bridewell, because more than the intellectuals, they were concerned about institutional reform. Their commitment to the reformed faith boosted their determination and zeal, but their preoccupation with nuts-and-bolts matters of law and order predated the writings of Vives and the break with Rome.

The evidence supports Foucault's contention that there were "linkages and homologies which connect penal power with other areas of governance and discipline."[131] The wider significance of Bridewell is evident in the justifications for its foundation and in the institutional changes that accompanied it. Much of the humanistic rationale for hospital reform was about matters of public order, health, crime, and citizenship. But contrary to Foucault, their reasoning was not always about political power. An economic argument was employed in discussions to make the the poor productive. Nor was thinking about crime thoroughly secular. The humanists' and Protestants' belief in the value of compulsory labor developed from theological and ethical critiques of voluntary poverty. Both took the line that forced labor would make better Christians of the poor, although humanists were less keen than Protestants to take the critique to its logical conclusion of dissolving monasteries and hospitals.

The widespread acceptance of the new penal theory supports the arguments of historians and sociologists who see a consensual campaign to civilize morals.[132] Even though it might have strengthened his case for "linkages and homologies," Foucault did not document this consensus, especially the role of civic leaders, whose views on public order often anticipated and generally concorded with those of the humanists and clerics. Bridewell was just one item on more ambitious political and cultural agendas, which further supports Foucault's position. Most immediately, it was part of London's thorough-going hospital reforms, which were made along the lines that Vives envisaged for Bruges. The city presented the scheme as a rationalization of facilities for all types of poor, and it was an ambitious reorganization. Besides former church lands, it was supported by collections in the parishes and livery companies.[133]

Foucault was also correct to argue that the creation of bridewells had legal and judicial significance beyond hospital reforms. For nearly three centuries, bridewells policed the large dependent labor force of servants and apprentices. The young worker who stole, disobeyed, or ran away was frequently among the inmates of the bridewell. Further, the institution embodied the kinds of law reform called for by More and Vives, whereby officials prosecuted petty criminals before they became felons and used remedial tactics rather than just corporal punishment. Bridewell represented, too, an extension of legal authority and policing over a host of minor offenses, above all prostitution and the protean crime of vagrancy. The assertion of city suzerainty over moral lapses bothered officials of the Marian church; Bridewell's extensive powers of arrest violated the Magna Carta, Sir Francis Bacon asserted.[134] But this enlargement of authority was consistent with the beliefs of the leading players. The censors proposed by Vives and Starkey would have exercised wide jurisdiction over people's moral and social behavior and would undoubtedly have been instrusive. Judging by the city's official records in the half-century before Bridewell was founded, this kind of policing was what its elites wanted.

It is possible, nevertheless, to exaggerate the pervasiveness of bridewells. Conditions favoring their foundation might be present, but they still might not be established. Many Catholic authorities were critical of able-bodied beggars but stopped short of wholesale bans and eschewed policies of incarceration and hard labor. There is undeniably a danger of overstating the bridewells' impact on the poor and the criminal. The vast majority of paupers were never imprisoned; hard time in a bridewell was for petty offenders rather than the simply destitute. Outside of London, most bridewells were small, with at most a couple dozen inmates. Although theoretically indefinite, sentences were usually short, with a few days the norm and at most a month in Elizabethan London. The main obstacle to greater numbers and longer stays were the rising numbers of offenders, which grew rapidly as London attracted huge numbers of immigrants. From the 1570s, more and more inmates were simply "punished and delivered" to their home parishes; by the late 1590s, this was the fate of the great majority.[135]

Merely because a movement or institution fails to meet all its objectives does not mean it lacks historical significance and interest. Even if it did not work according to plan, Bridewell represented new thinking on crime and punishment and established an institutional pattern that lasted until the birth of the modern penitentiary. Most importantly, Bridewell can be understood historically, and its story sheds light on the period when it was founded. Foucault missed an opportunity to discover the historical origins of early modern imprisonment, which would probably have strengthened his case for its wider significance. Instead of examining "the social context or moral foundations," he focused on "technologies of penal power" and the presumed outcomes of new forms of "penal technology,"[136] which were only part of the story and, from the historian's perspective, not the most important.

NOTES

1. Bridewell Hospital Court Books, volume for 1559–62, fol. 75b (microfilm copies in Guildhall Library, London; Bethlem Royal Hospital and the Maudsley Hospital). I am grateful to the clerk and the governors of Bridewell Royal Hospital for permission to consult the documents and to quote from them. Spelling and dates

have been modernized. In this chapter "Bridewell" refers to the London foundation of 1553; "bridewell" and "house of correction" refer generically to the institution.

2. Bridewell Hospital Court Book, 1559–62, fol. 81a.

3. John H. Langbein, "The Historical Origins of the Sanction of Imprisonment for Serious Crime," *Journal of Legal Studies* 5:1 (January 1976): 38.

4. Joanna Innes, "Prisons for the Poor: English Bridewells, 1555–1800," in *Labour, Law, and Crime: An Historical Perspective*, ed. Francis Snyder and Douglas Hay (London, 1987), 77–78.

5. W. J. Ashley, *An Introduction to English Economic History and Theory*, 4th ed. (London, 1906), Part II, 376; Rainer Baehre, "From Bridewell to Federal Penitentiary: Prisons and Punishment in Nova Scotia before 1880," *Essays in the History of Canadian Law: Volume III: Nova Scotia*, ed. P. Girard and J. Phillips (Toronto, 1990), 166–68.

6. Clifford R. Shaw, *The Jack-Roller: A Delinquent Boy's Own Story* (Philadelphia, 1930), 172; E. G. O'Donoghue, *Bridewell Hospital, Palace, Prison, Schools*, 2 vols. (London, 1923, 1929), 2:231, 234–35; Alfred J. Copeland, *Bridewell Royal Hospital, Past and Present* (London, 1888), 96, 106.

7. Lawrence Stone, "Madness," *The Past and the Present Revisited* (New York, 1987), 291–92.

8. Pieter Spierenburg, *The Prison Experience: Disciplinary Institutions and Their Inmates in Early Modern Europe* (New Brunswick and London, 1991), 31.

9. David Garland, *Punishment and Modern Society: A Study in Social Theory* (Chicago, 1990), 131.

10. E. M. Leonard, *The Early History of English Poor Relief* (Cambridge, 1900), 26–40; Beatrice Webb and Sidney Webb, *English Poor Law History, Part One: The Old Poor Law* (London, 1927), 27ff.

11. Leonard, *Early History*, 39.

12. G. Rusche and O. Kirchheimer, *Punishment and Social Structure* (New York, 1939), 42, 45, 50, 65, 68.

13. Spierenburg, *The Prison Experience*, 115ff.

14. *Thirty-Second Report of the Commissioners for Inquiring Concerning Charities, Part VI. City of London* (London, 1840), 393.

15. Spierenburg, *The Prison Experience*, 116–22; S. C. Ratcliffe and H. C. Johnson, eds., *Warwick County Records. Volume I. Quarter Sessions Order Book, Easter 1625 to Trinity 1637* (Warwick, 1935), 267.

16. Dario Melossi and Massimo Pavarini, *The Prison and the Factory: Origins of the Penitentiary System*, transl. Glynis Cousin (London, 1981), 3, 5, 22–23.

17. Innes, "Prisons for the Poor," 46–49; also A. L. Beier, "From Forced Labour to Labour Discipline: England, 1350–1800," unpublished paper, 11th International Economic History Congress, Milan, 1994.

18. Bridewell Court Books, volumes for 1597–1604, 1604–10.

19. J. A. Sharpe, *Crime in 17th-Century England. A County Study* (Cambridge, 1983), 151; Innes, "Prisons for the Poor," 85, 99, 105, 114.

20. Pieter Spierenburg, "The Sociogenesis of Confinement and its Development in Early Modern Europe," in *The Emergence of Carceral Institutions: Prisons, Galleys and Lunatic Asylums, 1550–1990*, ed. Pieter Spierenburg (Rotterdam, 1984), 30–31; Spierenburg, *The Prison Experience*, 25–26.

21. Spierenburg, *The Prison Experience*, 24–25, 274, and sources cited there;

André Zysberg, "Galley and Hard Labour Convicts in France (1550–1850)," in *The Emergence of Carceral Institutions*, ed. Pieter Spierenburg, 78–79; Melossi and Pavarini, *Prison and Factory*, 73.

22. B. Geremek, "Renfermement des pauvres en Italie (XIV–XVIIe siècles): remarques préliminaires," *Histoire économique du monde méditérranéan, 1450–1650: Mélanges en l'honneur de Fernand Braudel* (Toulouse, 1973), I, 208ff., though Geremek documents very little "enclosure" of the poor before the late sixteenth century, and even then it was limited in extent. Cf. Brian Pullan, "Support and Redeem: Charity and Poor Relief in Italian Cities from the Fourteenth to the Seventeenth Century," *Continuity and Change* 3 (1988): 194, 197–99; and his *Rich and Poor in Renaissance Venice* (Oxford, 1971), 257–58.

23. Geremek, "Renfermement des pauvres," 213–14. For a house of correction opened in Rome in 1703, see Luigi Cajani, "Surveillance and Redemption: The *Casa di Correzione* of San Michele a Ripa in Rome," in *Institutions of Confinement: Hospitals, Asylums, and Prisons in Western Europe and North America, 1500–1950*, ed. Norbert Finzsch and Robert Jütte (Cambridge, 1996), 301–24.

24. Langbein, "Imprisonment for Serious Crime," 45.

25. Marjorie K. McIntosh, "Local Responses to the Poor in Late Medieval and Tudor England," *Continuity and Change* 3:2 (1988): 225–33.

26. *Folie et déraison: Histoire de la folie à l'Âge classique* (Paris, 1961), 77–78, 81–83 (I have used the original French edition instead of the English translation *Madness and Civilization: A History of Insanity in the Age of Reason* (New York, 1965), which, although abridged by the author himself, omitted substantial portions of the original text); Ignatieff, *Just Measure of Pain*, 12–13. For further development of the crisis explanation, but with reservations, see M. Ignatieff, "State, Civil Society and Total Institution: A Critique of Recent Social Histories of Punishment," in *Legality, Ideology and the State*, ed. D. Sugarman (London, 1983), 195–96.

27. S. Rappaport, *Worlds Within Worlds: Structures of Life in 16th-century London* (Cambridge, 1989), 132, 405. With the base period of 1457–71 being 100, flour prices in 1547–49 averaged 125, and in 1550–53, 291 (my calculations).

28. F. J. Fisher, "Commercial Trends and Policy in 16th-century England," reprinted in F. J. Fisher, *London and the English Economy, 1500–1700* (London, 1990), 82.

29. C.S.L. Davies, "Slavery and Protector Somerset: The Vagrancy Act of 1547," *Economic History Review* (2nd ser.) 19 (1966): 538.

30. Susan Brigden, *London and the Reformation* (Oxford, 1989), 492–94, 496; Ian W. Archer, *The Pursuit of Stability: Social Relations in Elizabethan London* (Cambridge, 1991), 243; see also Slack, "Social Policy," 95–97; Roger B. Manning, *Village Revolts: Social Protest and Popular Disturbances in England, 1509–1640* (Oxford, 1988), 199.

31. Foucault, *Folie*, 64–65, 67–68, 71.

32. Of course, his book *Discipline and Punish: The Birth of the Prison* (Paris, 1975; Engl. transl., New York, 1978) caused great controversy but concerns a later development.

33. H. C. Erik Midelfort, "Madness and Civilization in Early Modern Europe: A Reappraisal of Michel Foucault," in *After the Reformation: Essays in Honor of J. H. Hexter*, ed. Barbara C. Malament (Philadelphia, 1980), 259.

34. Stone, "Madness," 291–92.

35. Roy Porter, *Mind-Forg'd Manacles: A History of Madness in England from the Restoration to the Regency* (London, 1990 ed.), 78; Paul Slack, *Poverty and Policy in Tudor and Stuart England* (London, 1988), 16 n.27; Spierenburg, *The Prison Experience*, 10.

36. A. L. Beier, *Masterless Men: The Vagrancy Problem in England, 1560–1640* (London, 1985), 51–57, 166; A. L. Beier, "Poverty and Progress in Early Modern England," in *The First Modern Society: Essays in English History in Honour of Lawrence Stone*, ed. A. L. Beier, D. Cannadine, and J. M. Rosenheim (Cambridge, 1989), 214.

37. Foucault, *Folie*, 64–67, 71, 73–74, 80, 86–87.

38. Ibid., 64–65; cf. (on chronology) Midelfort, "Madness and Civilization," 253, 257; Stone, "Madness," 271.

39. M. Mollat, *The Poor in the Middle Ages: An Essay in Social History* (London, 1986), 233, 243–47, 258–59; quotation (p. 293) from Miri Rubin, *Charity and Community in Medieval Cambridge* (Cambridge, 1987), 289–93, 296–98; Geremek, "Renfermement des pauvres," 208ff.

40. Foucault, *Folie*, 58ff.

41. Although Foucault cited E. M. Leonard in his bibliography (*Folie*, 662–72), he missed the Webbs' work, as well as that of Thorsten Sellin, *Pioneering in Penology: the Amsterdam Houses of Correction in the 16th and 17th Centuries* (Philadelphia, 1944); cf. Midelfort, "Madness and Civilization," 257; and Stone, "Madness," 271.

42. Garland, *Punishment and Modern Society*, 162 (quotation).

43. Jeffrey Weeks, "Foucault for Historians," *History Workshop* 14 (autumn 1982): 111.

44. This is the crux of chaps. 1–3 of Lawrence Stone, *The Past and the Present Revisited*, 2nd ed. (New York, 1987).

45. Information from the late A. H. John, London School of Economics and Political Science.

46. Foucault, *Folie*, 662–72; cf. Stone, "Madness," 274; and Spierenburg, *The Prison Experience*, 10.

47. This is the main issue dividing Lawrence Stone and Foucault in their exchange in *The New York Review of Books*, March 31, 1983, 42–44, reprinted in Stone, *The Past and the Present Revisited*, 283–94.

48. Weeks, "Foucault for Historians," 110.

49. R. Muchembled, *L'invention de l'homme moderne. Sensibilités, moeurs, et comportements collectifs sous l'ancien régime* (Paris, 1988), 155, 163–64, 166–70, 201.

50. Spierenburg, *The Prison Experience*, 17, 31.

51. The *locus classicus* is Natalie Z. Davis, "Poor Relief, Humanism, and Heresy: The Case of Lyon," in *Studies in Medieval and Renaissance History*, ed. William M. Bowsky (Lincoln, Nebr., 1968), 217–20, 231, 235, 245, reprinted in the collection of her essays, *Society and Culture in Early Modern France* (Stanford, 1975), chap. 2.

52. Margo Todd, *Christian Humanists and the Puritan Social Order* (Cambridge, 1987), 17, 30 (quotation), 33–39, 40–41.

53. Paul A. Fideler, "Poverty, Policy and Providence: The Tudors and the

Poor," in *Political Thought and the Tudor Commonwealth*, ed. Paul A. Fideler and T. F. Mayer (New York, 1992), 199–201, 205.

54. Paul Slack, "Social Policy and the Constraints of Government, 1547–58," in *The Mid-Tudor Polity, c. 1540–1560*, ed. Jennifer Loach and Robert Tittler (London, 1980), 98–99 (quotations).

55. Spierenburg, *The Prison Experience*, 27–28.

56. Archer, *The Pursuit of Stability*, 168.

57. E.g., Webb and Webb, *English Poor Law*, 48–49; Leonard, *Early History*, 31–32; W. K. Jordan, *The Charities of London, 1480–1660* (London, 1960, repr. 1974), 193; W. K. Jordan, *Edward VI: The Threshold of Power* (London, 1970), 221–23. The latter account gives the greatest individual influence to Ridley.

58. Slack, "Social Policy," 109–11, 115.

59. Spierenburg, *The Prison Experience*, 27–28.

60. Archer, *The Pursuit of Stability*, 168, 252–53.

61. F. R. Salter, ed., *Some Early Tracts on Poor Relief* (London, 1926). 97. Salter's source was apparently S. M. Jackson, *Huldreich Zwingli: The Reformer of German Switzerland* (London, 1901), 225 n., who misquoted Heinrich Bullinger, *Reformationsgeschichte nach dem Autographen* (Frauenfeld, 1838–40), I, 228–30. The reference in question is actually in Bullinger, p. 231. The most recent discussion of Zwinglian policies toward Zurich's poor gives no indication that incarceration took place: Lee Palmer Wandel, *Always Among Us: Images of the Poor in Zwingli's Zurich* (Cambridge, 1990), *passim*.

62. Spierenburg, *The Prison Experience*, 22; Jean-Pierre Gutton, *La société et les pauvres. L'exemple de la généralité de Lyon, 1534–1789* (Paris, 1971), 268, 272, 284.

63. Spierenburg, *The Prison Experience*, 16; Sellin, *Pioneering in Penology*, 18–19. This chapter's arguments about the novelty of London's Bridewell and the preeminent role of Protestant magistrates in its creation tend to go against the view favoring continuity in social regulation between medieval and early modern periods recently articulated by Marjorie McIntosh, *Controlling Misbehavior in England, 1370–1600* (Cambridge, 1998), although she cites the institution on p. 25. See also the "Symposium: *Controlling (Mis)Behavior*," *Journal of British Studies* 37:3 (July 1998): 231–305.

64. R. R. Betts, "Constitutional Development and Political Thought in Eastern Europe," in *New Cambridge Modern History: The Reformation*, ed. G. R. Elton (Cambridge, 1965), 2; 476; B. Geremek, *Poverty: A History* (Oxford, 1994), 191, 193.

65. Most studies of early Tudor humanists ignore their interest in the poor and criminal classes, but see Joan Simon, *Education and Society in Tudor England* (Cambridge, 1967), 160–62.

66. Plato, *The Laws*, transl. and ed. Trevor J. Saunders, (Harmondsworth, 1970), 443, 445. For Plato's influence, see David S. Berkowitz, ed., *Humanist Scholarship and Public Order: Two Tracts Against the Pilgrimage of Grace by Richard Morison* (London, 1984), 116, 269–70; also T. F. Mayer, ed., *Thomas Starkey: A Dialogue between Lupset and Pole*, Camden Fourth Series, vol. 37 (London, 1989), 108.

67. Robert Jütte, *Poverty and Deviance in Early Modern Europe* (Cambridge, 1994), 108, 113.

68. Jean-Pierre Gutton, *La société et les pauvres en Europe (XVIe–XVIIIe siècles)* (Paris, 1974), 104, noticed that imprisonment was on Vives' agenda.

69. There is no satisfactory English edition of the tract. The most recent is used here: Alice Tobriner, ed., *A Sixteenth-Century Urban Report* (Chicago, 1971), 38–43. But Tobriner gives no indication of the text from which the translation is made and, as in other translations, does not include Book I of the tract. Other translations are by Margaret M. Sherwood, Studies in Social Work, no. 11 (New York, 1917), and Salter, *Early Tracts*, 1–31. Sherwood and Salter both provide summaries of Book I.

70. Tobriner, *Urban Report*, 38.

71. Ibid., 40.

72. Ibid., 52.

73. Ibid., 35, 55.

74. Ibid., 36, 55.

75. Ibid., 36, 44, 55.

76. Ibid., 36–37, 55–56.

77. Ibid., 36.

78. Ibid., 55–56.

79. E. L. Surtz and J. H. Hexter, eds., *The Complete Works of St. Thomas More* (London, 1965), 4:191.

80. *Dialogue between Lupset and Pole*, 60–62, 100–105, 136.

81. Public Record Office, SP 6/7/fol. 71; British Library, Royal MS.18.C.VI.13b.

82. Elton, *Reform and Renewal*, 122–24; *Statutes of the Realm* (London, 1963), 3:329, 558; 4:i, pp. 5, 115.

83. Tobriner, *Urban Report*, 33, 43–44; further background is in Salter, *Early Tracts*, 2.

84. Webbs, *English Poor Law History*, 40.

85. Repertories of the Court of Aldermen, Corporation of London Records Office (hereafter Rep.), 2/200a, 201a, 204b; 3/11b, 98b, 189b, 190a.

86. Rep. 3/190a-b, 192a, 221a.

87. Journal, Court of Common Council, Corporation of London Records Office, 3/208 (indexed, but not found in original text); Rep. 1/41b.

88. *Memoranda, References, and Documents Relating to the Royal Hospitals of the City of London* (London, 1836), Appendix, 1–3.

89. McIntosh, "Local Responses," 237 n.7, makes the point, citing C. Barron, that able-bodied beggars were the subject of London legislation as early as 1366. But late medieval statutes did not attempt to reform offenders through imprisonment and forced labor.

90. Rep. 4 (no foliation—date 11 June 1520); 5/198a. A further group was arrested in 1539: Rep. 9/226b.

91. Rep. 6/9a.

92. Rep. 11/364a, 394b; 12 ii/7 July 1552, 501a, 554a; 13 i/40b, 43a, 52b–53a, 59a, 66b 75a, 115a; Archer, *Pursuit of Stability*, 239.

93. Rep. 11/364a, 394b.

94. Thomas Bowen, *Extracts from the Records and Court Books of Bridewell Hospital* (London, 1798), Appendix, p. 7.

95. E. Power and R. H. Tawney, eds., *Tudor Economic Documents* (London, 1924), 2:307 (hereafter *T.E.D.*).

96. Fideler, "Poverty, Policy and Providence," 206ff.; Neal Wood, "Foundations of Political Economy: The New Moral Philosophy of Sir Thomas Smith," in *Political Thought and the Tudor Commonwealth*, ed. Paul A. Fideler and T. F. Mayer (New York, 1992), chap. 5.

97. Quoted by Martin Bucer, *A Treatise, How by the Word of God, Christian Men's Alms Ought to be Distributed* (n.d.), 6; see also Thomas Lever, *Sermons*, ed., Edward Arber, English Reprints (London, 1870), 84.

98. Lever, *Sermons*, 77–78.

99. J. M. Cowper, ed., *The Select Works of Robert Crowley*, Early English Text Society, extra series, vol. 15 (1872), 14–15.

100. Bucer, *A Treatise*, 16–17, 24.

101. J. M. Cowper, ed., *Henry Brinklow's Complaynt of Roderyck Mors . . . and The Lamentacyon of a Christen Agaynst the Cytye of London, made by Roderigo Mors*, Early English Text Society, extra series, vol. 22 (London, 1874), 90; idem, *Four Supplications, 1529–1553 A.D.*, Early English Text Society, extra series, vol. 13 (London, 1871), 79; Cowper, *Crowley*, 166.

102. See the useful compendium in C. H. Williams, ed., *English Historical Documents, 1485–1558* (London, 1967), 5:271 (T. Becon); 277 (anon.); 293 (Tyndale); 299 (Starkey); 304, 306, 309 (Crowley); 325 (Brinklow); 341, 352, 354–6 (Latimer). The humanist position is spelled out in Morison's *A Remedy for Sedition* (1536), reprinted in Berkowitz, *Humanist Scholarship and Public Order*.

103. S. J. Herrtage, ed., *England in the Reign of King Henry the Eight. Part I. Starkey's Life and Letters*. Early English Text Society, extra series, no. 32 (London, 1927), letter to Henry VIII from Starkey, xlvii–lxiii; *Henry Brinklow's Complaynt . . . and The Lamentacyon*, 47–48, 89–90.

104. Clement Armstrong, *Drei volkswirthschaftliche Denkschriften aus der Zeit Heinrichs VIII von England* (Göttingen, 1878), 48–49, 54–55. Both Crowley and Brinklow addressed publications to Parliament: *English Historical Documents, 1485–1558*, 313, 325.

105. Compare Vives' institutional blueprints, cited above, with those in *Henry Brinklow's Complaynt*, 50–52.

106. For a stirring account see J. J. Scarisbrick, *Henry VIII* (London, 1968), 520–26.

107. See Vives, above; Richard Morison on poverty as a cause of sedition, *Humanist Scholarship and Public Order*, 128–29; Starkey, *Dialogue Between Lupset and Pole*, 102. Both writers blamed bad education for idleness and sedition.

108. *T.E.D.* 3:51 (Lever: prices); 57 (Crowley: rents); 90 ff. (Armstrong: trade); G. L. Corrie, ed., *Sermons of Hugh Latimer*, Parker Society (Cambridge, 1844), 98–102 (high rents and food prices); cf. G. R. Elton, "Reform and the 'Commonwealth-Men' of Edward VI's reign," *The English Commonwealth, 1547–1640: Essays in Politics and Society* (Leicester, 1979), 23–38, for a negative assessment.

109. *Dictionary of National Biography* (1917 ed.), 13:957–58.

110. Simon Fish, "A Supplication for the Beggers," in *Four Supplications*, 8, 13–14, 70; Cowper, *Henry Brinklow's Complaynt . . . and The Lamentacyon*, 47–48, 89–90; *Statutes of the Realm* (London, 1963 ed.), 4:24.

111. Brinklow, *Lamentacyon*, 79–80, 90; Corrie, *Sermons of Hugh Latimer*, 64; Lever, *Sermons*, 29–30, 32–33, 77–78, 81–82.

112. Corrie, *Sermons of Hugh Latimer*, 63–64.

113. *D.N.B.* (Grafton); Joseph Ames, continued by T. F. Dibdin, *Typographical Antiquities; or the History of Printing in England, Scotland and Ireland* (London, 1816), III, 270–315 (Berthelet), 421–33 (Grafton); and for Berthelet, see Berkowitz, *Humanist Scholarship and Public Order*, 25, 40, 42.

114. Neither Ridley's sermon nor the king's letters appear to survive in manuscript. The sermon's dating is uncertain, although most authorities prefer the early months of 1552: Jasper G. Ridley, *Nicholas Ridley: A Biography* (London, 1957), 285–86 (and sources cited there); Lever, *Sermons*, 78.

115. Brigden, *London and the Reformation*, 479; Bowen, *Extracts*; Appendix, 8; *T.E.D.*, 2:312; George Townsend, ed., *The Acts and Monuments of John Foxe* (London, 1847), 7:559–60.

116. *T.E.D.*, 2:312. Ridley himself implied that London took the initiative before he wrote to Cecil. For stylistic purposes, the order of the quotations reverses the original. The dating of this document is problematical. It first appears in John Stow, *A Survey of London*, ed. John Strype (London, 1720), 2:176. Cf. Ridley, *Ridley*, 287–88, who is otherwise often in error. For Cecil, see Jordan, *Edward VI: The Threshold of Power*, 500–501.

117. "Petition of the Mayor, Aldermen, and Commonalty of the City of London to King Henry the Eighth, in the 30th year of his reign," *Memoranda, References, and Documents Relating to the Royal Hospitals of the City of London*, Appendix, 2 (order of quotations reversed from original). The original documents are in the Corporation of London Records Office, Journals of the Court of Common Council 14/fols. 129–30 (*Memoranda*, Appendix, 1); and in the British Library, Cotton Manuscripts, Cleop. E.4, p. 222 (Bowen, *Extracts from the Records and Court Books of Bridewell*, Appendix, p. 1). The versions printed by Bowen and the *Memoranda* differ substantially, with the latter containing a second part that is wholly excised by Bowen but appears in Journal 14/129–30.

118. "Petition," *Memoranda*, 1, 3.

119. Bowen, Appendix, 7–8. I have been unable to trace a manuscript version of this document or even other published versions. J. A. Kingdon (*Richard Grafton: Citizen and Grocer of London*, London, 1901, p. 52 n.) states that the Charity Commissioners had seen the original for their report in 1840 but said that it "cannot now be found."

120. The wills are in the Public Record Office, PROB 11/—Ayliffe (26 Ketchyn: 1556); Barne (13 Noodes: 1558); Blundell (49 Chaynay: 1557); Bowes (3 Stonarde: 1565); Gresham (28 Ketchyn: 1554); Hill (33 Loftes: 1560); Judde (58 Noodes; 54 Welles: 1558); Lodge (29 Brudenell: 1583); Marshe (16 Loftes: 1557).

121. Peter Clark, *English Provincial Society from the Reformation to the Revolution: Religion, Politics and Society in Kent, 1500–1640* (Hassocks, 1977), 76.

122. See *D.N.B.* entries for Chester and Grafton. Berthelet left a will, but I have been unable to trace it. It is incompletely cited by Cyril Davenport, *Thomas Berthelet. Royal Printer and Bookbinder to Henry VIII* (Chicago, 1901), 51–53.

123. Clark, *English Provincial Society*, 58, 76, 420 n. (for a discussion of criteria). There is confusion about the identity of one signatory, who is variously identified as "Mr. Brown" and "Mr. Broome," but who was almost certainly al-

derman Sir George Barne, identified by Ridley as instrumental in creating Bridewell: *Acts and Monuments of John Foxe*, 7:559–60.

124. PROB 11/38, fol. 186b; Clark, *English Provincial Society*, 420 n.75, for the definition of radicalism. Cf. J. D. Alsop, "Religious Preambles in Early Modern English Wills as Formulae," *Journal of Ecclesiastical History* 40:1 (1989): 19–27 and sources cited there.

125. Brigden, *London and the Reformation*, 472; Archer, *The Pursuit of Stability*, 250–51.

126. *T.E.D.*, 2:306–11 (italicized in original).

127. *Acts and Monuments of John Foxe*, 7:560.

128. *T.E.D.*, 2:307–8.

129. *Memoranda*, 62–63, 75.

130. *Thirty-Second Report of the Commissioners for Inquiring Concerning Charities, Part VI. City of London* (London, 1840), 390–91 (for various uses of the term "continuance," see *The Oxford English Dictionary*).

131. Garland, *Punishment and Modern Society*, 131.

132. Whether the rejection of voluntary poverty and adoption of compulsory labor originated with humanists or Protestants seems moot and not terribly important, since both groups held these positions.

133. Rationalized in *T.E.D.*, 2:306–8; Leonard, *Early History*, 26–31; Mercers Company, Acts of Court, 1527–1560, fol. 281a.

134. Slack, "Social Policy and Constraints," 112; Beier, *Masterless Men*, 169.

135. Beier, *Masterless Men*, 164–69; Archer, *The Pursuit of Stability*, 218, 240–41.

136. Garland, *Punishment and Modern Society*, 131.

Blackmail as a Crime of Sexual Indiscretion in Eighteenth-Century England

Antony Simpson

For students of sexual behavior and gender relations, the law is of obvious and unique importance as a social construct. This is particularly true for explorations of historical research settings not productive of social surveys or other artifacts of contemporary public opinion. The law is dynamic and a consequence of its particular place and time. It demonstrates what society (or at least some powerful group within it) *does* about particular behaviors considered deviant, not just what it says and appears to think about them. Appreciation of society's attitude toward behaviors defined as criminal must accordingly be informed by an understanding of patterns of application of the law as well as its substance. This is true for all crimes but especially those whose proscription reflects moral values of varying popular strength. Reliance on legal substance alone can lead to conclusions that are ill-informed and even inaccurate. Deviant behaviors can be condemned, even criminalized, over time in what appears to be a very consistent fashion, but treated by the legal system very differently at different points in time in ways not indicated by changes in the content of the law.

An instance in point, and one of some relevance to the analysis presented here, concerns the crime of sodomy in English law. Between 1533 and 1861, this was a capital offense.[1] Although the legal requirements for the proof of this crime changed somewhat during this period, its punishment was determined by the same capital statute. However, policies in the application of this statute changed considerably within this period. Few prosecutions were brought before the 1800s, even fewer convictions were obtained and fewer executions carried out. It has been suggested that more than fifty homosexuals were put to death in England and Wales between 1800 and 1835, far more than were executed in the entire eighteenth century.[2] Intensification of homophobia in the early nineteenth century is clear: Execution is certainly a powerful social reaction. It is also a reaction hard to glean from other sources, just because condemnation of homosexuality, as expressed in novels, the press, and other popular sources was common and extreme from at least the late seventeenth century onward.[3] The very powerful difference between the two periods appears to be that before the end of the eighteenth century, society's hatred of male homosexuals[4] was apparently not strong enough to provoke use of the gallows.[5]

Early nineteenth-century interest in executing sodomites, even those engaging in consensual activity, has been widely used to associate the rise of homophobia with a variety of factors associated with societies in the midst of industrialization and modernization.[6] Use of executions in this context has therefore been used to underpin theories about the social circumstances that support intensified homophobia as well as to determine when this feeling gained legal expression. For this reason alone, use of executions as the prime indicator of such feeling warrants attention. One superficial problem is engendered by the sheer drama of the gallows and the apparent suddenness with which society came to use this means to express antihomosexual sentiment. Attention is certainly commanded by the image of a legal system with recognizably modern features fairly abruptly deciding to put to death perpetrators of usually victimless crimes. The fact that this occurred at a time when execution rates were falling, particularly for those capitally convicted of nonviolent offenses,[7] makes the image even stronger.

There are earlier activities within the English criminal justice system that suggest that the growth of this sentiment long preceded the routine imposition of the death penalty on homosexual miscreants. Waves of police activity directed at "molly houses" (pubs frequented by gays) and outdoor gay meeting places occurred regularly in London throughout the eighteenth century and were accompanied by mass prosecutions. As these grew in frequency as the century wore on,[8] it could be argued that they represented much earlier interest in invoking the criminal law to punish homosexual conduct. This may be true. However, the circumstances of these efforts make it unclear whether it was homosexuality or simply unacceptable public conduct that was being punished. Moreover, prosecutions of this kind undertaken in the first half of the century were largely supported by the Societies for the Reformation of Manners, organizations concerned with immoral conduct of all kinds and which by no means limited their attentions to the gay world.[9] Most important, the misdemeanor convictions frequently obtained from these waves of interest carried the relatively minor penalty of a few months' imprisonment (although occasionally the pillory): nothing remotely comparable to the death penalty.

The drama of the early nineteenth-century executions undoubtedly serves to direct attention to the nature of the behavior being punished and the overwhelming force of society's reaction to it. There was, however, another kind of capital offense that was directly linked to homosexual misconduct. Under certain circumstances blackmail became a capital offense in the last quarter of the eighteenth century and one that attracted far more prosecutions than ever did the crime of sodomy and resulted in a great many more executions. This development in the criminal law certainly reflected extreme distaste for homosexuality but was most closely linked to the protection of the reputations of heterosexual men from allegations of homosexual conduct. In the analysis that follows it is shown how the offense of blackmail was, in certain specific circumstances, transformed from a misdemeanor into a capital felony. Blackmailers using allegation of homosexuality as their stock-in-trade were alone among extortionists in having their activities redefined and incorporated within the capital crime of robbery. This quite dramatic change occurred through the courts and not through the legislature. In this sense it represents one instance of the ability of a common law system to respond quickly to concerns that are popular in origin or political in significance. It also represents the strength of popular attitudes against homosexuality and, accordingly, against those who extorted money under threat of allegation of its practice.

EXTORTION

Blackmail[10] in general remained a misdemeanor in this period and one, moreover, extremely difficult to prosecute successfully. It was subsumed within the common law offense of "extortion." This was limited originally to crimes involving abuse of public office for material gain, but between the beginning of the eighteenth century and the beginning of the nineteenth, it was expanded to include those who extorted under threat of prosecution. In 1805, such a threat was no longer acceptable as the basis for a misdemeanor charge of extortion. Between 1805 and 1843, when Lord Campbell's Libel Act was passed, there was very little basis for bringing a misdemeanor prosecution for extortion that did not involve misuse of public office.[11] In fact, the law regarding extortion as a misdemeanor was largely a dead letter in the century before this, as very few prosecutions for it were ever brought.[12] One form of blackmail was made a capital felony by statute early in the eighteenth century. The Waltham Black Act of 1722 (repealed, against strong opposition, in 1823) created a tremendous number of capital felonies. Included among them was extortion through a written communication in specific circumstances where violence or damage to property was threatened.[13] Although this act certainly established the principle of extortion as a capital crime, it must be regarded purely as a powerful legal weapon intended for the protection of the persons and property of rural landowners. It did not initially protect against threats to prosecute or damage to reputation. In 1757, it was amended to allow extortion by letter to be prosecuted under certain circumstances as a noncapital felony.[14]

One should not conclude from the generally undeveloped state of the law of extortion that this kind of criminal activity was rare in eighteenth-century England. In fact, it was rife. Civil suits and criminal prosecutions were thought to frequently constitute stages in processes of extortionate negotiation, and the two were often combined to address the same alleged tort or offense. Corruption within the court system of London was believed to be widespread (at least in those areas of the Metropolis outside of the city). Paid perjurers were known to frequent both civil and criminal courts. Occasional scandals revealed well-organized and apparently ongoing conspiracies among police officers and other thieftakers to frame innocent parties (or entrap others) for capital crimes in order to collect reward money.[15]

Citizens and jurists at this time were well aware of this state of affairs. Their apparent acceptance of it was at least in part conditioned by different, and definitely premodern, expectations of their legal institutions. Processes of "making up" an injury by offer of money and usually a public apology were traditional and understood. Although these had no formal place in the law, they achieved informal acceptance within the law and demands for compensation made by crime victims were, when these came to light in the courts, not necessarily regarded as instances of venality. Cases of sexual assault were commonly associated with defense allegations that the prosecutions were brought primarily to encourage defendants to pay off their supposed victims. Such claims, when believed by the courts in cases of rape or its attempt, were regarded variously as attempts to extort or to gain fair compensation for a real injury. In either case, such blackmail attempts were not regarded as a serious matter by the courts, except when allegations of them clearly had been fabricated by the accused. The very few who were convicted for extortions of this nature were not severely punished. This was undoubtedly in part because the efforts of these extortionists were overwhelmingly unorganized and amateurish in approach. However, there is also a strong body of evidence to suggest that men at this time were not generally concerned by the threat of being blackmailed for sexual misconduct, real or imagined—at least when the allegations were of a heterosexual nature.[16]

Extortion under accusation of "unnatural vice" was regarded in a very different light. These quite different reactions to allegations of different forms of sexual misconduct are suggestive of the modern working-class attitude toward manhood, in which a man's image is not necessarily damaged (perhaps the opposite) by heterosexual peccadilloes but is seriously tainted by the weakness associated with less conventional tastes. Legal expression of these reactions to accusation of homosexual misconduct was reflected in the unusual development of the law of robbery.

ROBBERY

Robbery in general was a crime that attracted considerable attention in this period. During the eighteenth century as a whole, convicted robbers constituted roughly one-third of all those executed in London and Middle-sex.[17] Whether or not it was accompanied by actual assault, robbery was then considered as the most significant crime against the person. It is likely that much contemporary fear of it was motivated less by the thought of robbery itself than by the fear of the violent potential of this crime. (In this unique sense, eighteenth-century reactions to this crime were probably much as they are today.) Given the large volume of robbery cases prose-cuted, courts and jurists had plenty of opportunities to develop precise definitions of what constituted robbery as a capital crime.

Hale defined robbery as "the felonious and violent taking of any money or goods from the person of another, putting him in fear, be the value thereof above or under one shilling."[18] It therefore included three elements. Its perpetrator, as with all felonies, had to have acted with *animus furandi*, or felonious intent. He had to have actually taken something from the victim's person, and he had to have done so by "putting him in fear," that is, with violence or threat thereof.[19] There were few legal difficulties with the first two of these requirements. Intent could be established by any of a variety of indicators, showing that the accused desired to permanently de-prive another of his property. The value of the goods did not matter, there was no minimal amount. Taking had to be from the person.[20]

Defining "putting in fear" was trickier. Actual violence qualified for this but the level of violence so needed was very slight. Snatching a purse out of someone's hand, but without touching the victim, was held violence enough to justify a capital conviction for robbery.[21] Threat of violence was no less acceptable. The many highwaymen who were convicted after lev-eling pistols at the unwary on Bagshot Heath and Shooters Hill did not usually offer actual violence and most probably did not threaten it in so many words. The display of a weapon made a nod as good as a wink. However, the import of any such threat had to be of a particular kind. It had to be sufficient to produce fears in the victim for his physical safety. These fears did not have to be very powerful; they just had to be there.[22] Those raised by a boy who asked for money politely, but with a mob at his back and during the Gordon Riots, were held to warrant a capital conviction.[23] A man who accepted money from a woman attempting to divert him from his object of rape was held to be a robber. It was held that, even though robbery had not been his motive, the money had not been offered voluntarily and was only offered because the victim had been put in fear.[24] Threats against property were held to constitute putting in fear in a 1780 decision but only in circumstances where the victim was given cause to also fear for his personal safety.[25]

In one sense, then, the eighteenth century was generous in interpreting a broad range of threats as sufficient to put someone in fear and, therefore, be tantamount to actual violence in their effects. There were nonetheless some strict limitations. Fear had to be of violence that was *immediate*. By this understanding, the "highwayman who gives you the choice of 'your money' now, or 'your life' next week, is not a robber."[26]

More important, threat of prosecution was held to be insufficient to induce fear of a capital kind. As noted earlier, an 1805 decision disallowed this kind of threat as a basis for misdemeanor prosecutions for extortion and therefore limited the relief for victims of this crime afforded by the law. However, this principle already applied in cases of felony. In Knewland's Case, heard in the Old Bailey in 1796, a woman brought a robbery prosecution against two men who had held her under restraint and forced her to pay them money by threatening to charge her with theft. Their conviction was overturned by the Twelve Judges,[27] who found the level of threat to amount to no more than simple duress, suitable as a basis for a civil suit only and not a criminal prosecution. In discussing this case, the Judges emphasized an important distinction: "Terror is of two kinds; namely, a terror which leads the mind of the party to apprehend an injury to his person, or a terror which leads him to apprehend an injury to his character."[28] This last did not constitute a sufficient basis for a capital prosecution in this circumstance.

It is, however, significant that the Judges defined both types of injury as "terror." They did so because there was by this time (1796) a unique circumstance in which threat of damage to character *could* be equated with the physical putting in fear necessary to support a capital conviction for robbery. This was if the threat concerned allegations of homosexual behavior. Such threats constituted the only exception in a legal tradition that was otherwise quite strict in regarding force as an essential ingredient of the crime of robbery. Recognition of this was clear in the Knewland decision, although the exception did not apply. Injury to character was discussed with the strict proviso that allegations of "sodomitical practices" were the *only* acceptable substitute for force or its threat in cases of robbery.

This principle had not always existed. Richard Noke was tried and acquitted of robbery in 1751, after he detained John Burk, a servant, and extorted money from him by threatening to prosecute him for sodomy. Burk was undoubtedly ill-used when in Noke's custody, and witnesses testified to seeing him beaten. The court, however, believed that it was the threat of prosecution and not this application of violence that had induced Burk to pay up. The judge directed an acquittal because such a threat was not then equated to putting in fear and no robbery had therefore been committed. He said, in effect, that Noke had been charged with the wrong crime and ordered him tried at the next session for extortion. Noke was accordingly tried, convicted, and sentenced to a year in prison.[29]

A similar case was heard in 1774. William Rooke was prosecuted for robbery by Joseph Fowle, a lawyer's clerk, after extorting money from him in St. James' Park under color of threat to prosecute for the usual crime.[30]

Rooke, a member of a gang, had observed the time-honored practice of following his victim home after the initial transfer of cash and of contacting him on at least two subsequent occasions to obtain further sums. Fowle eventually reported the matter to the Bow Street Police Court. A trap was laid for Rooke, and the next time he called, Fielding's men were on hand to observe the transaction. There was no question as to the facts of the case as these could be attested to by independent witnesses. Rooke's acquittal was directed simply because no violence or threat of it had been offered, and no robbery was, therefore, considered to have been committed. The case did not go to the Twelve Judges, because the court clearly had no doubts as to the clarity of the principle of law involved. Fowle had to be content with the judge's recommendation that he undertake a misdemeanor prosecution for extortion.

The spectacle of a professional blackmailer getting off the hook so easily was enhanced by a similar, and related, case heard in the same sessions of the Old Bailey. Professionals also were involved, and the three men charged included none other than the energetic William Rooke.[31] However, this case showed a greater appreciation of the legal difficulties involved in prosecuting for robbery under circumstances in which both violence and its threat were absent. The committing magistrate had some problems in advising the prosecutor, William Pretty, as to what charge to file. Robbery was rejected, as the element of violence was not present. In the end, the capital charge of stealing in a dwelling house was filed (at least one of the several payments extorted from Pretty had been made in his home). This was the charge sent to the grand jury and on which the three accused (Clarke, Pullen, and Rooke) were tried. The three were acquitted. It is not made clear in the report of the case just why this was so (the Twelve Judges did not address this case either). However, it is clear that an attempt to incorporate extortion within this category of theft would have created substantial legal difficulties. Stealing in a dwelling was a capital form of larceny. As such, its proof required a taking without the consent of the owner.[32] It is questionable whether this was so in this case. Pretty gave the money to his tormentors. The fact that his consent was forced does not mean that it was withheld. Whatever the reason, William Rooke once again walked free, this time in the company of his business associates. The public was once again treated to the sight of professional criminals practicing an especially odious trade with apparent immunity from legal retribution.

Shortly after this, the law of robbery underwent drastic revision. The first major case in this regard was that of Jones, heard in the Old Bailey in 1776.[33] Jones was tried for robbery in circumstances very similar to those of the first Rooke case, with the important difference that the accused was convicted. This different verdict is even more striking in that Jones, unlike Rooke, had not threatened to prosecute his victim, Mitchell Newman. The nature of the threat was contained in the order "Damn you, Sir, stop! For if you offer to run, I will raise a mob about you." An allegation of homosexual behavior was followed by the demand "A present—a present—you must make me a present."[34] Money duly changed hands.

HOMOSEXUAL CONDUCT

In this case, apparently for the first time ever in an English court, allegation of homosexual practices was considered as the single exceptional circumstance to the rule that force or its threat was a definitive characteristic of the crime of robbery. Character assassination of this peculiar sort had at this point in history become so terrifying that the jury felt able to convict Jones because "they thought that such an accusation would strike a man with as much or more terror than if he had a pistol at his head."[35] This view was upheld by the Twelve Judges, who firmly stated their belief that violence, actual or threatened, was not necessary to support a conviction for robbery when this unique type of character threat was demonstrated.

Jones' case has been widely, and correctly, cited as the first occasion on which this revolutionary legal principle was stated and applied.[36] There are, however, one or two difficulties with using the example made of Thomas Jones as the benchmark in this area of law. In the first place, there are a number of earlier cases in which, although some limited physical violence was offered, threatened attack on character in this way was considered as an important aggravating circumstance.[37] It is hard to know just how courts and juries weighed this additional factor. The fact of such accusation, and the possibility that it was true, may have exerted a greater influence on the outcomes of cases than the sparse record of the court suggests.[38] Second, there *was* violence offered to the victim in the Jones case and in another heard shortly after it.[39] This alone could have been used to justify conviction. The Judges admitted this in their discussion of the Jones case but qualified it by stating the new rule that this traditional characteristic of the capital crime of robbery would not in the future have to be present if allegations of homosexual conduct were applied in its stead. The Jones case should therefore be considered properly as a statement of a new principle for future rather than immediate use.

The first instance in which a conviction of this nature was sustained in circumstances where violence was expressly *negated* was in 1779, in the case of James Donelly (variant spellings).[40] In this, the trial court and the Judges acted upon the uncomplicated belief that accusation of unnatural propensities was "equivalent to actual violence; for no violence that can be offered could excite a greater terror in the mind, or make a man sooner part with his money."[41] There were some disturbing features of this well-publicized and most sensational case. Donelly, a publican, had extorted money from the Hon. Charles Fielding, Eton schoolboy and son of the Earl of Denbigh, under threat of prosecuting him on the supposedly false charge of sodomy. The affair came to light when Donelly later encountered Fielding's brother in the street and, mistaking him for his victim, repeated his demands.

Donelly was never executed, even though the judge told him at his sentencing that he had considerably aggravated his case by accusing the two principal witnesses of perjury and the committing magistrate, Sir John Fielding (no relation to the parties prosecuting), of subornation of perjury. Robert Holloway, a contemporary observer of the *demi-monde* at the beginning of the nineteenth century, tells us that Donelly was Charles Fielding's hired lover and that when this fact came to the attention of Fielding's father, the earl, he successfully petitioned the Privy Council for Donelly's reprieve.[42] Initially, the upholding of Donelly's conviction on capital charges by the Twelve Judges was a popular decision.[43] Support for Holloway's contention is given by the indications that Donelly's reprieve, in the face of confirmation of his conviction by the Twelve Judges, reflected a switch in informed public opinion. He was then described by one newspaper as "condemned *unlawfully* by due course of law, and rescued by the Crown from the Twelve Judges."[44] However, it was certainly not the new principle of law that was being challenged here, but rather the propriety of its application in this murky instance.

In the years that followed, the principle was tightened and streamlined. In the case of Staples, heard in the Old Bailey very shortly after that of Donelly, a threat to prosecute for an unnatural crime was considered to be fully the equivalent to standard forms of threat. Staples was convicted and hanged.[45] Hickman's conviction, obtained in 1784 and upheld by the Judges,[46] cleared up any doubts that might have lingered after Donelly regarding the equation of violence and character assassination. Fielding, Donelly's prosecutor, had claimed that he had experienced some fears for his personal safety, even though his persecutor had neither offered nor threatened violence. It was the Judges who decreed that this factor was immaterial in this instance. Hickman's prosecutor, however, expressly denied any such apprehension. Fear of damage to his character alone motivated payment and recognition of the capital nature of this in an undiluted form in the upholding of this conviction by the Twelve Judges.[47] The Hickman case therefore put the emphasis on attack on character rather than threat to prosecute. Because of the clarity of its circumstances, Hickman was the case most usually cited after 1784 to make this point.

The distinctive nature of accusation of homosexuality as character assassination having been firmly established in the law, later cases came to address other alternatives to it and to violence in cases of robbery. In generally rejecting these, the courts in effect reinforced the primacy of the view that this kind of character attack carried a power qualitatively different from any other kind of nonviolent threat. Later cases generally served to emphasize even more strongly the importance of a man's reputation as a heterosexual male as a unique and precious object in the law.

In 1794, the Judges knocked down the blackmail conviction of James Reane on the grounds that the victim had parted with his money for the purpose of bringing a capital prosecution and not out of fear for his person or character.[48] This emphasis on protection of character was restated in 1820 when, in Fuller's case, the Judges for some reason addressed an almost identical circumstance and reached an identical finding.[49]

Elmstead's case, decided in 1802, in one sense extended Hickman, as the Judges upheld the conviction even though the victim's only consideration in handing over the money was to protect his job. In doing so, the Judges gave recognition to at least one practical consequence of damage to character. This outcome was not considered altogether satisfactory, however, and three of the Twelve Judges expressed the minority belief that Hickman should not be taken as a binding legal precedent.[50] An 1808 case dealt the doctrine a more serious blow. The conviction of Cannon and Coddington was upheld, even though the prosecutor had felt himself in no physical danger. He *was* afraid of being prosecuted, which was the threat offered to him. Against the reasoning in the Staples case (see above), the Judges explicitly rejected the notion that a threat to prosecute for sodomy could be equated to the evidence of violence usually required in successful prosecutions for robbery. In taking this position, the Judges were undoubtedly following the principle established in 1796 in Knewland's case. This established the principle that threats to prosecute for capital crimes could in general not be used as a basis for a prosecution for blackmail as robbery. More damaging to the Donelly/Hickman doctrine was the Judges' finding in Cannon and Coddington that the victim's fear of damage to his character would not in itself have justified a capital conviction. This robbery conviction was upheld, but only because the defendants, misrepresenting themselves as police officers, had taken the victim into what he believed to be official custody. In the eyes of the Judges, this constituted "forcible restraint," which they thought *did* constitute a physical threat sufficient to support a conviction.[51]

Setbacks to the new definition of robbery were not serious and were only temporary. Most are seen best as necessary efforts to develop and refine a new concept in law and to tailor it to fit more established principles that applied in the legal interpretation of robbery. The 1802 case of Jackson, Shipley, and Morris, for example, simply affirmed a basic precept of robbery in law (and one noted earlier), that any fear induced by the robber had to be *immediate*. The victim of these three had paid up after having had ample "opportunity of applying to magistrates and others for assistance." Because of this the conviction was overturned.[52]

Cannon and Coddington upheld a conviction but at the same time appeared to strike at the heart of the Donelly/Hickman focus on the protection of character. However, the Twelve Judges' decision in this addressed a hypothetical circumstance not actually present in the case in point. Moreover, their thinking on this does not appear to have been followed in later years. A man named Cane was executed a couple of years later under circumstances in which threat of prosecution was the sole weapon of extortion.[53]

This confused situation was quite temporary, and the wheel quickly turned back. In 1818, James Egerton was convicted at the Old Bailey in a case that involved issues very similar to those raised in the Elmstead case of 1802 (see above). In both, it was the victim's fear of losing a job that were his paramount consideration in acceding to blackmail, and he had no fear of being arrested, prosecuted, or otherwise unjustly punished. Egerton's victim took seriously only his tormentor's threat "that he would swear to his master that the prosecutor wanted to take diabolical liberties with him." Judges in Elmstead had expressed some worry about whether the Hickman precedent of 1784 was binding. In Egerton, Hickman was affirmed explicitly as good law and the principal case in point. One of the Twelve, Baron Graham, had been one of the doubters in Elmstead. This time around he stated that although he believed the Hickman decision to be wrong, he would, then and in the future, support the contrary opinion of the majority.[54]

No significant ruling challenging the legality of construing blackmail under accusation of homosexuality as robbery was made after this date. This new form of robbery had become established by case law. As was common at this time, legal innovations introduced by the courts eventually came to be clarified by statutory enactment. The Extortion Acts of 1823 and 1827[55] extended the circumstances under which attempts to extort could be prosecuted as single (that is, noncapital) felonies. This enabled victims to circumvent the well-known difficulties of misdemeanor prosecutions in those cases in which money had not actually changed hands. At the same time, these acts effectively increased the penalties attending conviction and, as the table shows, prosecutions under them were attended by a very high rate of success.[56]

Only the 1827 act appears to have been drafted with the deterrence of homosexual blackmail in mind. This is suggested by its modification of the earlier legislation to make attempted extortion under accusation of "abominable predelictions" *alone* a variety of attempted robbery. Moreover, it was not just those who alleged homosexual conduct of a *criminal* nature who were addressed. The wording of the act made allegation of virtually any sort of commitment to a homosexual way of life a single felony, when made for the purposes of extortion.

By 1827 then, misdemeanor prosecutions for any sort of blackmail, sexual or otherwise, were certainly possible but were very hard to bring successfully because of the unacceptability of threats to prosecute. The 1823 act made all extortion demands communicated by letter into a single felony, when made under accusation of a crime.[57] It also considered a broad range of demands made in person and incorporated them within the single felony of attempted robbery. The 1827 act changed this by defining attempted blackmail with homosexual connotations alone as attempted robbery. These acts were quite loosely interpreted, and there is evidence that non-capital prosecutions were successfully undertaken under them when the capital form of the offense had occurred.[58] In this sense, they provided prosecutors with an alternative to capital prosecution, perhaps to be used in cases where a jury might be reluctant to invoke the death penalty. However, the acts cannot be seen as representing a more lenient attitude toward blackmailers. Incorporation of homosexual blackmail within the capital crime of robbery was specified in one section of the 1827 act, and capital prosecutions continued under it.[59]

Statute law had caught up with case law. In fact, it had gone beyond it. Since "abominable extortion" was now a form of robbery by statute, questions regarding the extent to which the victim had been put in fear were no longer relevant. This made capital prosecutions easier, as all that now had to be proven was the nature of the allegation and the handing over of money or other property. The decision taken to overturn the decision in Reane's case (see above) and others where victims parted with money for reasons other than fear of loss of reputation no longer applied. Reane's conviction would have been upheld if the case had been heard in 1827 instead of 1794.[60]

Blackmail as a felony thus became embedded in both statute and case law as a crime closely linked to homosexuality. The amount of time and energy spent on it by trial courts, the Twelve Judges, and eventually, the legislature over half a century, beginning in the 1770s, suggests this area of law to have been of more than slight importance. The careful and continuing separation of blackmail involving homosexuality from all other forms of extortion[61] further suggests this crime to have been viewed in a particularly odious light. This view could only have been supportable in a society that had come to disparage homosexuality (at least in men) with an intensity that was unique.

The question remains as to whether this kind of blackmail was pervasive enough to warrant the extreme legal penalties that came to be brought against it. No answer to this can be definitive. Blackmail is an inherently secretive activity. It involves both victim and victimizer in a conspiracy of mutual shame that both have reason to preserve from public view. Scholars of this crime in today's world are cagey about giving estimates of its prevalence, although they agree that it rarely comes to the attention of the courts.[62] Nonetheless, it is acknowledged that its link to homosexuality yet remains.[63]

For the time and place studied here, a stronger conclusion can be drawn.

It is suggested that blackmail of this nature was prevalent, and this prevalence was encouraged by the beliefs of a society that had come to hold homosexuality in the strongest contempt. Three groups of evidence can be used to support this contention. The first concerns the sudden and sustained interest of the law in this crime and is documented above. The second concerns the organized and professional nature of blackmail attempts of this kind, and the third is represented by the large volume of such cases that came before the courts and the way they were treated by the courts.

As noted earlier, the civil and criminal courts of eighteenth-century London were widely held to be corrupt and amenable to various kinds of manipulation for personal profit. These efforts were not, however, generally seen to be associated with crime that was professional and organized. One exception to this was the entwined activities of thieftaking, dealing in stolen property, and prosecuting capital crimes for financial reward. However, when scandals associated with these came to public attention, parties involved were punished to the fullest extent of the law.[64] Tolerance of such corruption between scandals was probably due to the fact that it primarily involved members of the criminal underworld and had little effect on the lives of most honest citizens. Blackmail under allegation of sexual assaults directed at females was rife but it was not the focus of professional criminals and was not generally taken very seriously.[65]

Homosexual blackmail was directly aimed at the respectable classes. A commonly stated belief was that such blackmail was only attempted on those guilty of the behavior of which they were accused. This was the opinion of experts such as Robert Holloway and Richard King.[66] It was also the opinion of Jeremy Bentham.[67] Also widespread was the belief that the considerable number of prosecutions for homosexual blackmail (see below) actually greatly understated the extent of the problem. It was thought that bringing a prosecution of this nature actually served to throw doubt on the morality of the victim.[68] The paradox of this popular association of victimization and guilt was that heterosexual men could be made just as vulnerable to extortion as homosexuals. Nor did an exalted position protect a man from this crime. Reputation was at this time regarded as a valuable and a personal commodity by all classes and was regarded as something to be earned and not inherited through a privileged background.[69] This scenario, and the attendant population of well-off potential victims, was tailormade for professional criminals.

A detailed example, showing both the vulnerability of the innocent, and the sophisticated and organized nature of the crime, is provided by the circumstances of the sustained victimization and related suicide of Lord Castlereagh in 1822. Castlereagh, a prominent member of the government,[70] was in the habit of strolling home from the House in the evening through St. James' Park. Occasionally, he would treat himself to the attractions of one of the young ladies to be encountered there, and, after spending an hour in her company at some nearby hotel, he would wend his way homeward. One night he was unfortunate. He picked up a woman, but at the point when he discovered that she was, quite literally, no lady, the hotel room door burst open and he found himself in the grip of a gang of extortionists. Castlereagh cut his throat some weeks later, after harassment by this gang proved an intolerable addition to his other burdens of mental instability and domestic unhappiness.[71]

The account of Castlereagh's victimization in this version of the badger game indicates the professional nature of the activity. It was slick, well planned, carried out for long-term profit, and involved a number of conspirators. Contemporary accounts of similar crimes, when they are sufficiently detailed, show similar characteristics.[72] A further indicator of blackmail as organized crime are the long careers enjoyed by some blackmailers. George Milward, himself a convicted homosexual, was charged twice for extortion and twice for "sodomitical practices" between 1760 and 1778 and eventually was convicted. His career presumably lasted at least eighteen years.[73] Reference was made earlier to criminals such as the Browns and William Rooke who, before the law of blackmail was revised, practiced their trade with relative impunity in the 1760s and 1770s. Such people existed long after their form of blackmail had become a capital offense.[74] This can only be explained by many victims being discouraged by the publicity and related social costs of bringing a prosecution.

PROSECUTORIAL ENERGY

Although contemporary opinion may have been that this crime was underreported, by today's standards it appears to have occupied a great deal of the time of the courts. This finding is one of implication. The problem with attempts to quantify prosecutions of this nature is that they are usually included with other robbery prosecutions and not identified as cases of blackmail. It is impossible to determine exactly how many of the hundreds of people charged with robbery in the Old Bailey between 1776 and 1830 were in fact being prosecuted for capital blackmail. In Table 1 forty-four prosecutions of this nature have been identified in this period. The conviction rate of 93 percent was extraordinarily high: The conviction rate for accused robbers as a whole rarely exceeded 50 percent.[75] Extortionists convicted of robbery were, moreover, much more likely to face the gallows. In London (the city and Westminster) and Middlesex, the execution rate for all convicted robbers averaged 14 percent between 1776 and 1804 and between 1811 and 1830.[76] As the table shows, the execution rate for blackmailers was several times greater than this.

There is every indication that the figures included in this table grossly underestimate the true extent of capital blackmail prosecutions. Court records and press reports from the period can be exasperatingly cryptic, and it is undoubtedly true that even important cases of this nature cannot now

Table 1
Felony Prosecutions for Blackmail Identified as Heard in The Old Bailey, 1776–1830

Part I

(1) Year	(2)	(3)	(4)	(5)
	Capital Prosecutions			
	Number Prosecuted	Number Guilty	Proportion Guilty	Number Executed
1776	1	1		1
(1777)	3	3		?
(1778)	1	1		0
(1779)	2	2		1
(1780)				
1781				
1782				
1783	1	1		0
1784	1	1		0
(1785)	2	2		?
(1786)	2	2		2
1787				
1788				
1789				
1790	2	2		?
1791				
1792				
1793				
1794	2	2		0
(1795)				
1796	1	1		0
1797				
(1798)	1	1		0
1799				
1800				
1802				
1803				
1804				
(1805)	3	3		0
1806				
1807				
1808	2	2		?
1809				
(1810)				
(1811)	1	1		1
1812				
1813				
1814				
(1815)	1	1		0
(1816)	1	1		1
(1817)	2	1		?

Table 1 (continued)

Part II

(1) Year	(2) Number Prosecuted	(3) Capital Prosecutions Number Guilty	(4) Proportion Guilty	(5) Number Executed	(6) Non-Capital Prosecutions Number Prosecuted	(7) Number Guilty	(8) Proportion Guilty
1819	3	3		?	1	1	
1820	3	3		2	1	1	
1821	1	1		1			
1822	1	1		?	2	2	
1823							
1824							
(1825)	4	2		0	2	2	
(1826)					1	1	
(1827)	1	1		?	1	1	
(1828)					1	1	
(1829)					1	1	
(1830)							
Totals	44	41	0.93	8	12	12	1.00

Note: For reasons discussed in the text, these figures undoubtedly greatly understate the numbers of prosecutions of this kind. Thus the figures should be used to evaluate conviction and execution rates and not the volume of such cases coming before the courts.

For those years marked in (parentheses), newspapers have also been searched.

Proportion of capitally convicted who were executed in those twelve years for which accurate data are available: 9 out of 24 = 0.38

Source: Old Bailey Proceedings, 1730 through 1830; Annual Register, 1758 through 1830; and Gentleman's Magazine, 1731 through 1830. The following texts (cited in full elsewhere in this chapter) were also searched: Carrington & Payne, Reports of Cases Argued; East, A Treatise; Leach, Cases in Crown Law; Russell & Ryan, Crown Cases Reserved; and Woolrych, The History and Results.

be identified as such.[77] Nonetheless, there is one strong body of evidence to show that a high proportion of accused robbers in the Old Bailey were blackmailers. Humphry Woolrych's compilation and analysis of early judicial statistics was published in 1832 and based on Parliamentary manuscripts since destroyed. His account of robbery cases gives some idea of the size of the dark figure of extortion. In considering executions for robbery in London and Middlesex, he separates the number of "abominable extortionists" from other robbers in two years only: 1820 and 1821.[78]

In 1820, two of the eleven robbers executed were extortionists; in 1821, one of ten. If we assume that this proportion of 15 percent was reflected in overall robbery prosecutions in this court, abominable extortion begins to loom large. Of the total of 133 people prosecuted for robbery in these two years, more than twenty could well have been extortionists. This seems a more powerful indicator of antihomosexual taboos than the relatively few sodomites prosecuted on capital charges. In 1820 and 1821, three men were prosecuted for sodomy in the Old Bailey; none were convicted. Between 1776 and 1830, fifty-eight accused sodomites were tried on capital charges. Twenty-one (36 percent) were convicted and fifteen of these (71 percent) were hanged.[79] If we accept the Woolrych proportion of 15 percent, we find that it was alleged blackmailers, not sodomites, who featured most heavily in capital cases involving homosexuality. Between 1776 (the year of the Jones decision) and 1804, 721 people were *convicted* of robbery in all its forms; two or three times this number would have been prosecuted. Between 1811 and 1830, 483 robbers were convicted.[80] Each year then, there were probably three or four extortionists among the twenty-five or so robbers convicted in the Old Bailey. A conviction for sodomy occurred only every two or three years in this court. Convicted extortionists and sodomites had comparably high chances of being executed, much higher than did robbers as a group (see above). Sodomy continued to be a capital offense until 1861. The death penalty for "abominable extortion" was lifted much earlier, in 1837. However, executions in both categories ended around the same time.[81]

The view that it was accusation of homosexuality, and not its practice, that was obsessive is supported by the fact that, in reality if not in theory, the predilections of the victim had considerable bearing on the outcome of a case. James Donelly, it will be remembered, managed to get off in the end, not because he was innocent of the crime, but because it was discovered that his prosecutor had been his lover. The results of the 1760 trial of the Browns have been mentioned in this context, as has the case of Robert Harrold, reprieved in 1778 because of suspicion about the behavior of the prosecutor. Anyone prosecuting an extortionist of this kind had a strong investment in the outcome of the case. His own reputation, as well as the defendant's life, hung in the balance. Many victims must have sympathized with Henry Sharpe, porter and extortion victim, who paid up in 1790 because "I was afraid of my character which is my bread."[82]

It is, therefore, hardly surprising that the most common defense of extortionists was that their victim's behavior had indeed conformed to the accusations made. This was not, strictly speaking, a proper defense in law. The commission of one crime was never thought to justify the commission of another. This was an old common-law principle in general operation[83] but not one specifically applied by the Twelve Judges to cases of blackmail until 1824. In that year, the Judges upheld the conviction in Gardner's case, even though there were strong indications that the prosecutor had behaved in the manner alleged by the defense.[84]

This principle was of relatively little help to the prosecution as most blackmailers made accusations of behaviors which were not in themselves criminal acts. This was a difficult point. Homosexual activities other than sodomy and attempted sodomy (an indictable misdemeanor) were in theory not against the law until 1885.[85] In practice, eighteenth- and early nineteenth-century courts interpreted attempted sodomy (often under the

rubric "assault with intent to commit sodomy" or "sodomitical practices")
very broadly. Prosecutions for this misdemeanor were used successfully to
convict men of propositioning and other forms of homosexual misconduct.[86] The principles embodied in Gardner's case were (as some earlier
examples of the reprieve process suggest) not taken seriously by juries, the
courts, or the Privy Council either before or after 1824. In the following
year, James Dovey and Roger Adams were convicted capitally after a spirited defense devoted almost exclusively to documenting the allegation that
the prosecutor, Hugh Jones, was dedicated to the *frottage* of young boys
in crowds. They appear to have been convicted only because they were
disbelieved. It was planned to execute them one day earlier than others
capitally convicted at the same sessions "in order that public attention
might be drawn in a peculiar manner to the enormity of their offence."
However, when evidence was later produced suggesting that their allegations were true, they were reprieved.[87]

From this it is clear that rights of both defendants and victims in capital
cases of extortion were very loosely enforced. This was not unusual in the
general run of things in the courts of this time and could sometimes be
helpful to the victim. The prosecution could often, and in the face of an
ancient legal principle, introduce evidence that the defendant(s) had been
charged with similar crimes before.[88] However, this flexibility was rarely
advantageous for the prosecution. Professional criminals could often do
more with innuendo and perjury than a prosecutor could do with the truth.

CONCLUSION

The above analysis shows that intense animadversion to homosexuality
showed itself in the English courts from the 1770s, three decades earlier
than is usually supposed. Such intensity is measured by me (as by others
in rather different contexts) as willingness to impose and carry out death
sentences for behavior linked to it. It should not be supposed that society
before the 1770s was particularly tolerant. Reference was made earlier to
periodic raids on gay meeting-places and the consistent way in which the
misdemeanor of attempted sodomy was broadly interpreted in law to prosecute a broad range of homosexual conduct. The taint of homosexuality
was something to be feared throughout the eighteenth century, and there
are many examples of wealthy and aristocratic men being socially ruined,
even hounded out of the country, following such smears.[89] Gangs of professional extortionists, too, were a problem for homosexuals (and for heterosexual men) long before this kind of blackmail became a capital felony.[90]

The point is, however, that before the 1770s, society's contempt for homosexuality was rarely translated into lethal action against its practice and
never against mercenary allegations of it. The low level of capital prosecutions of sodomites was undoubtedly due, not to any great tolerance of
them, but to an unwillingness to take their lives.

This finding is undoubtedly of some historical interest. A larger significance does, however, attach to it. Many explanations of the sudden emergence of virulent antihomosexual feeling have emphasized the circumstances of English society at the very beginning of the nineteenth century. Focus on this setting is justified by its characteristics as the earliest, and perhaps most dramatic, historical example of a society undergoing rapid transformation through the modernization process. Tightened attitudes toward gender relations in general, and homosexuality in particular, are viewed as adaptations to this transformation. An emerging market economy requires a workforce educated to exercise self-control, competitiveness, sobriety, and restraint in dealing with others. Bureaucratic structures (then largely staffed by males) require an organizational personality that is impersonal, unemotional, and cold. Any form of social interaction that embodies lack of restraint subverts the impersonality of the work setting and impedes the socialization of a society transforming itself into a modern world. Unrestrained sexual interaction in general is subversive in this context. Sexual interaction between males is even more so, as it is they who dominate the industrial workplace and its related administrative structures.[91] From these perspectives, the rapidity with which homophobia emerged paralleled the rapidity of the modernization process. It is regarded as part of a general movement toward social control that emphasized the family as the control unit and traditional sex roles within it. Emergence of new areas of power acting upon the psyche are comprehensible in Foucaultian terms as influences that become self-sustaining and ultimately beyond the full control of any dominant social group.[92]

Explanations of restrictions in sexual freedom that apply specifically to England at this time generally refer to the sudden politicization of moral conduct. Class conflict at the very end of the eighteenth century and the early decades of the nineteenth escalated to a point when many feared armed insurrection along the lines of the French Revolution. It is believed that the privileged classes came to associate immorality with revolutionary sentiment and the questioning of accepted moral standards with the questioning of the political status quo.[93] It is also argued that, in making such realizations, the upper classes began a conscious effort to moderate their own licentious behavior in order to justify their position and to set a good example for their social inferiors.[94] The spread of these new standards was reinforced by a growing middle-class presence in the cities and by the demands of a modernizing economy.[95]

Although these explanations undoubtedly have strength, they do not really explain the lethal homophobia documented here as having become established long before the beginning of the nineteenth century. England went through considerable social and economic changes between the 1770s and the 1800s. In the 1770s it had neither bureaucracies nor much of a commitment to a modern market economy. By the first decade of the 1800s, it was well on the way to both.[96] Neither was the 1770s an especially politicized decade. Fears of popular insurrection only arose in Britain after the storming of the Bastille in 1789 raised the real possibility of revolution a little closer to home.[97]

The emergence of lethal homophobia was undoubtedly encouraged by the modernization process, but it is clear from this analysis that its origins precede it. There is some reason to believe that an "ethos of masculinity" developed in eighteenth-century England, a phenomenon with lower-class roots but also strong appeal to the cultural baggage of upper-class and other men. Social structures that attach great importance to traits considered masculine are notoriously unforgiving to those men whose appearance and behavior fails to exhibit these traits.[98]

Regardless of the value of this concept in this context, this study of one area of the criminal law demonstrates that extreme animosity toward homosexuals in English history has a rather longer history than conventional approaches have suggested. The approach taken here is perhaps illustrative of the larger point, that uses of the criminal law as social indicators are best informed by an appreciation of the law's scope and subtlety in addressing conduct that is considered infamous as well as criminal.

NOTES

An early version of this chapter was presented at the annual meetings of the American Society of Criminology, Atlanta, GA, October 1986.

1. Francois Lafitte, "Homosexuality and the Law: The Wolfenden Report in Historical Perspective," *British Journal of Delinquency* 9 (1958): 8–19.

2. See A. D. Harvey, "Prosecution for Sodomy in England at the Beginning of the Nineteenth Century," *Historical Journal* 21 (1978): 939–48. In London and Middlesex, eight sodomites (out of twelve convicted) were executed between 1699 and 1800; fourteen (out of eighteen convicted) were executed between 1801 and 1828; see Humphry Woolrych, *The History and Results of the Present Capital Punishments in England; To Which are Added, Full Tables of Convictions, Executions, Etc.* (London, 1832), 144–45. Four of the early executions were carried out between 1725 and 1730 and were products of the campaigns of the Societies for the Reformation of Manners; Alan Bray, *Homosexuality in Renaissance England* (London, 1982), 89–93.

3. Discussion of attitudes expressed in these popular sources is included in Antony E. Simpson, "Masculinity and Control: The Prosecution of Sex Offenses in Eighteenth-Century London" (Doctoral dissertation, New York University, 1984), 693–741, *passim*. David F. Greenberg includes a review of the literature addressing English social and legal attitudes and reactions in the seventeenth and eighteenth centuries, *The Construction of Homosexuality* (Chicago, 1988), 323–42.

4. This finding does not apply to lesbians. Lesbian activities never have been against English criminal law and usually have been largely ignored by English society; Susan S. M. Edwards, *Female Sexuality and the Law: A Study of Constructs of Female Sexuality as They Inform Statute and Legal Procedure* (Oxford, 1981), 43–45.

5. There are strong indications that eighteenth-century prosecutors, committing magistrates, and grand juries preferred bringing charges that did not carry the death penalty; see Simpson, "Masculinity and Control," 445–48, 453, 462–63, and accompanying tables.

6. See, for example, Jeffrey Weeks, *Sex, Politics and Society: The Regulation of Sexuality since 1800* (London, 1981).

7. Philip Jenkins, "From Gallows to Prison? The Execution Rate in Early Modern England," in *Crime, Police and the Courts in British History*, ed. Louis A. Knafla (Westport, Conn., 1990), 129–49.

8. Organized raids, followed by prosecutions, of molly houses occurred in London in the 1720s; Bray, *Homosexuality*, 89–93. Raids of these establishments and of gay meeting places occurred regularly throughout the century and well into the following century; Simpson, "Masculinity," 483–500.

9. Edward J. Bristow, *Vice and Vigilance; Purity Movements in Britain since 1700* (Dublin, 1977); Randolph Trumbach, "London's Sodomites: Homosexual Behavior and Western Culture in the Eighteenth Century," *Journal of Social History* 11 (1977): 1–33.

10. The word blackmail originally meant payment coerced from farmers in the north of England by border reivers (bandits). It acquired its modern meaning early in the nineteenth century. Before this, the broader term "extortion" was generally used. The word "blackmail" did not appear in the English law until the Theft Act of 1968; Mike Hepworth, *Blackmail: Publicity and Secrecy in Everyday Life* (London, 1975), 7.

11. Antony E. Simpson, "The 'Blackmail Myth' and the Prosecution of Rape and its Attempt in London, 1730 through 1830," *Journal of Criminal Law and Criminology* 77 (1986): 101–50; W.H.D. Winder, "The Development of Blackmail," *Modern Law Review* 5 (1941): 21–50.

12. In another context I have identified twenty-three prosecutions for conduct amounting to extortion heard in the Old Bailey and the City of London Quarter Sessions between 1740 and 1830. Prosecutions were for conspiracy, perjury, or criminal libel. None was for extortion or its attempt. Less than half resulted in convictions; Simpson, "The 'Blackmail Myth,' " 120–21.

13. A. H. Campbell, "The Anomalies of Blackmail," *Law Quarterly Review* 55 (1939): 382–99; E. P. Thompson, "The Crime of Anonymity," in *Albion's Fatal Tree: Crime and Society in Eighteenth-Century England*, ed. Douglas Hay, Peter Linebaugh, John G. Rule, E. P. Thompson, and Cal Winslow (New York, 1975), 255–308. A detailed discussion of the substance of the Black Act, and the patterns of its application, is included in Thompson's *Whigs and Hunters: The Origin of the Black Act* (New York, 1975).

14. A single felony prosecution could be brought against anyone "threatening to accuse any person of any crime punishable by law with death, transportation, pillory, or any other infamous punishment, with a view or intent to 'extort or gain money, goods wares, or merchandizes." (See 30 Geo.II. c. 24 s.1.) It was certainly used against those attempting to extort under allegation of homosexual conduct; see *R. v. Major*, Old Bailey, 1796, in Thomas Leach, *Cases in Crown Law, Determined by the Twelve Judges, by the Court King's Bench, and by the Commissioners of Oyer and Terminer and General Gaol Delivery; from . . . 1730, to . . . 1815*, 4th ed. (London, 1815), 2:772–74.

15. For a discussion of the prevalence of "blood money" conspiracies (and of public awareness of them) throughout the eighteenth century, see Sir Leon Radzinowicz, *A History of English Criminal Law and Its Administration from 1750. Volume 2: The Clash Between Private Initiative and Public Interest in the Enforcement of the Law* (London, 1956), 301–46.

16. Simpson, "The 'Blackmail Myth.' "

17. Simpson, "Masculinity," 842–44.

18. Sir Matthew Hale, *Historia Placitorum Coronae: The History of the Pleas of the Crown* (London, New ed. 1800), 1:532.

19. Decision of the Twelve Judges in *R. v. Donelly* (or Donally), reported in the *Old Bailey Proceedings* (hereafter *OBP*) sessions beginning 19 May 1779.

20. Sir William Blackstone, *Commentaries on the Laws of England* (Oxford, 1765–69), 4:230–32.

21. *R. v. Stride, Miles, and Rudd, OBP*, sessions beginning 2 July 1777 (Case No. 407); *Morning Chronicle*, 5 June and 8 July 1777; *Morning Post*, 21 November 1777. All were convicted, and two of the three executed.

22. "Yet this putting in fear does not imply, that any great degree of terror or affright in the party robbed is necessary to constitute a robbery: it is sufficient that so much force, or threatening by word or gesture, be used, as might create an apprehension of danger or oblige a man: to part with his property without or against his consent"; Blackstone, *Commentaries*, 4:242.

23. *R. v. Taplin OBP*, sessions beginning 28 June 1780 (308); Edward H. East, *A Treatise of the Pleas of the Crown* (London, 1803), 2:712.

24. *R. v. Blackham*, 1787, in East, *A Treatise*, 2:711–12.

25. *R. v. William Brown*, Old Bailey, 1780, in East, *A Treatise*, 2:731. The victim was also advised to give the money "if he would keep the blood within his mouth."

26. Winder, "The Development," 30.

27. The Twelve Judges constituted an informal grouping of judges from the Old Bailey and the assizes of the major criminal courts; only the Court of King's Bench was not represented. The Twelve met on a regular basis to address problematic cases brought to them by their members. It was *not* an appellate court as there was no outside access to it. Decisions of the Twelve were supposedly binding and well documented within the law. This body was a major influence on the development of the law in this period; Sir James F. Stephen, *A History of the Criminal Law of England* (London, 1883), 1:311–12.

28. *R. v. Knewland and Wood*, Old Bailey, 1796, in Leach, *Cases in Crown Law*, 2:721–33, at 730.

29. *R. v. Noke, OBP*, sessions ending 7 December 1751 (33); Corporation of London Sessions *Minute-books* (hereafter *LSMB*), January 1752 (CLRO SM 107–34).

30. *R. v. Rooke, OBP*, sessions ending 13 July 1774.

31. *R. v. Clarke, Pullen, and Rooke, OBP*, sessions ending 13 July 1774.

32. Blackstone, *Commentaries*, 4:230.

33. *R. v. Thomas Jones alias Evans,* "*OBP*," sessions beginning 21 February 1776; Leach, *Cases in Crown Law*, 1:139–42.

34. William O. Russell and Charles S. Greaves, *A Treatise on Crimes and Misdemeanors*, 3rd ed. (London, 1843), 1:885–87.

35. Russell and Greaves, *A Treatise*, 2:886.

36. Sir James Stephen, for example, refers to this case in just this way: *A History*, 3:149.

37. For example, *R. v. Brown and Brown*, Old Bailey, 1760, discussed in *R. v. Thomas Jones, OBP*, sessions beginning 21 February 1776 (211); *R. v. James Brown*, Old Bailey, *Lloyd's Evening Post and British Chronicle*, 16–19 September and 10–12 October 1763.

38. In the 1760 *Brown* and *Brown* case, one defendant was acquitted and the other convicted but reprieved, probably because of the court's obvious suspicion of the sexual preferences of the prosecutor.

39. In a 1778 case that did not go before the Twelve Judges, Robert Harrold, alias Hutton, was convicted of robbery under circumstances of the "abominable allegation" and some limited violence; *OBP*, sessions ending 3 July, 1778; Leach, *Cases in Crown Law*, 1:199. Harrold was later reprieved, and he and one of his confederates subsequently convicted of conspiracy at Westminster Quarter Sessions; *London Evening Post*, 11–14 July 1778.

40. *R. v. Donelly*, Old Bailey, 1779, in East, *A Treatise*, 2:715–28; Leach, *Cases in Crown Law*, 1:193–99.

41. Leach, *Cases in Crown Law*, 2:198.

42. Robert Holloway, *The Phoenix of Sodom, Or the Vere Street Coterie* (London, 1813), 37–38.

43. "God only knows what numberless robberies of this kind would have been perpetrated by these detestable wretches on timorous minds, if their Lordships had been of a different opinion"; *Annual Register* 31, Part 1, (1779): 209.

44. *London Evening Post*, 2–4 September 1779.

45. *R. v. Staples, OBP*, sessions beginning 20 October 1779 (487); *London Evening Post*, 12–14 and 21–23 October, and 4–7 December 1779.

46. *R. v. Daniel Hickman*, Old Bailey, 1784, in East, *A Treatise*, 2:728–29; Leach, *Cases in Crown Law*, 1:278–80.

47. Leach, *Cases in Crown Law*, 1:218.

48. *R. v. Reane*, Old Bailey, 1794, in East, *A Treatise*, 2:734–36; Leach, *Cases in Crown Law*, 2:616–19; Russell and Greaves, *A Treatise*, 2:890–92.

49. *R. v. Fuller, OBP*, 2 December 1819; William O. Russell and Edward Ryan, *Crown Cases Reserved for Consideration; And Decided by the Twelve Judges of England, From the Year 1799 to the Year 1824* (London, 1825), 408–11.

50. Russell and Greaves, *A Treatise*, 2:795.

51. Russell and Ryan, *Crown Cases Reserved*, 146–48.

52. *R. v. Jackson, Shipley, and Morris*, Nottingham Assizes, 1802, in East, *A Treatise*, 2:xxi–xxiv; Leach, *Cases in Crown Law*, 2:618.

53. *The Times*, 21 February 1811.

54. Russell and Ryan, *Crown Cases Reserved*, 375–77.

55. 4 Geo. IV c.54 s.5 and 8 Geo. IV c.29 ss.7 and 9. For discussion of these acts, see Winder, "The Development."

56. This probably reflected the growing reluctance on the part of early nineteenth-century juries in general to bring in guilty verdicts for capital offenses other than murder. Single felony prosecutions naturally would have had much greater chance of success. The table also indicates that single felony prosecutions for blackmail began before passage of the 1823 act. This reflects the greater will-

ingness of courts and juries to consider attempts to blackmail as species of attempted robbery. There is also little doubt that many of these single felony prosecutions represented cases in which a capital offense had been committed but in which the victim (or the committing magistrate) was unwilling to seek the death penalty.

57. The conviction of a man who extorted by a letter accusing his victim of making homosexual "overtures" was overturned in 1824 because the behavior alleged did not constitute one of the crimes specified in the act; R. v. Thomas Hickman, Leicester Assizes, 1824, in William Moody, *Crown Cases Reserved for Consideration; And Decided by the Judges of England. From the Year 1837, to the Year 1844* (London, 1839–44), 1:34–38. If extortion had occurred in person, it could have been prosecuted capitally as robbery if money had changed hands and as a single felony if it had not.

58. For example, *R. v. Whitney*, OBP, 4 April 1823 (518); *R. v. Denman and Mould*, OBP, 9 April 1825. See also the table and the comments on it in the text and in note 56.

59. William Baker was capitally convicted of robbery under these circumstances shortly after the 1827 act was passed; *OBP*, 6 December 1827; *The Times*, 30 November and 7 and 13 December 1827.

60. Sir John Jervis, *Archbold's Summary of the Law Relative to Pleading, and Evidence in Criminal Cases,* (5th ed. (London, 1834), 224–27.

61. An 1837 statute (I Vic. c.87 s.4) continued this trend to its logical conclusion by making blackmail under these particular circumstances a separate and distinct crime from robbery. See also R. v. John and James Taunton, Old Bailey, 1840, in Moody, *Crown Cases Reserved*, 2:118–20.

62. Joseph Isenbergh characterizes its present incidence as "not readily knowable"; "Blackmail from A to C," *University of Pennsylvania Law Review* 141 (1993): 1,905–33, at 1,909. Richard A. Posner's search of the more than three million (primarily appellate) cases in *Westlaw* yielded only 124 instances of blackmail; "Blackmail, Privacy and Freedom of Contract," *University of Pennsylvania Law Review* 141 (1993): 1,817–47, at 1,841–43.

63. Posner calls exposure of homosexuality "a classic blackmail threat" and suggests that up to 10 percent of American homosexuals have been blackmailed at least once in this way; "Blackmail, Privacy." A similar view was held in Great Britain by the Wolfenden Committee, although this was expressed at a time when homosexual behavior was still illegal; Great Britain, Committee on Homosexual Offences and Prostitution, *Report* (London, 1957), 39–41. Post-Wolfenden support for this belief is, however, provided by Hepworth, *Blackmail*, 42, *passim*.

64. Radzinowicz, *A History of English Criminal Law*, 307–46. See also Gerald Howson, *Thief-Taker General: The Rise and Fall of Jonathan Wild* (New York, 1970).

65. Simpson, "The 'Blackmail Myth.' "

66. Robert Holloway, *The Phoenix of Sodom*; Richard King, *The New Cheats of London Exposed: Or, The Frauds and Tricks of the Town Laid Open to Both Sexes* (London, 1780), 91.

67. Jeremy Bentham's Essay on "Paederasty," ed. Louis Crompton, *Journal of Homosexuality* 3 (1978): 383–405; 4 (1978): 91–107.

68. For example, one account deplored the low number of prosecutions for this

crime and attributed it to victims' fear of being "suspected of impure associations," *The Times*, 13 January 1829.

69. Social emphasis on reputation and character was reflected in the criminal process. John M. Beattie discusses the great extent to which the courts valued this quality in the defendants, prosecutors, and witnesses who came before them; *Crime and the Courts in England 1660–1800* (Princeton, 1986), 440–49.

70. At the time of his death he was the Foreign Secretary. He was Secretary of State for War for a long period during the Napoleonic Wars.

71. H. Montgomery Hyde, *The Strange Death of Lord Castlereagh* (London, 1959), especially 182–90.

72. One such account documents the persecution of Edward Walpole, brother of Horace; *A Genuine Narrative of the Conspiracy of Kather, Kane, Alexander, Nickson, Etc. Against the Hon. Edward Walpole, Esq.* (London 1751). Another group was said to have victimized over 500 men; *R. v. Jones, OBP*, sessions beginning 21 February 1776 (211). When arrested, a third was found to have used up one quire and a half (36 sheets) of paper in writing blackmailing letters to "Gentlemen of Distinction"; *Whitehall Evening Post, Or, London Intelligencer*, 20–22 November 1755. Examples such as this are documented for the entire century.

73. *R. v. Milward, LSMB*, January 1765, May 1766, July 1778; Corporation of London *Sessions Files*, December 1760 (CLRO SF 768–1123).

74. Between August 1826 and March 1828, William Tomes was involved in three blackmail attempts that resulted in his name being widely publicized. In spite of this, he apparently never was convicted of a related crime; *The Times*, 7 August 1826, 13 August 1827, 28 March 1828.

75. The conviction rate for all those accused of robbery in the Old Bailey between 1776 and 1804 and between 1811 and 1830 was 27 percent. Between 1811 and 1830 alone it was 47 percent; Simpson, "Masculinity," 842–44.

76. Ibid.

77. Reports of the landmark Egerton case (see above) appearing in *The Times* and in the *Old Bailey Proceedings* do not identify it as one of blackmail; *The Times*, 24 September 1816.

78. Woolrych, *The History and Results*, 159.

79. Simpson, "Masculinity," 829–31.

80. Ibid., 842–44.

81. The last execution of a sodomite appears to have been in 1835; Harvey, "Prosecutions," 941.

82. *R. v. Platt and Roberts, OBP*, sessions beginning 8 December 1790 (35).

83. Blackstone, *Commentaries*, 4:27.

84. *R. v. Gardner*, Gloucester Assizes, 1824, in F. A. Carrington and J. Payne, *Reports of Cases Argued and, Ruled at Nisi Prius n the Courts of King's Bench and Common Pleas and on the Circuit, from . . . 1823, to . . . 1841* (London, 1825–41), 1:479.

85. Lafitte, "Homosexuality," 18–19.

86. Simpson, "Masculinity," 464–82.

87. *R. v. Dovey and Adams, OBP*, 18 February 1825; *The Times*, 27 March and 18 April 1825.

88. For example, *R. v. Platt and Roberts, OBP*, sessions beginning 8 December 1790 (35). General statements of this rule regarding the inadmissibility of the "gen-

eral disposition" of the defendant to commit the crime in point do, however, suggest that it was applied with considerable flexibility in both civil and criminal cases. For instance, see Jervis, *Archbold's Summary*, 109–13.

89. William Benbow, *The Crimes of the Clergy, Or the Pillars of Priest-Craft Shaken* . . . (London, 1823); Christopher Sykes, *Black Sheep* (London, 1982), 240–50.

90. A series of trials in 1744 showed that such gangs had long operated in St. James's Park: *R. v. Shaddows and Ruggles; R. v. Ruggles, Smith, and Cheworth; R. v. Smith, Jackson, and Pinker, OBP*, sessions beginning 5 December 1744. James Dalton, street robber and avowed homophobe, boasted in the 1720s of victimizing men in this way as a matter of routine; *A Genuine Narrative of All Street Robberies Committed since October Last, by James Dalton, and his Accomplices* (London, 1728), 31–32. When convicted of extortion in 1735, "Small Coal Moll" Partridge's long career in this area was attested to by the fact that he or she had been a witness at a trial for sodomy nine years earlier, as a result of which three men were hanged; *Select Trials for Murders, Robberies, Rapes, Sodomy, Coining, Frauds, and Other Offences: At the Sessions-House in the Old Bailey . . . from the Year 1720 to 1732* . . . (London, 1734/35), 2:193–97; *Country Journal: Or, The Craftsman*, 25 October 1735. Concern for extortion is indicated by amendment of the Black Act in 1757, to incorporate some of its forms (see note 14 and accompanying text). In 1779 (the year of the Donelly decision), the Lord Chief Justice "with great energy observed that it was a specious mode of robbery (that) of late grows very common"; quoted in Lafitte, "Homosexuality," 16.

91. For a review of these and other theories relating homophobia to the requirements of an emerging modern world, see Greenberg, *The Construction of Homosexuality*, especially 347–96 and 434–54, and Weeks, *Sex, Politics and Society*.

92. See Michel Foucault, *Discipline and Punish: The Birth of the Prison*, trans. Alan Sheridan (New York, 1977), and particularly, *The History of Sexuality. Volume 1: An Introduction*, trans. Robert Hurley (New York, 1978).

93. Bristow, *Vice and Vigilance*, 32–44.

94. Eric Trudgill, *Madonnas and Magdelens: The Origins and Development of Victorian Social Attitudes* (New York, 1976), 159–203.

95. Lyn H. Lofland, *A World of Strangers: Order and Action in Urban Public Space* (New York, 1973).

96. Asa Briggs, *The Age of Improvement, 1783–1867* (New York, 1959).

97. Trudgill, *Madonnas and Magdelens*, 29–34, 166–67.

98. For exploration of the "masculinity ethos" see Simpson, "Masculinity." For an extended summary of it, see Simpson, "The 'Blackmail Myth.' "

Henry Mayhew and the Criminal Classes of Victorian England: The Case Reopened

David Englander

Mr. Henry Mayhew, called in; and Examined.
q.3471. Mr. Monckton Milnes. WHAT is your occupation? I am an author.
q.3472. Have you given much attention to the question of crime and criminals . . . ?—Yes . . . I have been attending to the subject, directly and indirectly, for the last six or seven years. I have attended to it not only by association with the criminals themselves, but also by employing persons in collecting information and making general statistics for me. I have generally two clerks continually engaged upon that subject. I have also in visiting the prisons.
q.3473. Did anything lead you especially to take an interest in that subject?—Nothing more than it being part of my business so to do; it is part of my profession. I am devoting myself to an inquiry among the lower orders of people generally, and I have taken such steps as I believe to be necessary for studying their characters, and their habits and dispositions, simply, so to speak, in a scientific point of view. [*2nd Report of the Select Committee of the House of Commons on Transportation* 1856 (296), XVII.]

The Henry Mayhew, who appeared before the Select Committee on Transportation in 1856, was a celebrated figure who had established himself as something of an authority on social questions. His reputation rested in no small part upon the close relations he enjoyed with the criminal classes. The police, he told Honorable Members, "know very little, so to speak, of the homes and inward feelings of the criminals, and generally speaking have but little consideration of them."[1] With our author it was otherwise. "Upon what experience do you found all these opinions?" asked Sir John Pakington. "I mean your actual experience of the criminal class." "Being among them, and continually seeing them," Mayhew replied.[2] "Although I have had them in my home," he continued, "they have never taken a sixpence from me. I never lost a sixpence by the most desperate criminals, and I never knew a man tell me an untruth." [3] But it is Mayhew the sociologist who attracts most scholarly attention. Mayhew the criminologist, by contrast, remains a subject in search of a historian. Not that his writings are unknown or unused. Far from it. Were we so dull as to create one, our citations index doubtless would confirm his status as a standard source for criminal justice history. Students of criminal ecology, having rescued him from the condescension of positivist criminology, commend his insights and the originality of his contribution. [4] Others hold Mayhew in such high regard as to make him "the essential foundation" of their work. [5] Skeptics, in the main a charitable lot, tend to itemize his errors, counsel caution, and tread carefully. Tobias, though dubious about aspects of Mayhew's over-elaborate classification of the criminal class, concludes that "there is no doubt that he was describing something that really existed." Emsley is not so sure. The contradictions and confusions in the scheme of classification raised questions in his mind about Mayhew's methods and possible misrepresentation of the information he received. [6]

The most devastating piece of criticism, though, comes from F. B. Smith, who, in an extraordinary piece of detection, traced one of Mayhew's convict informants through the archives in Tasmania and London and was able to show disturbing discrepancies between the artful dodger as represented in Mayhew's report and the criminal described in judicial records. The implication of this case is not that Mayhew should be handled with care but that he should not be handled at all! [7] Such a conclusion would be rash. One case does not supply a basis for generalization. Besides, there are other ways of looking at Mayhew's writings and other questions to ask of them. The growth of interest in the study of punishment, criminal justice, and social regulation, for example, suggests an alternative framework within which Mayhew's work might be located. [8] Mayhew's criminological writings not only have much to say about the cultural and intellectual life of Victorian England, but they also enable us to make more sense of Mayhew himself.

Henry Mayhew baffled his contemporaries as still he baffles us. A literary hack and humorist, and a master of scissors-and-paste journalism, he was also the author of an acclaimed sociological inquiry that is vivid and compelling and a major contribution to empirical studies of poverty. Biographical details are few and contradictory. One contemporary had him dying in relative obscurity; another dwelt upon his well-attended funeral and continuing popularity. Athol Mayhew began work on a study to set the record straight. But the son, like the father, was better at projecting studies than finishing them, and the "connected account" of Henry Mayhew's "literary labours" remained unwritten. [9] It is the metaphor of the social explorer in a distant land that seemed to summarize Mayhew's identity and achievement. "He was," said one obituarist, "the originator of that school of journalistic philanthropists of which Mr Besant and Mr Sims, Mr Clark Russell and Mr James Greenwood, are now the popular representatives."[10]

In his prime, though, he was more than that. G. J. Harney, editor of the Chartist journal, the *Red Republican*, readily commended Mayhew's "excellent letters" on "Labour and the Poor."[11] Jevons considered him essential reading. Workers, thrust from under the shadows, cast him as their liberator. More effusive still was the Reverend Robert Montgomery, who declared that *London Labour and the London Poor* had opened his eyes and his heart to the suffering in their midst.[12] Beatrice Webb, by contrast, dismissed his work as "good material spoilt by bad dressing."[13] "It is really a mass of incidents of low life, told with dramatic intensity and simplicity by the actors themselves," wrote a like-minded critic, "but it fails to gather up its facts into any connected statement, or to point the way towards any solution of one of the greatest problems of modern civilization."[14] Modern assessments are equally varied. One school criticizes his allegedly maverick methods, the unrepresentative character of his material, and the unreliability of his conclusions.[15] Another insists that his work has been ignored, his achievement undervalued, and his stature diminished. An army of redressers has rediscovered, revised, and reprinted, in whole or in part, the missing items that, it is claimed, restore his reputation as one of the most creative and significant of social investigators.[16]

The difficulty with all such assessments is that they are based upon a highly selective reading of Mayhew's writings. Skeptics, reliant in the main upon the published text of *London Labour and the London Poor*, have no problem in exposing its undeniable deficiencies. No less partial are their critics, who, though seeking to extend the canon by inclusion of the letters serialized in the *Morning Chronicle*, are still prone to abstract from the millions of words that he published only a fraction of his output. The tendency, common in all forms of Mayhew criticism, to detach the author from the totality of his writings does, however, create problems. The Harrison-Himmelfarb view emphasizes the faults at the expense of the virtues. The alternative view, though, is equally misleading. The Mayhew, rediscovered and reclaimed for posterity, is the Mayhew of 1849–50, the irreverent social investigator, whose curiosity, sympathy, insight, and imagination carried him almost beyond the boundaries of political economy. The Mayhew presented by E. P. Thompson and Eileen Yeo has sloughed off the ideas and attitudes of his bourgeois origins and harnessed the commercial considerations of the jobbing journalist to a higher social purpose. The Mayhew thus created was uniquely close to working people and their immediate concerns, trusted for his commitment and counsel, and at least deserving of consideration for a place in the pantheon of the proletariat. The question, then, naturally arises: Why did he proceed no further?

It has been suggested that Mayhew simply was not bright enough to convert his empirical observations into meaningful social theory. Eileen Yeo tells us that he lacked the colossal brain of a Marx necessary for such a purpose and so never realized his true potential. We are thus left with a "Mayhew moment" or a turning point that failed to turn.[17] E. P. Thompson, her collaborator, though keen to rehabilitate the author of *London Labour and the London Poor* as a systematic sociologist, was uncomfortably conscious of additional defects in Mayhew's makeup. For Thompson, indeed, the problem was one of personality rather than of intellect and of the coexistence of a set of approved enlightened activities alongside certain socially regressive attitudes and opinions. The latter, however, were not addressed. The likelihood of having exaggerated the triumph over social origins, and the consequent recognition that the distance between Mr. Mayhew and Mr. Podsnapp was not so great after all, was simply too difficult to contemplate. Mayhew's chauvinism, pomposity, and prudishness were noted as regrettable lapses without further comment.[18] The censorious exposure of cunning beggars and critique of indiscriminate alms-giving, which made *London Labour and the London Poor* recommended reading by the Charity Organization Society, or the numerous passages of commonplace middle-class moralizing that punctuate Mayhew's sociological writings, are either passed over in silence or dismissed as "uncharacteristic."[19]

Neither account is satisfactory. The suggestion that Mayhew's sociological writings were the product of some personal identity crisis that required him to step out with the middle class seems likely to remain an interesting but undocumentable speculation. His sociological and nonsociological writings, taken in tandem, supply the basis for a rather different interpretation, which enables us to locate him within the mainstream rather than on the margins of middle-class social reform movements. Mayhew, it will be argued, is better understood not as some deracinated type but as a figure firmly rooted within his class and its outlook. The unknown Mayhew is not the Mayhew of the *Morning Chronicle*, nor the foreigner-hating, flag-waving, anti-Semitic, puffed-up Englishman whose bourgeois prejudices persisted in spite of his experiences as a social investigator. Mayhew was both. There was no dual personality; they are two sides of the same coin. Once this is appreciated, the the task of revision can begin.

JOURNALIST AND SOCIAL INVESTIGATOR

Henry Mayhew was born on 25 November 1812, the son of Joshua Mayhew and his wife, Mary Ann Fenn. His father, a successful London solicitor, was a stern, autocratic paterfamilias; his mother, a mere cipher. Seven of the seventeen Mayhew children were boys. All joined their father's practice and all, with one exception, abandoned the law for journalism. From the little we know of them, the brothers Mayhew appear to have been spirited sorts who disregarded their father's wishes—but not his allowances—to pursue literary and theatrical interests, turning out popular farces, almanacs, comic novels, travel accounts—anything for which there was a ready market—and contributing to regular newspapers and journals while participating in the founding and editing of miscellaneous money-making ventures. Most were failures. None of the Mayhew brothers had any business sense; two were bankrupts, and all seem to have experienced a good deal of financial insecurity. In the case of the eldest, it led to tragedy. Thomas Mayhew, editor of the radical *Poor Man's Guardian*, who died by his own hand in 1834, was also unusual in his complete identification with the popular radical movement. The descent of his siblings was less steep.

Headstrong Henry, having dropped out of respectable society, fell into a middle-class bohemia where he came into contact with Thackeray, Dickens, and Douglas Jerrold, whose daughter, Jane, he married in 1844. It was a comfortable, convivial, and creative environment peopled by dramatists, journalists, and witty, talented types, meeting in pubs and clubs, scribbling satires, and dreaming up all sorts of theatrical and literary projects.[20] Some faces were familiar. The illustrated comic weekly, *Figaro in London*, which Mayhew edited between 1835 and 1839, was owned by his Westminster contemporary and one-time partner Gilbert Beckett. *Punch*, the climax of such ventures, was founded in 1841, and although Mayhew was ousted from the editorial chair in 1842, he continued his association with the journal until 1845. Twelve months later, Mayhew, like Beckett before him, was bankrupted. The next three years witnessed a desperate casting around for cash. There followed several pot boilers, written in collaboration with his brother Gus, before fortune again smiled in October 1849, with the invitation from the editors of the *Morning Chronicle* to act as the metropolitan correspondent for its national investigation of "Labour and the Poor."

With this appointment began the three serial inquiries, conducted during the next five years, which together constitute the Mayhew survey as it will be described below. In 1849–50, Mayhew produced some eighty-two letters for the *Morning Chronicle*, about a million words in all, devoted primarily to the condition of the London manufacturing trades. In the next two years, he published the equally weighty *London Labour and the London Poor*, an investigation in sixty-three weekly parts of the metropolitan street trades. Included on the wrappers was a correspondence column, which foreshadowed the attempted critique of political economy that was developed in *Low Wages*, a separate part-work, also published in 1851, which folded after four issues. The same fate befell the *Great World of London*, a projected panorama, which appeared in monthly installments between March and November 1856. Its most substantial legacy, the partially finished survey of the prison population, was later completed with outside assistance and published in book form in 1862.[21] All three inquiries were closely connected. About a third of the material published in the *Morning*

Chronicle was incorporated in *London Labour and the London Poor*, which also supplied the key reference for the sequel, *The Criminal Prisons of London.*[22]

Mayhew's brief was to provide a reliable account of the earnings of laboring London. The survey population for this purpose included:

all those persons whose incomings are insufficient for the satisfaction of their wants—a want being, according to my idea, contra-distinguished from a mere desire by a positive physical pain, instead of a mental uneasiness, accompanying it. The large and comparatively unknown body of people included in this definition I shall contemplate in two distinct classes, viz., the *honest* and *dishonest* poor; and the first of these I propose subdividing into the striving and the disabled—or in other words, I shall consider the whole of the metropolitan poor under three separate phases, according as they *will* work, they *can't* work and they *won't* work.[23]

The trades were largely self-selecting. The weavers of Spitalfields, dock-laborers, and slop clothing workers, universally acknowledged as paradigmatic low-wage trades, supplied an obvious starting point. Attention then shifted to those artisanal trades where, in consequence of the reorganization of the social relations of production, the degradation of working conditions and deterioration of living standards was most pronounced. Included here were the tailors, hatters, boot and shoemakers, carpenters, joiners, and cabinet makers; excluded were the metal and engineering trades, precision manufacturers, and printing and paperwork. Unskilled laborers and service workers were underrepresented. Domestic service, the largest single source of employment, was omitted.[24]

The want of "trustworthy information" that supplied the rationale for the inquiry posed formidable problems.[25] The growth of the statistical movement, as Michael Cullen has shown, was an expression of middle-class anxieties provoked by the narrow informational basis of the Condition of England Question.[26] Mayhew, though not part of any of the various social reform networks, was closer to the mainstream than is sometimes suggested. The great parliamentary inquiries of the period did not pass over him as the Angel of Death had passed the Children of Israel. Mayhew, like Engels, was an assiduous reader of official publications. The reports of police authorities, poor law commissioners, the registrar-general, factory inspectors, and other regulatory agencies were scrutinized for evidence and argument, and their strengths as well as their defects readily were exposed. The blue-book sociology that framed the values, assumptions, and concepts of contemporaries also supplied the point of departure for his particular method of social inquiry. The possibilities of a scientific representation of the social order obtained through detailed direct personal testimony seized his imagination. Mayhew's solution was to combine the ethos and interrogative approach of the royal commission with the reporting skills of the journalist. The technique, perfected in *London Labour and the London Poor*, enabled him to justify the work as "the first commission of inquiry into the state of the people undertaken by a private individual, and the first 'blue book' ever published in twopenny numbers."[27]

The sanitary science, which in London, as in Paris, thrived on the panic provoked by the conjunction of cholera and crime and the displaced fears of social change expressed by them, provided another point of reference. Mayhew, who had spent time in the French capital, knew of the work of the public hygienists, and wrote as though his readers might be familiar with Thenard's researches or with toxicologists like D'Arcet, whose work was published in the *Annales d'hygeine publique*.[28] Here, too, perhaps, he first encountered the work of Alexander Parent-Duchatelet, a one-time editor and authority on sewerage and industrial hygiene, who was also the author of *De la prostitution dans la ville de Paris* (1836), which Mayhew cites with approval.[29] Parent-Duchatelet's extraordinary study of the pathology of Paris reveals an intellectual framework of public inquiry that was well in advance of developments in England. Parent-Duchatelet was remarkable in his use of social statistics and in the path-breaking application of field observation and personal interview to social research. The point at which Mayhew read the Frenchman remains to be established. What is clear, though, is that he fully shared contemporary concerns in respect of the connection between laboring and dangerous classes. His survey, defined as a fact-gathering exercise on wages and incomes, addressed a particular debate on poverty and criminality and the reestablishment of social order.

The requirements of the work led him into strange company. Laborers were summoned by cab to the newspaper offices; testimonies were taken at public meetings, in the workplace, in private interviews held in trade societies, and in small gatherings in low-lodging houses. Mayhew consorted with coal heavers and convicts, spoke with street walkers and slop workers, fraternized with beggars, visited the poor at home, and even received them in Mrs. Mayhew's parlor! The extraordinary rapport that developed between writer and audience found expression in the letter columns of the *Morning Chronicle* and in the pathetic appeals from distressed needlewomen, the wives of impoverished railway guards, and like-minded correspondents, who cast him as a finder of jobs and distributor of alms.[30] These roles he was not willing to perform. Mayhew's mission, as he himself defined it, was to act as an intermediary between the classes and to explain to one half how the other half lived. The keeping of low company was a requirement of social science, not evidence of weakened class loyalties. "To this middle class we ourselves belong," he wrote, "and, if we ever wandered out of it, we did so but to regard the other forms of life with the same eyes as a comparative anatomist loves to lay bare the organism and vital machinery of a zoophyte, or an ape, in the hope of linking together the lower and the higher forms of animal existence."[31]

The powerful and compelling quality of the Mayhew survey, though it drew something from his widening social sympathies and the use of open-ended questions, owed more to the ways in which the interviews were written up. Mayhew insisted that the experiences told to him were taken down on the spot and "repeated to the public in the selfsame words in which they were told to me."[32] The language of the poor it may have been; spontaneous it was not. To be sure, the actors were unscripted, but the production was carefully staged. Cues were given and the audience prepared for the lines about to be delivered. Eileen Yeo and Anne Humphreys have noted also the heightened effect created by the elimination of the reporter's questions and the presentation of each interview as if it were an autobiographical statement in the "voice" of the worker.[33]

Mayhew was assisted by his brother Augustus and two former London city missionaries, who acted as stenographers. He also employed a "clerk" to help with the preparation of statistics and collation of information.[34] Interviews generally began with questions about wages and working conditions. No reliable wage series existed when Mayhew began his inquiry. Employers small and large, who paid the lowest wages, were generally uncooperative. Workers, though helpful, were poor record keepers, "and it is only with considerable difficulty and cross-questioning that one is able to obtain from them an account of the expenses necessarily attendant upon their labour, and so, by deducting these from the price paid to them, to arrive at the amount of their clear earnings."[35] Mayhew, in an attempt to construct the average rate of wages, took extraordinary pains to secure reliable information. Assuming that his informants were "naturally disposed" to understate their earnings and that his readers expected them to do so, he explained his procedure thus:

My first inquiries are into a particular branch of the trade under investigation upon which the workman is engaged. I then request to be informed whether the individual has his or her work first or second-handed; that is to say, whether he or she obtains it direct from the employer, or through the intervention of some chamber or piece-master. If the work comes to the operative in question second-handed, I then endeavour to find out the prices paid for the work itself to the first hand, as well as the number of work people that the first hand generally employs. This done, I seek to be informed whether the work of the individual I am visiting is piece or day work. If day work, I learn the usual hours of labour per day, and the rate of wages per week. If it be piece-work, I request to be made acquainted with the prices paid for each description of work *seriatim*, the time that each particular article takes to make, and the number of hours that the party usually works per day. By these means I arrive at the gross daily earnings. I then ascertain the cost of trimmings, candles, and such other expenses as are necessary to the completion of each particular article; and, deducting these from the gross gains per day, I find what are the clear daily earnings of the individual in question. I then check this account by obtaining from the workman a statement as to the number of such articles that he can make in a week; and, deducting expenses, I see whether the clear weekly earnings agree with those of the clear daily ones. After this I request to know the amount of the earnings for the last week; then those for the week before; and then those for the week before that. Beyond this point I find that the memory generally fails. Out of the scores of operatives that I have now visited, I have found *only one* instance in which the workman keeps a regular account of his weekly gains . . .

When I have obtained an account of the clear earnings of the workpeople during such times as they are fully employed, I seek to procure from them a statement of what they imagine to be their weekly earnings, taking one week with another, throughout the year. Having got this I then set about to discover how often in the course of the year they are "standing still", as they term it. I inquire into the number and duration of "the slacks". This done, I strive to obtain from the operative an average of the weekly earnings during such times. I then make a calculation of the total of the workpeople's gains when fully employed for so many months, and when partially occupied for the remainder of the year. By this means I am enabled to arrive at an average of their weekly earnings throughout the whole year; and I then compare this with the amount I have previously received from them on the subject. . . . I finally check the whole account of their earnings by a statement of their expenditure. I generally see their rent-book, and so learn the sum that they pay for rent; and I likewise get a detail of their mode and cost of living inquired into, especially with regard to the truthfulness, industry and sobriety of the individual.[36]

The personal visits and lengthy interviews with operatives required to elicit income data were perhaps the most time-consuming part of the whole inquiry. The bias toward the skilled worker, which has drawn criticism in some quarters, owed as much to his developed record-keeping practices as to any other virtues. The comparative expenditure of time and effort in securing reliable information on earnings made Mayhew appreciative of the intelligent artisan and, above all, of the "Society" man, who could supply more readily standard list prices and other essential documents. One such informant, who "placed in my hands a variety of statistical papers connected with the trade," was, he concluded, "a person of superior understanding." The difference between those who stored information on paper and those who relied purely upon memory was for Mayhew and his associates a personal as much as a cultural consideration. "Indeed," he wrote, "the change from the squalor, foetor and wretchedness of the homes of the poor people that I had lately visited, to the comfort, cleanliness and cheerfulness of the operative tailors, has been as refreshing to my feelings as the general sagacity of the workmen has been instrumental in the lightening of my labours."[37]

Mayhew, though, was concerned with more than the calculation of wage rates. The survey, undertaken at a key moment in the transformation of the urban economy, recorded the changes in manufacturing activity associated with the expansion of the sweated industries. Captivated by the articulate artisans with whom he consorted, Mayhew developed a quite remarkable understanding of the cultural and material changes that flowed from the increasing degradation of labor. Before Marx, there were few who had a better grasp of its defining elements. Mayhew, who spent time in the workshops and petty manufactures, separates work into its constituent parts and proceeds from an analysis of the labor process to chart the changes in the division of labor in order to show how labor power has become a commodity organized and cheapened to suit the needs of its purchasers. He describes the disruption of the labor market, the expansion of the sweated, slop, or dishonorable sector, and the varying forms of work process, work organization, and wage payment that were applied to increase labor productivity.[38]

Mayhew's comparative method—the cross-checking of statements and juxtaposition of empirically grounded conclusions with received truths—did not yield necessarily reliable results, but it did make the investigator increasingly critical of official sources of information and the explanatory framework into which they were organized. In particular, he became skeptical of the representation of society as a spontaneous and self-adjusting order, and he began to doubt whether prevailing economic arrangements were either natural or necessary.[39] The gloomy implications of the Malthusian theory of population and its rationalization of the subsistence theory of wages struck him as both vicious and contentious. He took up arms against the wage-fund theory and ridiculed the view, imputed to J. S. Mill, that "there is no hope for the working men of this country until they imitate the Catholic priests and register vows in Heaven of perpetual celibacy."[40]

Mayhew not only documented the downward pressures on the artisan at work, but he also recorded the sense of loss experienced by the destruction of craftsmanship and the communities it sustained. The silk weavers of Spitalfields, "formerly, almost the only botanists in the Metropolis," with their once-flourishing entomological, floricultural, and mathematical societies, exemplify the severance of science and art and the despair among craft workers at the loss of skill, independence, and control.[41] He was just as concerned with the social relations of production, with the values, beliefs, and assumptions of his informants, with their traditions and memories, and with the connection between their work and their way of life. Taking his cue from the craft trades, he recorded the enormous cultural variations between skilled and unskilled occupations and how these distinctions affected their corporate consciousness and political outlook. He noted, with respect to the waterside trades, how regularity of habits was incompatible with irregularity of income. He notes, too, how different groups of workers respond to technical and economic change and the pressures that transformed coal whippers into special constables and costermongers into Chartists.

Mayhew knew the criminal class as Moses knew his Maker. "Scarcely a day passes," he told the Select Committee on Transportation, "but I . . . either see them or have communications from them."[42] His celebrated classification of "beggars, thieves, prostitutes, cheats and swindlers" into upwards of one hundred specific groups and his account of the criminal quarter were based on personal observation and personal testimony. *London Labour and the London Poor* includes more than a dozen life histories in which offenders recount their experiences, disclose their procedures, and detail their progression from juvenile delinquent to professional criminal.

Moving from the streets to the prisons and reformatories, Mayhew explored how the prison operated and how it was organized. *The Criminal Prisons of London*, which is simply an extension of the previous inquiry, provides a detailed description of penal institutions and, like its predecessor, includes statistical information of considerable interest. It also touches upon the evolution of the criminal, the deficiencies of police statistics, recidivism, and the causes of criminality. *The Criminal Prisons of London* is, however, a text that says as much about civil society as about the penal system. The prison population, so often viewed as an undifferentiated mass, is here disaggregated and presented as men, women, and juveniles whose condition highlights the place of punishment and prison in the social system. New punishment regimes were examined, the jails and methods of the organization of penal life scrutinized, and the prison assessed as both school and factory. Direct personal testimony taken from inmates, ticket-of-leave men, and young offenders as always makes compelling reading and reinforces the connection between prisoners and civilians.

SOCIAL INVESTIGATION AND SOCIAL THEORY

The disjuncture between the process of production and wealth creation as represented by political economy and the exploitation revealed by his investigations into the manufacturing trades raised questions that Mayhew felt impelled to answer. Having been led to the view that inadequate remuneration rather than inefficient expenditure was the principal cause of poverty, he switched attention from observation to analysis.

Apart from a well-thumbed copy of Mill's *Principles of Political Economy*, the key texts were those of Smith and Ricardo. Mayhew also read Charles Babbage's *Economy of Machinery and Manufacturers* (1832), Adam Ure's *Philosophy of Manufacturers* (1835), Chalmers, possibly McCulloch, and others.[43] Of the unorthodox economists, there was no mention. The writings of the Ricardian socialists, who between 1820 and 1840 advanced the claim of labor to the whole product of industry, seems to have passed him by. So he began with Mill's statement that the rate of wages was determined by the law of demand and supply and sought its refutation and reformulation from the standpoint of workers as observed in the productive process. His definition of wages as the ratio of the re-muneration of the laborer to the quantity of the work performed differed markedly from the orthodox view in which wages depended on the pro-portion between population and capital and enabled him to focus attention on employer strategies for controlling the labor process to show how the supply and remuneration of labor was affected by organizational systems, wage systems, and the mechanization of production rather than by any increase in population. His conclusion, badly summarized, was that over-work rather than overpopulation was the more influential cause of the surplus of labor.

Mayhew located the crux of the problem in a growing disequilibrium between the funds available for the maintenance of labor and the funds absorbed by capital. His conclusions, though, were almost as pessimistic as those of the classical economists. He envisaged a future of increasing competition in which the relentless downward pressure on wages and em-ployment provoked crises of overproduction and underconsumption, dis-tress, and disturbance. No relief was possible, he argued, until wages were made to better reflect the value created by the worker. Justice, rather than the market, should rule, and the workman should receive a fairer share of the "increased value that . . . [he] . . . by the exercise of his skill, gives to the materials on which he operates."[44] What was required, then, was a "new partnership" between "the man of money and the man of muscles."[45] The reconciliation of the classes through the development of an equitable wage system, he concluded, would best secure material and moral pro-gress.[46]

Mayhew's claim to revise economic theory in the light of the evidence he had collected—to be, in his own words, "the first who has sought to evolve the truths of the Labour Question by personal investigation"—rep-resents an aspiration rather than an achievement.[47] What had gone wrong? Scholarly approaches here are of two kinds. Some assert that Mayhew's "unreliability and lack of tenacity" accounts for the poverty of his theory; others direct attention to certain shortcomings in his assumptions and pro-cedures.[48] Mayhew, in the second approach, is presented as the victim of his own sources. His economics, it has been argued, express an artisan trade consciousness that helps to account for the uneasy shifting from fact to value to reach conclusions that do not proceed from theoretical consider-ations.[49]

Low Wages, Mayhew's attempt to gather his thinking into a general statement, is widely perceived as an exercise that displays his limitations rather than his strengths. "Mayhew's economic analysis," writes Gareth Stedman Jones, "consisted largely of antinomies—the disclosure of phe-nomena not easily accounted for, or indeed, even mentioned in the con-ventional economics of the period, accompanied by an inability or unwillingness to locate them in an alternative theoretical structure. Such an ambivalence made it unclear even to himself whether he was engaged in a critique of political economy or an extension of it."But whereas previous commentators have fixed upon Mayhew's alleged fecklessness to account for the abandonment of serious social analysis, Stedman Jones presents him as the victim of economic and political change, beached by the onset of mid-Victorian stability and thus deprived of the radical constituency that might have sustained his project.[50]

Plausible though it is, the interpretation rests on a counterfactual that cannot be tested. The outcome of the Mayhew survey, had it been undertaken at the beginning rather than the close of the 1840s, must remain a matter of conjecture. The extent to which Mayhew had been radicalized by his experience as Metropolitan Commissioner may also be questioned. It will be seen below that, for all his advances in respect of the labor question, he accepted far more of the assumptions of liberalism than he ever criticized. Mayhew's commitment to private property, support of emigration, qualified approval of trade unions, and liking for profit-sharing arrangements locate him squarely within the ranks of the enlightened middle classes. Even his concern with unequal exchange was connected with a continuing preoccupation with the formation of the dangerous and criminal classes. Thus Chalmers, whose opinions Mill considered erroneous, was mustered by Mayhew in defense of the principle that wages should be sufficient to prevent pauperism. The "immense mass of surplus labourers, who are continually vagabondizing through the country," he claimed, partly reflected the want of such a wage.[51] Viewed in the round, his theoretical interventions seem much more like an attempt to modify or moralize political economy rather than to replace it.

Mayhew's search for an organizing framework for his findings was not exhausted by his encounter with political economy. The need of an alternative anchorage became pressing after the break with the *Morning Chronicle* and the shift toward the street trades and the criminal classes. Those readily available did not at first seem promising. "The phrenologists alone have looked into the subject, but unfortunately they are theorists with a disposition to warp rather than discover facts," he wrote. Of ethnography he was equally critical. "Ethnologists," he observed, "have done little or nothing towards increasing our knowledge of the physical conformation of the predatory and vagabond races of the world."[52] It was the descriptive force and evolutionist assumptions of ethnography that caught his imagination. Two features were noteworthy: the division of mankind into two anatomically and morally distinct classes, the civilized settlers and the unproductive wanderers; and the parasitism of the latter upon the former. The similarities between the social order as portrayed by contemporary anthropology and that which formed the subject of his investigation seemed to Mayhew to constitute:

points of coincidence so striking that, when placed before the mind, makes us marvel that the analogy should have remained thus long unnoticed. The resemblance once discovered, however, becomes of great service in enabling us to us the moral characteristics of the nomad races of other countries, as a means of comprehending the more readily, those of the vagabonds and outcasts of our own.[53]

How well versed Mayhew was in the anthropology and travel literature of his day is uncertain. Mayhew himself, one literary scholar has recently noted, "is unspecific almost to the point of mystification about his ethnographic references."[54] *London Labour and the London Poor* acknowledges, but does not engage with, the writings of Pritchard, Lewis, and others. There was no good reason why it should. Ethnology, as presented here, was not a set of testable propositions, but a strategy that enabled the author to develop his role as social explorer and interpreter of the poor. Mayhew's borrowings were largely for purposes of illustration to underscore the scope for further reform, rather than as an invitation to further research.[55]

The nomadic poor are likened to primeval savages who are ruled by brute passions and animal appetites and live without structure and restraint. They are dangerous and depraved, restless and indulgent, improvident, licentious, and lewd. These people, unknown to the census enumerators, supplied the recruits to the vagabond hordes that were said to be roaming the country. Questions concerning numbers, though, were less urgent than the possibilities of redemption and rehabilitation. Here there were grounds for optimism. On closer inspection, Mayhew found regularities and system in the lives of the poor and showed them trying to create order and meaning out of the apparently meaningless chaos of their everyday existence. The significance of this discovery, however, has been obscured by a whiggish preoccupation with the origins of modern British sociology and the modern idea of culture. Of such things contemporaries knew little. Mayhew, who well understood the needs of his audience, had shown that, notwithstanding appearance to the contrary, the outcast poor might be susceptible to rational analysis and perhaps also to rational reform.

SOCIAL ANALYSIS AND SOCIAL ACTION

Scientist in spirit, and with a lifelong enthusiasm for chemistry, Mayhew had set out to apply the techniques of natural science to the study of social phenomena. "I have undertaken the subject with a rigid determination neither to be biased nor prejudiced by my own individual notions," he wrote. "I know that as in science the love of theorising warps the mind, and causes it to see only those natural phenomena that it wishes to see. . . ."[56] His self-image as an inductive reasoner, and self-declared role as a recorder of facts and register of opinions, untrammeled by partisan considerations, represents an intention rather than a description of his practice. His alleged empiricism was in fact filled with unexamined presumptions. Mayhew, though not himself a systematic thinker, was influenced by the association-ist psychology of the Utilitarians. Whether acquired by extensive reading and careful introspection or by simple exposure to blue-book Benthamism, Mayhew assumed that the pursuit of pleasure constituted the basis of hu-man motivation and welcomed the possibilities of enlightened social action that were built upon it. Chadwick's *Report on the Constabulary* of 1839, that "valuable Report," was for Mayhew a key text as much for its rea-soning as for its information and specific proposals. Benthamite traces were also evident in his plea for educational reform. *What to Teach and How to Teach It* (1842), subsequently became more pronounced.[57] His paper on the abolition of capital punishment, read to the Society for Promoting the Amendment of the Law in 1856, was a simple restatement of the Utilitarian view that capital punishment was inconsistent with that economy of bodily pain that should form one of the main objects of progressive penal policy.[58]

Empirical investigation, too, was influenced by the moral categories of Benthamite social analysis. Less eligibility supplied a perspective on social research as well as a basis for public policy. Mayhew shared with contem-poraries numerous preconceptions about poverty and the poor, and readily classified individuals as respectable and worthy or depraved and vicious. Thus the informants and respondents by whom he set such store were all located within the same evaluative framework. With the workshy, thriftless, and criminal elements he had no truck. "Those who desire to live by the industry of others, form no portion of the honest and independent race of workmen in this country whom Mr Mayhew wishes to befriend," he in-formed one correspondent. "The deserving poor are those who *cannot* live by their labour, whether from under payment, want of employment, or physical or mental incapacity, and these Mr Mayhew wishes, and will most cheerfully do all he can, at any time and in any way, to assist."[59]

The origins of these distinctions were also accountable in Utilitarian terms. Mayhew's analysis of the formation of laboring and dangerous clas-ses thus combined aspects of sensationalist psychology with an appreciation of the special circumstances of time and place. The genesis of criminality, though rooted in an impatience of steady labor, was primarily due to the neglect and tyranny of parents and masters, and a consequent failure to engender a love of industry.[60] Men and women, Mayhew believed, were born egoists. "Theft," he wrote, "is a *natural* propensity of the human condition and honesty an *artificial* and *educated* sentiment. We do not come into the world with an instinctive sense of the rights of property implanted in our bosom, to teach us to respect the possessions of others, but rather with an innate desire to appropriate whatever we may fancy."[61] Chadwick's formulation—"Crime is *mostly* the result of a desire to obtain property with a less degree of labour than by regular industry"—was also cited with approbation.[62] Prostitution, too, he believed, arose among those "who are born in labour for their bread, but who find the work inordinately irksome to their natures, and pleasure as inordinately agreeable to them."[63]

Mayhew's concern with the roots of criminality also led him to an appreciation of Mandeville's sensationalist hedonism. Apart from the irreverent tone and mordant wit, and the telling use of vignettes, anecdotes, and sketches—all of them no doubt congenial to the founding editor of *Punch*—it was the satirist-philosopher's assertion that pride was the key to social organization that caught his imagination. Mayhew, though he balked at the egoistic reduction of morality, found the idea of self-love as a socializing agent, capable of converting human animals into human beings, particularly pertinent to his inquiries. What was most suggestive about Mandeville's writing was the unfolding possibilities of moral progress through the balancing of the weaker passions against the stronger. The role of the legislator and moralist to promote such adjustments as were necessary to secure the continuing victory of reason over passion seemed equally apposite.[64] Mayhew, like the political economists who drank at the same trough, readily endorsed Mandeville's view that the desire to be admired, and the disinclination to be despised, constituted an insight of great importance in the shaping of social and market relations. The spirit of emulation, properly mobilized, Mayhew asserted, represented "one of the great means of moral government in a State." Its absence among the lowest social classes accounted for prostitution and crime.[65] Mayhew, though, did not believe that such people could not be reached. His proposal for the formation of self-regulating street-trading communities was a measure designed to channel restlessness into respectability.[66]

The idea of man as a creature of desires who seeks to satisfy them as abundantly as he can at the least cost to himself served to distance him from evangelical educational initiatives and allied strategies for social reform. Apart from a misguided preoccupation with externals, evangelical social action was, he believed, too narrow in its scope to address the labor question effectively. His attempts to demonstrate this empirically by a case study of the Ragged School Union brought down the wrath of the philanthropic establishment upon his head and opened the rift with his employers that was to culminate in his departure from the *Morning Chronicle*. Mayhew, though "pelted with dirt from every evangelical assembly throughout the country," declined to go down gently.[67] Charges against the "religious gentry" were repeated and embellished in subsequent publications. He scorned educational systems in which children were "duly taught to spell and to write and to chatter catechisms and creeds that they cannot understand" and condemned the influence of parson and chaplain as harmful. "No man," he wrote, "can have a deeper loathing and contempt for those *outward* shows of godliness—those continued 'lip services'—the everlasting 'praying in public places', which the revelation of our everyday's commercial and prison history teaches us to believe, constitute the flagrant 'shame' of the age."[68] In place of chaplain and bible worship he recommended "really good, sound wholesome, labour training."[69]

For Mayhew, it was the formation or nonformation of habits of industry that was central to his understanding of the social question. Mayhew, though he was not attached to any particular group or program, drew selectively upon the stock of ideas that formed the basis of middle-class radicalism and shared in full its civilizing mission. His belief that criminal behavior reflected a want of self-control due in large part to an unwholesome environment underscored the importance not only of the family but also of employment in the key initiary stages of social development. Apart from the production of necessities, work provided the most direct evidence of the subordination of the passions. For Mayhew, as for his contemporaries, an aptitude for labor was readily perceived as a direct measure of the restraint and discipline upon which social order rested. The tripartite division of the metropolitan poor into those that will work, those that cannot work, and those that will not work as the organizing principle of the Mayhew survey expressed middle-class fears of the growth of pauperization and the consequent descent of the laboring classes into the dangerous classes. The utilitarian roots of his thinking were also evident in his conception of work as a necessary form of suffering in which pain might be mitigated and industry encouraged through education, example, and deliberation.[70]

Mayhew's concept of education, though, was wider than that sanctioned by philosophical radicalism. Coleridge's insight into the complexities of the human intellect and feelings impressed him, and he in turn insisted upon the separation of learning skills and knowledge and was critical of those evangelical initiatives in which the two were confounded. "Of course," he wrote in respect of the rehabilitation of young offenders, "the teaching of reading and writing is a negative good; but it becomes almost an evil when people get to believe that it has any positive or moral religious effect, *per se*, and so to forgo . . . all education of the feelings, and principles, and even the tastes, of those confined within them. The most valuable of all schooling is surely that of the heart, and the next that of the hands, especially for the poorer classes, who are mostly the inmates of our jails. . . ."[71] Cooke Taylor's dictum that "reading and writing are no more education than a knife and fork is a good dinner" was quoted with approval on several occasions.[72] The cultivation of the feelings and education of the moral sentiments, he argued, supplied the basis for a curriculum that directly addressed the social crisis.

Mayhew the social investigator, who appeared as an expert witness before the select committee on transportation in 1856, was less marginal than is sometimes imagined. He was preeminently a man of the middle classes, a socially aware, compassionate and responsible citizen, ready to mount philanthropic initiatives—Loan Societies, Discharged Prisoner Aid Societies, etc.—and to press the case for reform and rehabilitation in accordance with the enlightened mainstream.[73] Mayhew spoke up for reformatory training for those who could benefit from it but also for more severe measures against the incorrigibles. "Transportation I think very valuable to old and confirmed offenders, people who are called vagabonds, and who have certain primitive notions of society upon them," he remarked, and added, "I think it is for the good of society to get rid of such people, and to send them into a primitive country, where vagabond habits are consistent as it were with liberty."[74] Mayhew, the Utilitarian, was almost equally as tough on the reformation of those who remained in the cells. "I do believe," he told the select committee, "that there is a dangerous humanitarian notion abroad, which would strip punishment of what appears to me to be its great and main element, namely penance."[75] Mayhew's view of prison as a training ground of work-discipline and moral improvement based upon a self-acting system of rewards and incentives is, as Martin Wiener has shown, best understood as part of the transformation of the criminal justice system and the reconstitution of punishment to create self-disciplined citizens from unrestrained low-lives.[76]

Why is it, then, that Mayhew's ideas have proved difficult to place? Mayhew's want of system and failure to locate his ideas within a coherent program of social reform suggest one line of inquiry. It is possible, however, that the difficulty lies in ourselves, in our assumptions about the Victorian middle classes, and Mayhew's place within them. To be sure, Mayhew's own humanity did get in the way of the Utilitarian precepts he was trying to uphold. But was that so unusual? Is it not likely that his alleged antagonism to a unified bourgeoisie makes him seem rather more marginal than was the case? In truth, we do not know. The teleological bias of histories of social science and the tendency of recent work to focus upon text rather than context diverts us from the more fruitful study of how his work was received and understood in his own day rather than how it is "read" in ours.

NOTES

I would like to thank Clive Emsley for his valuable comments on an earlier draft of this chapter.

1. *Select Committee on Transportation*, q.3502.
2. *Select Committee on Transportation*, q.3533.
3. *Select Committee on Transportation*, q.3503.
4. See, for example, L. Lindsmith and Y. Levin, "English Ecology and Criminology of the Past Century," in *Crime and Delinquency in Britain: Sociological Readings*, ed. W. G. Carson and Paul Wiles (London, 1971), 19–29; Terence Morris, *The Criminal Area* (London, 1957).

5. Kellow Chesney, *The Victorian Underworld* (London, 1970), 28, 30; see, too, James Bennett, *Oral History and Delinquency: The Rhetoric of Criminality* (Chicago and London, 1981), 11–62.

6. J. J. Tobias, *Crime and Police in England, 1760–1900* (Dublin, 1979), 59–60; Clive Emsley, *Crime and Society in England, 1700–1900* (London, 1987), 60–62.

7. F. B. Smith, "Mayhew's Convict," *Victorian Studies* 22 (1979): 431–48.

8. See, for example, Martin J. Wiener, *Reconstructing the Criminal: Culture, Law and Policy in England, 1830–1914* (Cambridge, 1990).

9. "The Late Mr. Henry Mayhew," *Illustrated London News* (6 August 1887), 158. Cf. "Mr. Henry Mayhew," *The Athenaeum* (6 August 1887), 181–82. Athol Mayhew's promised "Life and Times" became *A Jorum of "Punch"* (London, 1895), an unsatisfactory volume that centered on Mayhew's early career.

10. *The Athenaeum* (6 August 1887), 181–82. The connection is not fanciful: See Eileen Yeo, "Mayhew as Social Investigator," in *The Unknown Mayhew: Selections from the Morning Chronicle*, ed. E. P. Thompson and Eileen Yeo (Harmondsworth, 1973), 100–101. Some continuities are also identified in P. J. Keating, *The Working Classes in Victorian Fiction* (London, 1971).

11. *Red Republican* 21 (9 November 1850): 168.

12. T. W. Hutchinson, *A Review of Economic Doctrines 1870–1929* (Oxford, 1953), 33; Peter Razzell, ed., *The Morning Chronicle Survey of Labour and the Poor*, 6 vols. (Firle, 1980), 1:113. Hereafter cited as *MCS*. See too comments of "A Working Tailor" in *Red Republican* 12 (23 November 1850): 178; Answers to Correspondents No. 11, 22 February 1851, printed on bound wrappers of *London Labour and the London Poor*, nos. 1–63, 3 vols. (London, 1851) BL Pressmark, 8276 c.55.

13. British Library of Political and Economic Science, Passfield Papers, Beatrice Webb's (Manuscript) Diary, August 1887.

14. Anon, "Life and Labour in East London," *London Quarterly Review* 24 (1890): 316.

15. Ruth Glass, "Urban Sociology in Great Britain," *Current Sociology* 4 (1955): 43; H. J. Dyos, "The Slums of Victorian London," *Victorian Studies* 11 (1967): 13; B. Harrison, "London's Lower Depths," *New Society* (2 November 1987): 638; Gertrude Himmelfarb, *The Idea of Poverty: England in the Early Industrial Age* (London, 1984), 212–370.

16. See Anne Humphreys, ed., *Voices of the Poor: Selections from Mayhew's Morning Chronicle Letters* (London, 1971); E. P. Thompson and Eileen Yeo, eds., *The Unknown Mayhew, Selections from the Morning Chronicle* (Harmondsworth, 1973); Victor Neuberg, ed., *Selections from London Labour and the London Poor* (Harmondsworth, 1985), xii–xxiii.

17. Thompson and Yeo, *The Unknown Mayhew*, 84; Eileen Janes Yeo, "The Social Survey in Social Perspective, 1830–1930," in *The Social Survey in Historical Perspective*, ed. Martin Bulmer et al. (Cambridge, 1991), 53.

18. Thompson and Yeo, *The Unknown Mayhew*, 9–55.

19. On the popularity of *London Labour and London Poor* with middle-class philanthropy, see Gareth Stedman Jones, *Outcast London, A Study in the Relationship Between Classes in Victorian Society* (Oxford, 1971), 10; on the nonen-

gagement with the insensitive Mayhew, see Yeo, "The Social Survey in Social Perspective," 54.

20. On the situation of middle-class journalists without a university education or private income, see Nigel Cross, *The Common Writer: Life in Nineteenth-Century Grub Street* (Cambridge, 1985).

21. Henry Mayhew and John Binny, *The Criminal Prisons of London* (1862).

22. *Second Report of the Select Committee on Transportation*, 1856 (296), xvii, q.3472; Karel Williams, *From Pauperism to Poverty* (London, 1981), 238.

23. *MCS* 1:40.

24. Anne Humphreys, *Travels into the Poor Man's Country: The Work of Henry Mayhew* (Athens, Ga., 1977), 49.

25. *Morning Chronicle*, 18 October 1849.

26. Michael Cullen, *The Statistical Movement in Early Victorian Britain* (London, 1975).

27. Henry Mayhew, *London Labour and the London Poor*, 4 vols. (London, 1864), 1:xv. Hereafter cited as *LL & LP*.

28. See *MCS*, 1:134, 36.

29. See *Criminal Prisons of London*, 454–55.

30. Answers to Correspondents, Nos. 6 & 9; Thompson and Yeo, *The Unknown Mayhew*, 46–47.

31. Henry Mayhew, *German Life and Manners*, 2 vols. (London, 1864), 1:118.

32. *MCS*, 1:111.

33. Thompson and Yeo, *The Unknown Mayhew*, 71; Humphreys, *Travels into the Poor Man's Country*, 40.

34. "At the time when I was making an inquiry as to the tickets of leave," he later explained. "I sent a gentleman, my clerk . . . round the different haunts of the men. He visited by my instructions, and saw some 300 of the people, and his statement to me was, that he found the great majority of them engaged in certain street pursuits; generally selling certain things," *Select Committee on Transportation*, q.3504.

35. *MCS*, 1:170.

36. *MCS*, 1:170, 199–202.

37. *MCS*, 2:89, 93.

38. See Ralph Samuel, "Mayhew and Labour Historians," *Bulletin of the Society for the Study of Labour History* 26 (spring 1973): 47–52.

39. Answers to Correspondents, No. 50, 22 November 1851.

40. Answers to Correspondents, No. 14, 15 March 1851.

41. *MCS*, 1:51–63.

42. *Select Committee on Transportation*, q.3506.

43. J. B. Say, for example, is sometimes cited for his social observation rather than his economic theory. There are also references to Wakefield's work on cooperation, though it is not clear whether he read them in the original or at secondhand in J. S. Mill's *Principles of Political Economy*, ed. W. J. Ashley (London, 1909), 116–17.

44. Answers to Correspondents, No. 22, 27 September 1851.

45. Answers to Correspondents, No. 10, 15 February 1851.

46. *Low Wages, Their Causes: Consequences and Remedies* (London, 1851), 36–51.

47. Answers, No. 16, 29 March 1851.

48. The psychologistic approach is well illustrated by Anne J. Kershen, "Henry Mayhew and Charles Booth: Men of their Times?" in *Outsiders and Outcasts: Essays in Honour of William J. Fishman*, ed. G. Alderman and C. Holmes (London, 1993), 100; the methodogically centered approach is exemplified in the work of Karel Williams, *From Pauperism to Poverty* (London, 1981), 237–77.

49. Williams, *From Pauperism to Poverty*, 257–58. It should be noted, though, that Mayhew did sometimes attempt to locate the theory of overwork with the skilled trades. See, for example, *LL & LP*, 2:216–60, 297–338.

50. Gareth Stedman Jones, "The Labours of Henry Mayhew, 'Metropolitan Correspondent,'" *London Journal* 10 (1948): 80–85.

51. *LL & LP*, 2:236. On Mill's view of Chalmers, see *Principles of Political Economy*, 75.

52. Answers to Correspondents No. 11, 22 February 1851.

53. *LL & LP*, 1:2.

54. Christopher Herbert, *Culture and Anomie: Ethnographic Imagination in the Nineteenth Century* (Chicago and London, 1991), 208.

55. Wiener, *Reconstructing the Criminal*, 33.

56. *MCS*, 1:52.

57. Reference to Chadwick's report, include *LL & LP*, 3:369, 376–77; on the primacy of the pleasure principle in education, see Henry Mayhew, *What to Teach and How to Teach It* (London, 1842), 18.

58. See Society for Promoting the Amendment of the Law, *Three Papers on Capital Punishment* (London, 1856), 32–61. On his familiarity with associationist psychology, see Henry Mayhew, "What is the Cause of Surprise? and What Connection has it with Suggestion?" *Douglas Jerrold's Shilling Magazine* 6 (1847): 561–64.

59. No. 9, Answers to Correspondents.

60. *MCS*, 3:43–44.

61. *Criminal Prisons of London*, 408. "The habitual criminal I believe to be a person who has a direct aversion to earn his own livelihood; such men as I know are mostly marked by a directly vagabond spirit; an incapability to attend to any one particular subject or to pursue any one occupation," *Select Committee on Transportation*, q.3489.

62. *MCS*, 4:135; repeated in *MCS* 3:35.

63. *Criminal Prisons of London*, 454.

64. On Mandeville's social thought see the excellent assessment by M. M. Goldsmith, *Private Vices, Public Benefits* (Cambridge, 1985).

65. *Criminal Prisons of London*, 455–56.

66. *LL & LP*, 3:432–33.

67. On Mayhew and evangelical effort, see E. P. Thompson, "The Political Education of Henry Mayhew," *Victorian Studies* 2 (1967/8): 23–30. Quotation from *Criminal Prisons of London*, 390.

68. *Criminal Prisons of London*, 421.

69. Ibid., 421–22.

70. *MCS*, 3:42–48.

71. *Criminal Prisons of London*, 431.

72. *MCS*, 4:135; *Criminal Prisons of London*.

73. *LL & LP*, 1:105–6; 2:264; *Select Committee on Transportation*, qq.3584–86, 3590–11.

74. *Select Committee on Transportation*, q.3516.

75. *Select Committee on Transportation*, q.3521.

76. Wiener, *Reconstructing the Criminal*, 111–22, especially 118.

Consolidation of the Raj: Notes from a Police Station in British India, 1865–1928

Arvind Verma

The Raj syndrome has been a popular theme for a long period of time and appears to show no decline of interest. Research in the multifaceted aspect of the British rule over India is in fact attracting more and more researchers, and the voluminous output is building an impressive account of that era.[1] It was a period when the sun supposedly never set upon Britannia and India formed the jewel in the crown. However, it was a bruised jewel, since the Raj was established and sustained upon a brutal criminal justice system. The notorious "Kala Pani" (literally, "black water") prison at the Andaman island, the public floggings and humiliations, the labeling of more than 13 million people as "criminal tribes," and the terror unleashed upon the citizens are also memories that have become part of the Indian psyche. In this oppressive state, the creation and administration of the police system was an important factor that has not been as deeply examined. The manner in which a small number of British officers built the organization that enabled the hegemony of the Raj is as fascinating a saga to any student of the British Empire as anything else. The shaping of the police as an instrument of the Raj, one where native police officers without hesitation followed orders and baton-charged Gandhi's peaceful followers or shot to death young boys raising Indian flags, is a subject that requires much more research to be done.

The Indian police organization was established formally in 1861, and the subsequent years saw the gradual strengthening of this system through various administrative decrees and control mechanisms. These controls were largely exercised through a close supervision system in which the officers kept a tight administrative leash upon the subordinate police not only through rules and regulations but also through physical inspection of the personnel and offices and a plethora of records. In this control system, the inspection of the police station was an important regulatory mechanism that played a key role in wielding power upon the people through the police department. In these inspection notes, supervisory officers recorded their comments about the way the local police station was being administered, the social and political affairs of that area, the crime situation, and control strategies, as well as the performance and activities of the personnel.

This chapter examines the inspection registers of a police station in a north central part of India where Mahatma Gandhi first led the noncooperation movement that became the launching pad for India's independence struggle. First, we will discuss the objectives of the British in establishing the modern Indian police system, briefly describe the area under study, and point out the significance of these registers as an archival source about the working of the police department. Thereafter, the chapter will describe the inspection procedure and examine the comments made by the British officers about the crime phenomenon, offenders, functioning of the local police, and the social conditions of that time. We seek to interpret these in the larger context of colonial policies, for undoubtedly "the police and its functions are determined by the nature of the state which they serve and the theory upon which such a state is based."[2] The aims and objectives of creating a police force that consolidated the Raj will be found in the decisions and directions given by the British officers.

THE HISTORY AND ORGANIZATION OF POLICE IN INDIA

The roots of the present police system in India are generally credited to the British, but these can be traced back to the structure developed by the Mughals in the seventeenth century. "The British not only borrowed this structure but also took over the feeling tone of the Mughal administration—a mixture of great pomp and show combined with benevolent and despotic intervention."[3]

For almost two hundred years the British intervened only sparingly in the administrative structure of the country, keeping their purpose limited to the enhancement of their trading interests. The country continued to be governed by a host of judicial systems developed by the various kings, nabobs, and chieftains who ruled over the country in small principalities. Although, by the victory in 1757 at Plassey, the British had emerged as the de facto ruling power in India, they still did not assume the reins of government except around Bengal, where they were granted the *diwani* (tax collection) rights by the defeated Mughal emperor, Shah Alam II. However, in the absence of a well-established criminal justice system, especially a police organization, the task of maintaining law and order in the vast country was becoming difficult. Small bands of brigands, the menace of the thugs, and expensive demands on the military to supplement civilian forces were factors that were making the tasks of the East India Company extremely forbidding. The civilian police system was also an embarassment to the imperial power, for it was an organization that was neither effective nor able to keep the trading routes safe.

In a candid memorandum to the English Parliament in 1856, the company's directors acknowledged that "the police have hitherto remained the most faulty part of our system in India."[4] The memo grudgingly added, "The recognized defects of the system are, the low rate of pay and the consequent inferiority of the class of men who enter the police, and the disproportion of the strength of the force to the density of the population."[5] The court of directors of the company, in another internal note, also recorded

That the police in India has lamentably failed in accomplishing the ends for which it was established is a notorious fact; that it was all but useless for the prevention and sadly inefficient for the detection of crime is generally admitted. Unable to check crime, it is with rare exceptions, unscrupulous as to its mode of wielding the authority with which it is armed for the functions that it fails to fulfill, and has a very general character for corruption and oppression.[6]

Yet, instead of these considerations, it was the first war of independence (labeled as "mutiny" by some authors) staged by the Indians in 1857 that provoked the British to reorganize the police. The war forced the English Parliament to supersede the East India Company and assume the reigns of the country directly into their hands. The threat to the Empire necessitated the formation of the system, one that would ensure no repetition of the "mutiny" by their subjects rather than the obvious needs to rectify the defects of the organization. After the suppression of the war for freedom, there was substantial reduction in the total strength of the army, around 40 percent, but it was qualitatively transformed to include an increase of almost 60 percent in the number of British troops.[7] At the same time, it was clear that in view of the increasing political consciousness, the vastness of the country, the existing state of the communications, and the distrust in which the Indian troops were to be held in the future, even the reorganized army could not possibly be relied upon to ensure the safety and continuity of British rule.

The war radically changed the attitude of Englishmen toward Indians and, consequently, the aims and objectives of the British government as well. Mostly, those who sided with the British, like the Sikhs, Gorkhas, and Pathans, were declared the "martial race"[8] and the others, like Bengalis, were no longer to be trusted and ruled ruthlessly, if necessary. "The new spirit was cold, bureaucratic, optimistic and racially arrogant."[9] The suppression of the people was to take the first priority in the functions of the police, and this became evident even from the Indian Penal Code and Criminal Procedure Code enacted in 1860–61, a year before the police itself was reorganized. In the former, offenses against the state, including conspiracy to wage war, were given greater prominence. The commonest preoccupation of the police is with the offenses against the person and property, but these find places in the code only from chapter XVI onward.[10] Additionally, repressive regulations of earlier times, like the Bengal Regulation III of 1818, were continued and used freely to deport nationalist leaders. The offense of "sedition" was added as early as 1870 to further make the intention clear, and the Arms Act of 1878 made it illegal for any native to possess arms, even swords, thereby virtually disarming the country.[11]

Similarly, in the Criminal Procedure code, the chapters on security for the maintenance of public order, including the use of force by the police and military, take precedence over provisions for the investigation and trial of criminal offenses. Besides, the police were vested with so much power that the lowest functionaries, though illiterates and barely paid any salary, still had powers to arrest and detain any person for twenty-four hours. "The new police was so shaped in personnel, powers and procedures as to be a terror to the law abiding citizen."[12]

This new act was in sharp contrast to the reforms enunciated by Sir Robert Peel in England three decades before and even from the systems being established in the other colonies like Australia and Canada. The Indian Police Act of 1861 was primarily a mechanism to subjugate the people, and the traditional cooperation of the community was overlooked in the concerns for law and order. Moreover, the responsibility for all police work continued to be entrusted to officers who were ill-trained, ill-motivated, and had no roots in the community they were required to serve. The executive magistrate, a member of the Indian Civil Service, continued to be in control of the police at the district level and also retained judicial powers. "District administration under the 1861 arrangement thus became a despotism."[13]

The imperative need was to develop a sense of fear of authority in the entire population, and it was achieved through the system of police extending to every nook and corner of the country and serving as the first line of internal defense. The police commission, appointed in 1860 to suggest a reorganization of Indian police, was, not surprisingly, told to bear in mind that the "functions of police are either protective and repressive or detective" and that the "line that separates the protective and repressive functions of the civil police from functions purely military, may not, always, in India be very clear."[14] These considerations reigned supreme and were incorporated in the Police Act of 1861, forming the *raison d'être* of the British Raj in India.

THE STRUCTURE AND REORGANIZATION OF THE
INDIAN POLICE

In ensuring their objectives of keeping the populace subdued, the British did not have to change the basic structure and organizational ethos of the police department. The system functioning from the Mughal period continued under the British, where the local police department exercised control over 100 to 200 square miles of the country. The *darogha* (local police officer) was answerable only to the district magistrate, who himself managed an area more than 100 miles wide. Thus, except for the occasional brief period when the magistrate was touring his area, the *darogha* was his own master. "The darogha ruled as little kings in their own jurisdiction and reaped a rich harvest of bribes from all classes."[15]

The new Police Act formally established the Indian Police (IP), a superior police service in which the chief of police, called the inspector general (IG), exercised complete control over all the police forces in the province. He was assisted by a few deputy inspector generals (DIGs), and a superintendent of police (SP) was put in charge of the police department at the district level. The SP supervised the functioning of the police stations and the working of the lower-ranking native officers and was responsible for the discipline and internal management of the force under his control. In this management system, the British administrators, although playing only a supervisory role, exercised extraordinary powers and developed elaborate procedures to keep control over the subordinate officers. The superior police service was restricted to Englishmen, who enjoyed vast perks and privileges with a status surpassed only by the Civil Service. Until 1921, no Indian was admitted to this elite service, and even until 1947, the number of Indian officers in the service was proportionately small. The entire structure and organization of the police department was hierarchical with distinct similarities to the military in terms of ranks, dress, and organizational culture. The head constables wore stripes, and the subinspectors wore stars, while senior police officers were adorned with similar stripes and star insignias as their military counterparts.

In the new setup, the *darogha* was designated as the subinspector (SI), who, through training and regular inspection, was now expected to be disciplined and made more accountable. The British, therefore, only replaced the Mughal controllers and did not create a police that would work with the people. This new organization, superimposed over the old edifice, was made to resemble the military perhaps with the hope that its disciplinary nature may get transferred to the notorious subordinate structure. The constables and subinspectors continued to do all the common police duties of patrolling, investigation, keeping contact with the people, being responsible for providing security to the areas, and for apprehending those accused of breaking the law. The SP was expected to provide control over a

dozen or more of these police stations by frequent tours and formal inspections. Thus there was little change in the police organization. Yet the
1861 Police Act and the new supervisory structure were looked upon as a
means to transform the *darogha* into the smart officer of the Royal Irish
constabulary.[16]

The supervision involved a bureaucratic arrangement where control over
the police work would be maintained through frequent inspection of the
police stations. The senior officers were required to visit the station and
examine the personnel and records to ensure proper discharge of their duties. In addition, all information reaching the police station and every action
taken by the officers were required to be promptly reported to the police
headquarters. Since reports submitted to the headquarters were considered
generally unreliable, the police administrators attached greater importance
to the physical inspection of the police station, where all the records were
to be personally scrutinized by the visiting officers. These tours were considered the most important functions of the supervisory officers, especially
that of the district superintendent of the police. The proper working of the
police station has traditionally been acknowledged as the most important
concern of the police leadership, and these inspections were considered the
best way to supervise the work of the local police.

The police station was inspected frequently by all the senior officers from
the rank of circle inspector to deputy and assistant superintendents, SP,
DIG, executive magistrates, commissioners, and IG. In one sense, the responsibility of these senior officers was to ensure the proper functioning of
the police station under their charge. Thus the police station was theoretically under constant supervision, and this mode of control was taken to
be the best way to ensure that the police department was functioning properly and efficiently. The records kept at the police station consisted of a
large number of registers in which information about all the multifarious
functions of the local police had to be meticulously maintained. Scrutiny
of these registers was seen as a way to understand and control the work
done by these subordinate officers.

The military styles of the police force, the use of similar ranks and en-
signs, and the induction of army officers into the supervisory ranks for a
long time reinforced the true intentions of the Police Act of 1861—that of
making the police into an occupational army. Further, the subordinate officers and men were continued on the pattern of an old irregular force,
which even the East India Company had acknowledged as the "most faulty
part of their system." The low pay, little demand for education, and emphasis on maintenance of law and order rather than on service to the people
ensured that the police served the purpose of providing an economical
means of keeping the people of India under the British sovereignty. The
emphasis on the official records rather than some feedback mechanism
from the people encouraged the officers to pad the documents. Finally, a

style of administration where senior officers deliberately kept themselves at a distance from the native population ensured that the people had to submit to the extortionist ways of the *darogha*. "The machinery for the maintenance of British rule and the preservation of the Indian empire was thus consolidated and perfected as far as human ingenuity could permit."[17]

THE CHAMPARAN DISTRICT

Motihari is the district headquarters of the old district of Champaran, a name to conjure with the launch of the Satyagrah movement in India by Gandhi. This district is situated in the northeastern corner of Bihar province and had become important in the nineteenth century for indigo plantation by Europeans who reaped rich harvests by exploiting the peasantry. Motihari town had a population of less than 25,000 people by the turn of the century, but the place has considerable religious significance due to its association with the epic Ramayan. Champaran district borders Nepal, and its Terai area is still covered with lush forests. With its mild climate, Motihari was also a popular resort for tiger hunting during the British period.

THE NATURE AND SIGNIFICANCE OF THE INSPECTION NOTES

The inspection registers contain a summary of the supervisory officers' assessment of the working of the personnel, the maintenance of law and order, and the upkeep of all the records. As a permanent document, it is written sequentially, wherein each note also ensures the compliance of the faults detected by the last inspecting officer. Therefore, the inspection notes provide a chronological summary of all the important records of the police station, an assessment of the individual performance of the officers, the changing phenomenon of crime, its control mechanism, and the social problems of that area. As an official document maintained by senior officers, mostly in their own handwriting, these notes are invaluable for understanding the objectives and concerns of the police department, the crime situation, and even the nature of the state and society of that period. This period of study is based upon the archival records kept at Bihar police museum, Patna, where these inspection registers, bound in two volumes, are available from 1865 to 1928 with some intermittent gaps. The pages are not numbered but arranged chronologically according to the date or month of inspection.[18] Some notes were missing, some were in Urdu language, and in some cases the pages were torn. Some of these notes were brief, mentioning nothing more significant than "the working of the police station was found to be in order." In most cases, the inspection was very formal, beginning with the turnout of the staff to the scrutiny of every record of the station. Such detailed comments described the state of the police building, the uniforms worn by the personnel, the account of government money, the crime statistics, the success and failure of the investigations, and discussions of the performance of the officers. In this chapter, the reference to these notes will be made through the date of inspection that will serve as an index to the two registers.

GENERAL COMMENTS

The myth of the district officer keeping a sharp but benevolent eye upon every nook and corner of his district was built carefully as part of the Raj syndrome. While Kipling's writings eulogized their deeds, Woodruff presented them as "guardians" who were men "selected and trained . . . to imitate whatever is proper to their profession and to model themselves on brave, sober, religious and honorable men."[19] Yet, these notes reveal them as men who were ordinary, disdainfully bureaucratic, unconcerned about their subjects, superfluous in the discharge of their duties, and indifferent to their responsibilities. The police department, it appears, was run with little understanding and concern for the problems of the people. The consideration for proper supervision of the police work, the desire to improvise and improve, and above all an understanding of the great country that they were administering were all found lacking in their comments. The supervision and inspection that were essentially to check the depredations of the local police were superficial, and the officers appeared to exercise their responsibilities very casually. The control exercised over the subordinates was ineffective, and it is apparent that the records were maintained more to paint a serene picture than to reflect the actual state of affairs.

Despite the stress on regular inspections, even the visits to the police stations were sporadic and more for the record than for any meaningful exercise of control. An analysis of these tours and visits to the police station suggests that the inspections were infrequent with wide unaccounted gaps. There seems to have been little correlation with the rise in recorded crime figures and the periodicity of these visits. The correlation between the difference in monthly crime statistics and the number of days from one inspection to the next from the period 1868–83 (for which complete statistics were available) was found to be barely 6 percent showing no relationship at all.[20]

Even when the superior officers visited the station, the supervision was casual and brief. In September 1868, the DIG wrote that the SP had not been visiting as often as he should. The next week, the SP returned to correct the record and wrote, "During the month of June, July and August the station was visited by me *5 or 6 times* [underlined by SP himself] but I have no comments to offer regarding any of these visits!" At a later period, another SP, realizing the significance of registering his visit, stated, "Forgot to record because the notes went missing!" Most observations were little more than casual, with perfunctory comments about the building, the poor rate of detection, and the pillaging ways of the local constables. Rarely was any attempt made to analyze the data, to suggest preventive measures, to educate the subordinate ranks, or even to look beyond the truth of the official documents.

RAJ AS SYMBOLIC IMAGE

However, the most obvious concern of all the supervisory ranks that was apparent in the notes was the *appearance* of the police station and its subordinate officers. Most of the inspections began with the turnout of the personnel and an inspection of the premises. The British rulers seemed inordinately concerned with the general appearance and uniforms worn by the subordinate officers as well as the looks of the police station building. Almost every inspection included a strong comment about the upkeep of the police station and the turnout of the subordinate officers. Some illustrative comments are very revealing: On 20 December 1865, the SP recorded that he "found the police house clean and in good repair. The men's belts were not as clean as they ought to be." On 21 November 1867, the SP was again pleased to note that "the men were clean!" On 17 March 1868, the DIG was pleased to note that the building (premises) was in good shape, although "the books and registers are in unsatisfactory condition." The dress, too, came under close scrutiny, and the SP recorded angrily that the "constables wear the belt in a slovenly manner. I brought back a constable of this station who I found going out into the moffusil [rural areas] dressed most carelessly and dirty."[21]

These comments seem to imply that the general cleanliness of the station, the maintenance of its premises, and the correct manner of wearing the uniforms were major concerns of the supervisors. However, these should not be construed as an indication that the British officers of that period were very particular about the general appearance of their Empire. Except for those places inhabited or regularly visited by the administrators, the rest of the country was left to fend for itself. The municipal services, the general cleanliness of the cities and towns, even the public offices run exclusively by the "natives" remained dirty and ill equipped. Document after document of that era mentions the poor state of health of the population, the almost nonexistent medical services, the filth and open drainage in every population center, and the consequent high rates of mortalities.[22] Life expectancy, even by 1947, when the British left, was in the low fifties, and unhealthy conditions and infectious diseases were rampant. These notes themselves record the outbreak of disease-ridden calamities: "The town people in greater numbers had left their homes on account of the serious plague that had broken out in the town," mentions an entry by the SP in 1913.[23]

It was, therefore, an altogether different concern that operated in keeping the police stations as shining examples of tidiness. The intention was to create among the people a sense of awe in the police, to demonstrate an aura of grandiose superiority in the most important institution of the British Empire. All police buildings were of the bungalow style,[24] imposing structures in Victorian architecture that were constructed and maintained not for providing efficient service to the people but to keep them at a distance. With high ceilings to trap the hot air, the bungalow-style buildings had broad verandahs running all around where most of the official work was done. Typically, Indian police stations had no room for the citizens to sit and be received by the police personnel, though a large room for visiting supervisory officers and housing for subordinate personnel were always provided within the campus. In this, too, visible differences were created: rooms and dak bungalows (travelodges) for the British officers were spacious, well groomed, and separate from the crowded, poorly constructed rooms for the subordinates. The house for the station officer in charge and the barracks substituting as accommodation for the constables were small, poorly ventilated, and economically designed buildings.

The police stations had also a large compound with a curving path to the gate manned by an armed sentry. The imposing high walls of the station and the sentry generally succeeded to keep the people out, and if they did reach inside, constables kept them at a distance from the British police officers.[25] Quite disarmingly, the SP wrote, "In the station [building] there should be only one door for the whole station and at that door the sentry should be placed."[26] The overall effect was thus to maintain an aura of power and keep the police institution secure from the influence of the local people. Underneath the concern for the exposition of the police station and the proper turnout of the personnel was simply the objective to create a powerful, foreboding impact upon the local population.

As the inspection notes show, the formal comment upon the building, clothes, turnout, and even furniture was a standard feature of the inspection, and every inspection commenced with observations on these matters. That the police personnel remained inefficient and indifferent to the general problems of their areas was never a cause for dismissal, but their appearance was always a serious concern. Thus, not surprisingly, an assistant SP, the most junior British IP officer indignantly punished a constable who was found to be walking without his belt.[27]

INADEQUATE PROVISION OF RESOURCES

One of the frequent complaints against the British was that they were always reluctant to spend money on administrative needs and attempted to run the institutions in an almost impoverished manner.[28] The police perhaps were neglected even more in this respect, since they did not generate revenue and were confined to the limited role of maintaining British hegemony. The notes support this observation in several ways. For one, the police station officers were rarely given funds for running their stations and had to depend for every need upon the SP. The accounts register was closely scrutinized, and any undispersed funds resulted in a censure. The system was such that absolutely no money was entrusted in the hands of the officer in charge, and for every need he had to send requisitions to the SP's office.

Even in the exhortation to maintain the appearance of the police station, the desire to economize was overwhelming. For instance, the inspector (dated 18–20 December 1868) drew attention repeatedly to the poor state of the police station building, "there is no cooking shed and part of the back verandah has fallen in." Even the IG (chief of police) conceded, "I am not much struck by the appearance [either] of the station building."[29] However, nothing was done to repair the building, and three years later the SP attempted to remind him with the candid assessment that "The station house is as clean as it can be kept but it is a wretched building."[30] Incidentally, the building soon became unfit for occupation, and on the next inspection the DIG noted that "This station house is now being dismantled and being pulled down for the construction of a new station building. This is not before it was needed—I find that the District Superintendent undertook to build a new station for something under Rs. 1500/—This has (now) been constructed by the PWD [Public Works Department] at an estimated cost of more than Rs. 2000/,"[31] (which was high for its period).

The PWD, too, had police needs in low priority. By 5 January 1875, the DIG again noted that "The building is in my opinion not completed" and "I decline to allow the police to occupy it. At present the police live in a miserable place quite unfit for proper work." Yet, the police officers are directed to shift in the new premises on 9 January 1875, although the DIG noted that "one or two of the pillars are coming down. The finishing in several places appears to be of a very 'kutche' (loose) description. There is not sufficient ventilation in the lock up."[32] The British government kept a tight hold on the purse strings, though the officers were admonished again and again for the poor state of the premises. There were never sufficient funds to undertake the repairs and perhaps, as remains the practice, the officers themselves bore the costs of the necessary repairs and undoubtedly charged them to the people.

The harshest comment on the need to maintain austerity concerned the use of kerosene oil that was supplied by the SP's office for lighting purposes. The SP devotes a major portion of his inspection note to this matter. "The rate per bulb for lantern per month is 4 anna and 6 paise. The SI is making a bad precedent. The cost of the oil which he is spending at present will amount to Rs. 8/ where as the actual grant is only Rs. 5/ per month." The SP then goes on to inform of the experiment conducted at another station, where castor oil and kerosene were mixed in a certain proportion to give the best results. On the basis of the above experiment he observes that, "given the 13 bulbs for lantern here, calculating at the above rate 19 seers of such a mixture will be required for one months consumption,"[33] which was the monthly supply then fixed for the station. The officer in charge of the government's lanterns acknowledged that the SP's orders were being carried out, although it remained unclear whether he also educated himself about the experiment. Most probably he himself must have footed the bill for extra kerosene oil required by the police station. The practice in the police department since the very beginning had been not to depend upon governmental funds to run the basic needs of the police station. The officers themselves contributed money for these requirements, money which they obviously extorted from the population.

CORRUPTION AMONG THE PERSONNEL

That the subordinate officers were extorting money also appears to be an acknowledged fact by the British. The observations by the East India Company officers, as mentioned earlier, the general folklore about the *darogha* in various memoirs, and the scathing comments by the National Police Commission of 1902 mention the depredations in no uncertain terms. The interesting observation appears to be that this extortion was directed not only against the helpless citizens, who had few avenues to complain, but also against other lower functionaries of the government. For instance, the *chowkidar* (village watchman), who was placed under the local police and had a lower status, was also a victim of the subordinate officers' extortion. As a representative of the British administration in the village, the *chowkidar* was considered an important government functionary, and there was a strict requirement of proper uniform for him. The supply was made from public funds, and it was the responsibility of the subordinate officers to check regularly and ensure that it was kept in proper shape. Again, with increasing bureaucratization, the police department created a booklet to be maintained by the *chowkidar* in which government supplies given to him were recorded. Failure to keep these booklets resulted in fines and actions against the *chowkidars*, as noted in the inspections.

However, the local police used this rule for extortion and took money for providing these booklets. In his inspection note the SP records:

I regret to record that I have discovered that nearly every chowkidar has been charged one anna for his book. The WC (writer constable) of this station is on leave is the culprit. In some cases it has been taken for the price of the forms supplied to Panchayats [Village councils]. It would appear that this custom is not confined to Motihari as I met a chowkidar of Addapore Thanah [another police station] on the road this morning and on interrogating him indirectly he assured me he had paid the price of his book and that all chowkidars paid one anna yearly for their books.[34]

There is little mention in subsequent notes to suggest that any action was taken against the writer constable or that this practice could be curbed by the British authorities. Occasionally, the notes also mention complaints against officers and men, but again these records show that very little action was ever taken. Thus the SP noted that "constable Raj Bansee Singh has been in this area for long and wields great influence . . . he does as he likes."[35] Yet, this constable continues for several more years in the same area. So long as the local police served the British interests and did not become a burden upon the British purse, the administrators remained unconcerned about their failings, ill reputation, and depredations upon the people.

THE CRIME PHENOMENON

It appears that, initially, the British officers did not encounter an alarming situation in which the police were hard-pressed. The inspection notes mention frequently that "the situation is under control" and that "offenders are being apprehended." Therefore, the analytical notes about the crime phenomenon were brief and mentioned just the monthly statistics. For instance, early on, the SP could write, "Few cases occurred in the previous quarter and recovery is moderately successful."[36] Yet, the new administrators soon realized that "crime is concealed in this station,"[37] and "There is not much to be said about this return [of crime statistics] except that if it represents a true state of affairs it [calls] for congratulations!"[38] As the years progressed and problems became difficult to conceal, the subordinates were forced to submit more detailed statistics. The supervisory officers in these notes began drawing up different crime statistics under several heads for more elaborate comments on the crime situation. Crime data for monthly statistics under several categories were demanded and comparisons were done every quarter with previous years' figures. Comments on the distributions of specific crime types, comparisons within the smaller jurisdiction of the police station, and differentiation between rural and urban regions all evolved slowly as part of the inspection procedure, although the analysis remained perfunctory.

The data from the inspection notes clearly indicate the rising trend in the crime phenomenon as Figure 1 suggests.

In the early years of the police administration, the local police seemed efficient in apprehending those accused of the crimes, and the number of arrests per criminal incident remained high for quite some time. Similarly, the conviction and acquittal figures also show the apparent success of the British in maintaining hegemony over the vast countryside. Yet, by the

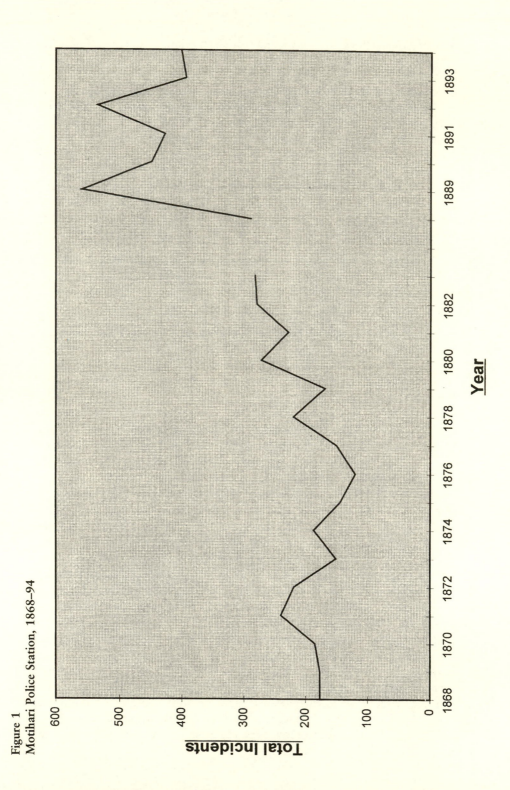

Figure 1
Motihari Police Station, 1868–94

1910s, the situation was deteriorating, and the crime figures also suggest that there were steep rises. However, increasing numbers do not seem to have bothered the administrators too much, for even when there were spurts in the crime figures the commentary did not appear to have changed significantly. For instance, in 1913, 169 crimes were recorded, as compared to only 88 in the previous year. The rise in burglaries, from 19 to 67 in just one year should have been considered alarming. Yet, even the DIG who visited the station during this period wrote in his brief inspection note, "The police station was inspected by the SP in December for 3 days but has lost his notes and so no remarks are on record." After noting the above crime figures in his handwriting, the only directions given were, "Both the sub-inspectors should take steps to provide themselves with serviceable ponies."[39]

Quite clearly, the crime phenomenon did not bother the supervisory officers. By the advent of the 1920s when Mahatma Gandhi's Satyagrah (quest for truth) had taken roots, "the problem of traditional crime, always of minor concern to the British government of India, had practically ceased to bother them, as the police got more and more involved in putting down civil disobedience and revolutionary activities."[40] Even crime statistics that were being kept elaborately in the inspection notes had been discarded for general comments.

However, as the British power started facing challenges and questions about its legitimacy, there was an increasing demand for more and more statistics from the operational units. Thus, new documents such as the "gang" register, the "dacoity" register, the "Khatian," or crime statistics, register, the burglary charts, and the crime maps were added to the existing records system to feed government's demand for more information. The problem of the escalating crime situation was to be handled by the management of crime statistics. Yet, the elaborate information that the officers demanded never was put to any effective use or to improve the situation. The efforts needed to examine minutely the crime figures, or to understand the etiology of crime and even to plan preventive operations never materialized. The supervisory officers bothered only to ensure that the more than three dozen different but overlapping registers were being updated and that statistics demanded by the growing bureaucracy were being supplied by the local police. The inspection of these records was only to look for improper or incomplete entries, and no attempt appears to have been made to analyze them. Clearly, despite easy access to every kind of crime data, the British officers displayed little zeal to combat the crime or even to check if the investigators made any use of this information.

For instance, the demand for more numbers to feed organizational demands led to the practice of keeping a separate register for deaths and births in the area by the local police from 1878 onward. Thus, even from the records maintained at the police station, it was possible to do more meaningful crime analysis, such as estimating the crime *rates* instead of total crime figures to examine annual fluctuations. Considering that the police administrators must have been aware of the work of Adolphe Quêtelet and A. M. Guerry with the European crime statistics,[41] it remains surprising that, despite the availability of population figures, not one officer ever bothered to work out the changes of crime on the basis of a standard rate. Even the high death rate never caught the attention of the administrators, although improper wearing of caps and belts continued to be commented upon. The attempt to probe the data for more meaningful supervision and, thus, better policing for the people was perhaps never the intention of the British administrators. Analysis of crime patterns, seasonal fluctuations, and geographical distribution of incidents, the basis of any professional police work, leaves no evidence in these notes. So long as the local police maintained the order in the Raj and kept the rumblings of the people from erupting in any threatening manner, the officers remained content with the paper performance of their rapacious policemen.

RAJ AND THE BORN CRIMINALS

"When we speak of professional criminals we . . . (mean) a tribe whose ancestors were criminals from time immemorial, who are themselves destined by the usage of caste to commit crime, and whose descendants will be offenders against the law, until the whole tribe is exterminated or accounted for in the manner of thugs."[42] This official British ideology formed the basis of the repressive Criminal Tribes Act (Act XXVII of 1871), providing for strong measures against almost thirteen million people until its repeal in 1947, when India attained its freedom. The act empowered the police to register the members of these tribes, maintain surveillance, and keep control over their movement. The regulations also gave powers to the police to inspect a suspect's house for any stolen property, and if any member was found outside limits of the prescribed area of movement, to apprehend him/her without warrant.

The notion that members of these tribes are criminals by birth was a part of the prevailing criminological theories, which became popular with the Italian school headed by Cesare Lombroso. His idea of a born criminal, who was moreover a biological throwback, found ready experimentation upon the roaming tribes, whose unsettled bohemian ways were contemptible amongst the educated and "cultured" people of India as well.[43] The crimes of theft and robberies were, moreover, seen as a challenge to the authorities, for these violated the sanctity of order that was the primary concern of the Raj. Therefore, there was little hesitation in the imposition of stiff sanctions "against the wanderers and vagrants who were outside the normal network of sedentary society."[44] That these official perceptions were inaccurate and that "an entire tribe cannot be criminal,"[45] sentiments expressed by several concerned people, still did not stop the passing of the act that placed wide-ranging disparate groups of differing cultural, economic, and social backgrounds in the criminal category.

Among several such tribes targeted by the new law, the group of people known as Magahiya Domes were placed perhaps at the rank bottom of the scale. The British image of a person from that tribe was: "his habits (are) so disgusting, his custom so debased, and his avocations so repulsive that he is viewed as less than human."[46] These sentiments naturally echoed in the comments of the police administrators of that area, and the official concern with this group stemmed from the police reports in the 1860s that described them as wandering tribes of Champaran and the neighboring Shahabad and Saran districts that these people frequented. That this tribe did not suffer much distress in the great famine of the 1870s was further proof of their "thieving ways" to Metcalf, the important commissioner of Patna division.[47]

The inspection notes contain several references to the Domes, and their presence in the district or nearby was always a cause for alarm. Thus, the SP commenting upon the failure of the local police to detect burglaries and thefts stated: "there is this to be said however that most of these are the handiwork of Domes and as such are extra difficult to solve."[48] The low detection rate is attributed again and again to the dreaded Domes, as once more another SP wrote: "Personally made inquiries and have come to the conclusion that for the majority of the crimes the Domes are responsible."[49] Again, on 11 December 1916, the SP wrote that the increase in the cases of thefts and burglaries in the town is "due to the gang of Domes" and laments that stringent action under section 109 and 110 Cr.P.C.[50] is not being taken. Their attitude and treatment is perhaps best reflected in the following comment: "The Mughiya Doms have given a wide berth lately. They are hunted down the moment they show themselves anywhere in this station."[51]

The ideology behind the "criminal tribes" was related undoubtedly to the notion of "dangerous classes" prevalent in contemporary Victorian Britain. Yet, unlike the Habitual Offender's Act passed in 1869 in England that covered only the convicted offender, the Indian Criminal Tribes Act encompassed the entire community. "Even India's criminals were not similar to England's."[52] These comments resulted in harsh action by the local police and reinforced the perceptions of colonial ethnography, the mentality of Raj in India.

NO CONTACT WITH THE PUBLIC

The officials rarely attempted to contact the people to obtain another picture of the situation than that provided by their own officers. This is perhaps most apparent in the case of unnatural deaths, where the subin-

Table 2
On Unnatural Deaths

Year	Un-natural Deaths
1868	22
1869	33
1870	31
1871	31
1872	50
1873	41
1874	42
1875	34
1876	28
1877	46
1878	58
1879	62
1880	32
1881	83
1882	98
1883	145

spector's pen would change a homicide into a death for which there was not even an inquiry. The administrative rules defined certain deaths as "unnatural" if they were not due to old age or disease. Examples of its kind were deaths from snake bites, fire, falling from trees, drowning, injury caused by an animal, and so on. The rules prescribed that a proper record be kept of all such deaths, and the police had to inquire in order to ensure that these did not involve any foul play. However, no further investigation was required if the local inquiry (to be done promptly) revealed that the death was indeed due to "unnatural" reasons and none could be blamed for it.

Table 2 displays the frequency of such deaths from 1868 to 1883, for which full details are available.

The figures clearly indicate that the fluctuations in such deaths were uneven and that some cases were definitely suspicious in nature. However, the senior administrators never bothered about any of these deaths as long as the officers categorized them as unnatural and included them in their statistics. If the inquiry officer ruled that such deaths were "unnatural," then no post mortem was required, a discretion that placed great power in the hands of the subordinate officers. It is quite probable that for pecuniary gains many homicides would have been suppressed by recording them as unnatural death, a practice common in the Indian police even today. Yet, not one single unnatural death was inquired into by any of the supervisory officers, the mere registration being considered sufficient for administrative purposes.

Several figures in these notes appear to suggest foul play. For example, deaths by snake bites appear to form a major proportion of unnatural deaths recorded in the inspection notes. Despite the fact that in the quarter July to September 1883, thirty-two deaths from snake bites were recorded as compared to an average of around two to three in similar quarters of previous years, the administrators remained indifferent to them. Similarly, the death of an indigo factory servant, alleged by his wife to have been beaten fatally by the guard, remained classified as unnatural, "for the local police inquiry suggested [that] there was no basis for the allegation."[53] That the indigo planters were ruthless in their control over the *ryats* [cultivators] and servants has been documented by several researchers.[54] Gandhi, too, substantiated these allegations in his detailed inquiries against the indigo planters. However, for the British police administrators, these so-called unnatural deaths never became murder or foul play, despite the glaring and obvious nature of these statistics. The policing concerns of the British administrators were limited; so long as there was no public outcry the authorities remained indifferent to the reality of the situation. This exercise in deception was part of the Raj syndrome, since genuine inquiries would have exposed the repressive nature of their administration. "Ideology became a servant for false consciousness, empty phrases and hypocrisy. It was decadence in the name of greater efficiency and order."[55]

PERFORMANCE APPRAISAL

The investigation work was never organized properly on scientific management principles to improve police effectiveness. The work load was always asymmetrically distributed, with "good" or "connected" officers taking most of the tasks and the stragglers or those out of favor being kept aside. As a means of consolidating their grip over the police apparatus, the senior officers strictly controlled the power exercised by the subordinates. Those who were obsequious, compliable, and obedient were given more responsibilities and occasions to display their authority over the people despite poor performance.

For instance, the entry dated 15 December 1868 reveals that in the year 1867 of the fifty serious cases registered at the station, subinspector I. Bannerjee investigated thirty-seven cases, while three other subinspectors and two inspectors combined investigated only thirteen cases. Similarly, in

1870, of a total of 186 cases registered, subinspector Raj Coomar Singh (35), Head Constable Nusrat Ali (57), and Constable Juddonath Sahai (29) shouldered investigation of 65 percent of the cases, while the rest, comprising one inspector, two subinspectors, and ten constables, were only entrusted with the remaining 35 percent of the cases. This discrepancy remains unexplained, even though subinspector Laxmi Charan Pandey and constables Kurim Singh, Feyda Hussain, and Nourangee Lall, as determined from the notes, obtained convictions for more than 90 percent of the people they arrested in their cases. From the inspection notes, it is also clear that these officers and men remained at the police station for the whole year, yet they were not entrusted with full responsibilities. The supervisory officers made no mention about this uneven distribution of work load and whether this affected efficiency. The extensive statistics mentioned in the notes[56] clearly indicate that such an evaluation was possible but was never attempted by the senior officers.

GANDHI IN CHAMPARAN

The police act stipulated that the police role was primarily one of providing various kinds of services to the people, including safety of person and property. The act also included several provisions where the police were expected to mitigate social problems. In fact, the "guardians" and their memoirs constantly talk about the "white man's burden" of educating the Indian society from the scrupulous demands of its marauding elite classes.[57] Yet, the British-controlled police never bothered about the injustices perpetrated upon the people by unscrupulous merchants and landlords. The police records, too, remain silent upon any such trepidation, painting a picture where the only "problem" was the danger from the "criminal tribes." Moreover, the police administrators followed a deliberate policy of not intervening in any matter unless brought before them through the official channels. Naturally, such a state of affairs gave tremendous powers to the subordinate officers, who would not record cases except on pecuniary grounds or at the behest of locally influential people. The importance of the local elite and their role in supporting the British rule has been suggested by many researchers.[58] Naturally, the British police would not entertain any complaint against them, and the horrendous cases of landlords' brutality, crimes against their *ryats*, were rarely recorded.

The inspection registers provide a striking example of this indifference to the injustices and exploitation going on in that period. These registers do *not* contain even a single reference to any of these problems, and moreover, they ignored Gandhi's visit to Champaran in the summer of 1917. The plunder and exploitation by the indigo planters of the Champaran district was notorious and certainly well known to the administrators. The literature of this oppression[59] and Gandhi's subsequent inquiries in this area revealed how the indigo planters of Champaran were exploiting the peasants and producing widespread suffering among them. However, the planters, mostly Europeans, exerted great influence in the district and "[even] expected the district magistrate to dance to their tunes."[60]

Supported by the Bengal Tenancy Act that gave permanent titles to the landlords and a sympathetic administration, the planters imposed the *"tinkanthia"* system upon the peasants, forcing them to cultivate indigo in three-twentieths of their holdings whether it was profitable or not. Even when indigo was becoming unprofitable on account of synthetic substitutes, the planters forced new agreements upon the cultivators to either pay enhanced rents or grow indigo on their land. Even though in most places this *tinkanthia* regulation was not enforceable, the planters continued to extort high rents from the peasants. The methods they used included beatings, incarcerations, impounding of cattle, preventing people from getting out of their houses, and levying illegal taxes on marriages, construction of houses, and more. The peasants even had to pay their landlords a tax called *"pararhi"* for sending the *"sahib"* to the hill station in summers. "The influence of the planters with the government and the officials was so great that the peasants dared not approach either the judicial or the executive authorities."[61]

Gandhi was invited by Kishore Babu to see the situation for himself and do something about it. He visited Motihari on 17 April 1917 and stayed there for the next six months, inquiring into the conditions of the peasants to assure for himself the truth of the grievances and allegations against the planters. He personally took down more than twenty thousand statements and, convinced of the injustices, staged his remarkable nonviolent agitation on behalf of the peasants. His struggles forced the government to appoint a Commission of Inquiry that finally abolished the hated *tinkanthia* and all other illegal levies.

Undoubtedly, these six months and subsequent years were momentous for the district and even the country. The civil disobedience movement had taken root and India had been stirred as never before.[62] Consequently, the Satyagrah at Champaran must have affected the life at Motihari, and one would expect such momentous events to affect the police and the district administration also. Yet, the inspection notes contain not even a *single* entry about Gandhi's visit or the social climate of that period. The British administrators continued to be concerned about those traditional crimes that were brought to their notice and were only bothered about fluctuations. The only entry that hesitatingly acknowledged the social problems of that area was a brief comment by the DIG Muzzafarpur stating: "Feelings between planters and Ryots: Good."[63] These "pretentious hauteur blissfully insulated a ruling minority from an India immediately beyond the different layers of khitmatgars."[64]

CONCLUSIONS

"The study of police is a way of seeing the mechanisms by which authority and control were exercised and maintained historically."[65] If this were to be true, then the objectives and the concerns of the British police officers that emerge from this study support the theme that policing was to be the bulwark for their Raj. These inspection notes provide a glimpse of how deviance was being defined and about the ways in which the police department was being created and strengthened. The official attitudes toward the offenders and the concern toward an image rather than the substance of the police functions clearly suggest that for British officers, the police role was limited to the maintenance of the Raj. Policing objectives were irrelevant to the society, and the personnel were brutalized deliberately and kept apart from the people. The police was to be more an impressive show of force to keep the people subjugated than an instrument of service to the society.

The Raj was built on force and whenever necessary had to be sustained by force. Kipling was perhaps more honest when he observed, "Never forget that unless the outward and visible signs of our authority are always before a native he is as incapable as a child of understanding what authority means, and where is the danger of disobeying it."[66] The British police officers were naturally more guarded and never stated their objectives in such plain terms, but they faithfully followed Kipling's advice. They ensured that the police department reflected the glory and power of the Raj. Modern, independent, and democratic India, where the same police system ironically is still continuing, must learn from these notes.

NOTES

1. The British Indian Raj has been examined from a host of perspectives ranging from the political dimension to the architectural styles of its buildings. The experiences of the British administrators and their memoirs, attitudes toward their subjects, the social and economic conditions under English rule, the lascivious life styles of the Maharajas, the great famines and impoverishment of the Indian people, the dress, fashions, cuisine, memsahibs, and the tiger hunt have all formed the fascination toward the Raj. Some of the memorable readings on these subjects can be found in the following: April Swayne-Thomas, *Indian Summer: A Memsahib in India and Sind* (Delhi, 1981); Evelyn Battaye, *Costumes and Characters of Raj* (New Delhi, 1982); Rudyard Kipling, *Kim* (London, 1901); Thomas R. Metcalf, *An Imperial Vision: Indian Architecture and Britain's Raj* (Berkeley, 1989); Jan Morris and Simon Winchester, *Stones of the Empire: Buildings of the Raj* (London, 1983); Michael Satow and Ray Desmond, *Railways of the Raj* (London, 1980); J. K. Stanford, *Ladies in the Sun: The Memsahib's of India, 1760–1860* (London, 1967).

2. George L. Mosse, ed., *Police Forces in History* (Beverly Hills, 1975), 4.

3. Bernard S. Cohn, *The Development and Impact of British Administration in India* (New Delhi, 1961), 8.

4. East India Company, *Memorandum of the Improvement in the Administration of India during the Last Thirty Years and the Petition of the East India Company to the Parliament* (London, 1968), 39.

5. Ibid., 41.

6. Cited in Anandswarup Gupta, *The Police in British India 1861–1947* (New Delhi, 1979), vi.

7. Ibid., 6.

8. Thomas R. Metcalf, *The New Cambridge History of India: Ideologies of the Raj* (Berkeley, 1994), 125–28. Cited hereafter as *NCHI*.

9. Cohn, *Development and Impact*, 10.

10. B. B. Misra, *The Administrative History of India 1834–1947: General Administration* (London, 1970), 540–48.

11. Peter Heehs, *The Bomb in Bengal: The Rise of Revolutionary Terrorism in India 1900–1910* (Delhi, 1993), 8.

12. Gupta, *Police in British India*, 74.

13. Misra, *Administrative History*, 538.

14. Imperial Gazetteer cited in Gupta, *Police in British India*, 7.

15. Philip Woodruff, *The Men Who Ruled India: The Guardians* (New York, 1954), 53.

16. Ibid.

17. Gupta, *Police in British India*, 194.

18. These registers, entitled *Inspection Registers: Motihari PS* are in two bound volumes. *Volume 1: 1865–1895* and *Volume 2: 1896–1928*. These will be cited as Inspection Register Vol. 1 or 2 with date of inspection serving as the index.

19. Woodruff, *Men Who Ruled India*, 21.

20. *Inspection Register*, Vol. 1.

21. Ibid., 4 April 1879.

22. See for example, Veena Talwar Oldenburg, *The Making of Colonial Lucknow 1856–1877* (Princeton, 1984); J. B. Harrison, "Allahabad: A Sanitary History," in *The City in South Asia*, ed. Kenneth Ballatchet and J. B. Harrison (London, 1980).

23. *Inspection Register*, Vol. 2, September 1913.

24. Anthony King, *The Bungalow: The Production of a Global Culture* (London, 1984).

25. Metcalf, *NCHI*, 177–78.

26. *Inspection Register*, Vol. 1, 3 August 873.

27. Ibid., Vol. 2, 28 November 1921.

28. Gupta, *Police in British India*, 250.

29. *Inspection Register*, Vol. 1, 5 March 1869.

30. Ibid., Vol. 1, 22 October 1872.

31. Ibid., Vol. 1, 18 February 1874.

32. Ibid., Vol. 1, 9 January 1875.

33. Ibid., Vol. 2, 6 November 1916.

34. Ibid., Vol. 1, 27 May 1879.

35. Ibid., Vol. 1, 23 February 1867.

36. Ibid., Vol. 1, 21 November 1866.

37. Ibid., Vol. 1, 23 February 1867.

38. Ibid., Vol. 1, 25–26 October 1877.

39. Ibid., Vol. 2, 21 March 1914.

40. Ted Robert Gurr, Peter N. Grabosky, and Richard C. Hula, *The Politics of Crime and Conflict: A Comparative History of Four Cities* (Beverly Hills, 1977), 574–75.

41. George B. Vold and Thomas J. Bernard, *Theoretical Criminology*, 3rd ed. (New York, 1986), 131–32.

42. Anand A. Yang, ed., *Crime and Criminality in British India* (Tucson, 1985), 109.

43. Ibid., 111.

44. Metcalf, *NCHI*, 122.

45. Testimony of D. N. Majumdar, Reader in Anthropology, Lucknow University, in *Report of the Criminal Tribes Inquiry Committee, United Provinces, 1947* (Allahabad, 1948), 53.

46. In Yang, *Crime and Criminality*, 120.

47. Ibid., 121.

48. *Inspection Register*, Vol. 1, 25 April 1877.

49. Ibid., Vol. 1, 17 May 1886.

50. These two sections provide for preventive detention under the law.

51. *Inspection Register*, Vol. 1, 10 August 1877.

52. Metcalf, *NCHI*, 125.

53. *Inspection Register*, Vol. 1, 12 June 1876.

54. See, for example, Ann B. Callender, *How Shall We Govern India? A Controversy Among British Administrators, 1800–1882* (New York, 1987), 118–22; E. Thomson and G. Garratt, *Rise and Fulfilment of British Rule in India* (Allahabad, 1966), 475; Woodruff, *Men Who Ruled India*, 54.

55. Suhash Chakraborty, *The Raj Syndrome: A Study in Imperial Perceptions* (Delhi, 1989), 156.

56. *Inspection Register*, Vol. 1.

57. See Eric Stokes, *The English Utilitarians and India* (Oxford, 1959); C. C. Eldridge, *England's Mission: The Imperial Idea in the Age of Gladstone and Disraeli* (Chapel Hill, 1973).

58. See Yang, *Crime and Criminality*, for instance.

59. Chakraborty, *Raj Syndrome*, 152; Raymond K. Renford, *The Non-Official British in India to 1920* (Delhi, 1987), chap. 11.

60. Woodruff, *Men Who Ruled India*, 54.

61. R. R. Diwakar, *Saga of Satyagraha* (Delhi, 1969), 124.

62. V. T. Patil, *Mahatma Gandhi and the Civil Disobedience Movement: A Study in the Dynamics of the Mass Movement* (Delhi, 1988).

63. *Inspection Register*, Vol. 2, 21 May 1925.

64. Chakraborty, *Raj Syndrome*, 2.

65. Yang, *Crime and Criminality*, 19.

66. Rudyard Kipling, "His Chance of Life," in *Plain Tales from the Hills* (London, 1921), 81.

The White Slave Trade and the British Empire

Philippa Levine

In this chapter, I want to redraw the contours of a historical problem with which most of us have at least a passing familiarity—the white slave trade or white slave traffic of the late nineteenth and early twentieth centuries. Though this is an issue with a surprisingly small historiography, it is nonetheless a phenomenon—or at least a catchphrase—with considerable currency. Generally, I don't think it would be unfair to say that historians, at any rate, see the white slave trade as symptomatic of a racialized *fin-de-siècle* moral panic that gripped most English-speaking countries in the late nineteenth century, a moral panic that ensued (not entirely surprisingly) at around the same time as organized women's groups began demanding a reevaluation of the rights of citizenship and at a moment after the American Civil War had failed to extend those rights fully in the New World. These are key sites for understanding the white slave trade as a historical representation, but I want to suggest some rather less familiar contexts that might help us reassess the issue usefully. My two new "flagposts" are crime and colonialism—crime because the sex industry has long been associated with criminal "justice" and the underworld, and colonization because, as I hope to be able to demonstrate here, the narrative of the white slave trade necessarily took on new meanings and representations when the ground shifted from "metropolis" to "colony."

Thinking about women's crime has not been an easy task for feminists. Quantitatively minded criminologists have dismissed female crime as statistically insignificant; a long line of commentators stretching back into the mid–nineteenth century have linked female delinquency to women's independence in an attempt to stem both; and the very binaries constructed around crime—moral and immoral, victim and perpetrator—have dogged attempts to reformulate and reconsider the behaviors we routinely associate with criminality.[1] To speak, then, of gender and crime is to offer important challenges to existing assumptions.

But prostitution, a frequently criminalized activity, falls outside the routine association of crime as a masculine activity. Erroneously but nonetheless generally called *the* women's crime, prostitution is one of the few arenas where arrest and conviction rates, popular imagery, and legal definition have focused almost exclusively on women.[2] And lurking in this equation is an essentialist notion of female disorderliness as a function of unbridled, uncontrolled female sexuality. In short, even where exercising the agency of crime, women are still subject to the controlling forces of their sexual nature.

In practice, of course, female prostitution is a good deal more complicated. It offers the prospect not only of women defined by their sexual nature but also of a more threatening vision of women actively putting that sexuality to work for their own benefit.[3] Prostitution, conceptually, is a double-edged sword, holding out the chance for female independence, on the one hand, and representing, on the other, the ultimate submission. Prostitution, thus, both *consolidates* gender roles, as a crime that stresses women as sexual objects, and *disrupts* gender roles because the women involved get paid, thumb their noses at strictures about criminality and femininity as well as "nice girl" mores, and thus move into a typology structured around active male rather than passive female behaviors.

In nineteenth-century Britain, this confusion—at a time of rigidifying gender roles—is evident in the considerable literature on the motives for female prostitution, which veered between harsh criticism of the woman actively abandoned to pleasure and sympathy for the hapless and passive object of male lust.[4] Was the prostitute a depraved monster and a specter of uncontrolled womanhood, or was she the public face of victimization at the hands of heartless men? My intention here is to investigate this tension between blame and helplessness, but through a wider set of boundaries than those merely of domestic mainland Britain, in order to get at not only the gendering of issues of responsibility in this period but also their racializing—specifically in British imperial contexts. I'm interested, then, in deepening our readings of the Victorian parameters of female disorder by a close attention to issues of race and colonialism.

A commission appointed to investigate the working of an 1867 ordinance regulating the Hong Kong prostitution trade asserted significant racial differences between an Asiatic and a European mode of commercialized sex, arguing that female prostitution in Asia was systemic in ways it was not in Europe. The Hong Kong–based commissioners argued:

Chinese prostitution is essentially a bargain for money and based on a national system of female slavery; whilst European prostitution is more or less a matter of passion, based on the national respect for the liberty of the subject; and further . . . these Chinese prostitutes of Hong Kong are as a whole, an extremely quiet, orderly and well behaved sort of people, not given to intemperance or excess; in one word, they are not "abandoned women" as the prostitutes of Europe only too frequently are.[5]

In essence, European prostitution could be explained as the unfortunate excess of wayward individuals driven by their passions, while Chinese prostitution was collectively acceptable and rested more on social approbation than on individual desires. Thus, while Chinese prostitutes were orderly and disciplined, theirs was a tyrannical culture that allowed no room for individual preference or temperament. In this reading, disorder was not individual in Chinese society, but endemic and, ironically, capable of producing a biddable if brutalized femininity.

Let us be clear here that while the colonial authorities insisted that statements such as this were dispassionate acknowledgments of cultural difference, there can be no doubt that they served principally and critically as racial markers. James Mill, in his *History of British India*, first published in 1817, made the treatment of women among different races and cultures a transcendent mark of adjudging superiority. "Among rude people the women are generally degraded, among civilized people they are exalted."[6] One essential feature of the way in which British colonialism marked out the racial hierarchies necessary to the maintenance of colonial rule connects us back, through an examination of prostitution, to the governing precepts of criminological theory and that is, the critical if misleading binary division between the masculine active and the feminine passive.

One fuzzy but fascinating area of investigation, invaluable in investigating this divide, is the so-called "white slave trade" or "white slave traffic." Often dubbed a fantasy of late Victorian fervidity, the white slave trade invoked an image of unsullied innocent young women kidnapped and coerced into brothels against their will to feed an ever-hungry male population with an unquenchable desire for young white female flesh.[7] It relied crucially on the depiction of women as passive victims given over to the active insatiability of a bigger and stronger power. While evidence of a large-scale human trade of this sort has never been satisfactorily established, its existence is quite simply *not* the point. Its rhetorical function, on the other hand—which stands at the meeting point of issues of race and sexual role—has never been questioned, nor has its impact on attitudes to female criminality in the nineteenth century. It is these that I will reconsider here in the light of notions of crime and sexual disorder.

The idea of a white slave trade had its prototype in both the popular and the pornographic literature of the eighteenth and nineteenth centuries. Lord Byron, at the turn of the century, racialized a penchant for lustful cruelty in his popular poem, *The Giaour*, which tells of a young girl, Leila, drowned for infidelity by the sultan who possessed her. Byron described the unfortunate Leila as "a soulless toy for tyrant's lust."[8]

The pornographic formula of the time involved a white virgin stolen by an Oriental potentate and subjected to his sexual attentions. In these tales, though the damsel begins by resisting, she ends up worshipping at the phallic altar.[9] The stock narrative of the later white slave trade panic, a device more of journalism than of pornographers or literati, ended in less celebratory fashion than the male fantasies of this earlier erotica, but it is hard to believe that such past masters of the exposé as William Stead (of "The Maiden Tribute of Modern Babylon") or Alfred Dyer were not exploiting much the same sensational medium, with their stories of girls plucked from their homeland to service faceless and unnumbered legions of men in inhospitably foreign environments.[10] The repeated rapes perpetrated by determined fictional sultans and the stream of brothel clientele bear some similarity in their representation of a perverted and racialized coercive sexuality.

The complex racial dynamics of empire, central to its sustenance given the fragile but critical declaration of white prestige, worked, however, to reframe the stock figures of the white slave trade narrative in suggestive ways. The most spectacular stories at home told of the "young country-faced girl" approached and, of course, finally seduced by a "flashy" man.[11] Less sensational versions presented young girls of slightly less impeachable character but still with enough moral sense left to want to step back from the brink at the last moment—but, of course, prevented from doing so by the profiteers. In most versions, it was foreign men, souteneurs, and their women companions—frequently Jewish or French—who instigated the "downward path" and made good from the young woman's misfortunes.

The two elements, then, on which this story relied were women's ultimate lack of choice, and the dangers associated with foreignness and foreigners. Women working as prostitutes were not the criminals of the white slave trade; they were unfortunate victims of a criminal class of procurers. Women's crimes were not, thus, of their own making; they could be pitied, they could be rescued, and they could be redeemed because though their morals were in peril, their feminine helplessness was not so much intact in this scenario as it was *definitional*. But if we turn our attention to commentators around the globe, rather than in Britain (or France or America, where the white slave trade was as celebrated as it was in Britain), a different picture emerges, one that suggests to me that the links between crime and race in this period are more complex and more critical than we have hitherto fashioned them.

The white slave trade was, of course, already and inherently about race, since it alluded to a slavery that some reformers claimed was more terrible than that experienced by Africans uprooted from their homes. But translated to the colonial context, the figure of the hapless and properly passive white woman sexually enslaved would not and did not work. For, as my earlier quotation about enslaved Chinese women suggested, such total passivity was the province not of "civilized" whites but of ignorant "natives." Thus what in London was represented as a commerce that shipped white women to the major colonial centers—India, Egypt, South America, South Africa—was given a very different spin by colonial authorities. Ann Stoler reminds us that "colonial cultures were never direct translations of European society planted in the colonies, but unique cultural configurations."[12] The reformulation of the white slave trade in this context stands as one bizarre but significant case study of that precise point.

Fanny Epstein was a young working-class Jew employed in the East London garment trade. When she and her belongings disappeared one day in 1891, the National Vigilance Association and her father were convinced that she had been abducted and was a victim of the white slave trade, but when Fanny was successfully located in Bombay, she told the European Police Commissioner there a very different story, impressing him with her "singular calm and self-possession."

I particularly questioned her, and more than once, as to whether she was being, or had been, coerced in any way, but she laughed at the idea and said she was entirely her own mistress and could do as she pleased. She expressed no contrition or regret for having left her father's house or for anything else she had done, nor did she show any horror for the position in which she there was.[13]

The Epstein case is unusual, insofar as it was pursued with some vigor by the social purity group, the National Vigilance Association, who finally prosecuted Alexander Cahn—whom they dubbed "a notorious trafficker in girls"[14]—for Epstein's procurement late in 1891, and because we have Epstein's own testimony to the police in India. Of course, it may be that she made her apparently unruffled statement under duress, but the attitude of the Police Commissioner toward her statement is not out of keeping with the shift in thinking about sexual slavery and about female criminality that I am arguing accompanied the move eastward.

Deborah Gorham, in an important and pioneering article on the white slave trade and child prostitution in England, points to the discomfort that otherwise sympathetic police officers felt toward the independence of the working-class child.[15] In the colonial context, those same indices of independence became not a mark of potential unruliness or delinquency so much as a symbol of whiteness and of civilization. European women engaged in prostitution in the East were, of course, a profound threat to white prestige and to the alleged safety of "respectable" white womanhood. But at the same time, and contrary to the sensationalism of stock white trade narratives, they were cognizant of their actions, exercising rational choice and free will, and were not subject to the bonds of slavery so crucial to the

Western picture of female helplessness. They may have been prostitutes, and in the case of Epstein, problematically Jewish, but they were still white and the vestiges of civilization thus clung to them. The Legislative Council of the Straits Settlements, debating the need for a Women and Girls' Protection Ordinance in the late 1880s, had no doubt as to that distinction. The Singapore legislators concurred in the wisdom of confining protective provision to "brothels which are exclusively occupied by Asiatic women. It is considered that European women need no special protection and are able to take care of themselves."[16]

It was, then, the indigenous women of various colonial possessions who were the unfortunate victims of the barbarity of sexual slavery, according to this doubly racialized version of the white slave trade story. A gubernatorial committee reporting on brothels in the Straits ten years later concluded that Chinese brothel inmates in Singapore and the Malay Peninsula "have absolutely no voice in any matter in connection with their own lives," while in contrast "European and Japanese women . . . come here avowedly to practice their profession and are willing to submit to the consequences thereof."[17] Singapore's protector of Chinese took the same view. The "young and helpless" Chinese girls of the brothels were, he said, "mere articles of trade or barter."[18]

In India, the scenario differed only slightly. In the 1870s, the Indian government gave serious consideration to legislation that would have prevented Indian dancing women—widely regarded as prostitutes by another name—from the common practice of adopting young girls whom they trained in their varied arts. The legislation was largely considered by colonial officials to be pointless and, more dangerously, to be capable of rousing strong indigenous protest. The deputy commissioner of Gurgaon, writing to his superior divisional officer in Delhi, was more succinct in his prose, but his view was typical among the majority who successfully opposed the legislation. "It must be remembered that the chief and almost universal amusement of the Natives is watching dances and hearing singing, and the performers are always women of immoral character brought up to the trade from their childhood."[19] In short, women were dedicated to "immorality" at an early age: They had no choice in the matter.

In a recent article on Victorian criminological discourse, Patrick Brantlinger and Donald Ulin point to the irony—and the fear—of a criminal freer than a respectable citizen bound by the fetters of the rule of law. They point to a decisive Foucauldian shift in early Victorian thinking from the criminal as agent to the criminal as a product of environment or birth.[20] The colonial version of this can be seen in the distinction between the self-made white prostitute and the voiceless and choiceless. Even translated to the shores of Britain, the "oriental" was a passive vessel of impurity and depravity. In the first eight pages of his account of missionary work among

Eastern seamen in London, Joseph Salter refers to the "helpless Lascar," "the poor helpless natives of India," and "the helpless Oriental."[21]

Contrast the descriptions of European women working as prostitutes in Asia. In his memoir of life in Singapore in the early years of the twentieth century, Alec Dixon remembered the European women as "street walkers of the florid, blowsy type, foul-mouthed harridans,"[22] R.C.H. McKie painted a similar picture: "They were tough unruly harridans these girls who sat on doorsteps below their heavy scented rooms and screamed their wares."[23] In both these descriptions, not only are the European women in control of their trade and hardened to it, as all the police reports also contend, but they were loud—they screamed and they swore. They were anything but voiceless.

At home, of course, in Europe, such women would have been consigned to the dustbin of delinquency, and increasingly, over the course of the century, their prostitution would have been seen as evidence of inherited feeble-mindedness or depravity. In the colonies, small though their numbers were, their position was more ambiguous, and their presence complicated the ways in which crime and disorder were perceived. Such women were clearly a problem—they undermined the respectability of imperialism, the specific roles assigned to European femininity, and the easy racial divides of imperial rhetoric.[24] Yet they were still European, and however great a problem their presence posed, they could not be treated as if they were the same as, or indeed as if they were, "natives."

This curious tension gave rise to an interesting realignment in ideas of disorder and criminality in colonial contexts. European prostitute women were professionals, and as such they appreciated the need for order and regulation. Thus, though the mass slavery that Chinese, Indian, and even Japanese women were said to endure was seen as deplorable, even in their passivity it was nonetheless indigenous women who represented disorder. White women who, in the metropolitan context, would have been subject to constant police surveillance and very probably to harassment and endless petty conviction—almost certainly on charges of disorderliness, a favorite charge against prostitutes in British police courts—were said by the colonial police to "give . . . very little trouble."[25] European women were magically transformed from marginal figures who had dropped out of femininity into business-like professionals, rationally appreciating the need for control and regulation of their business and gracefully submitting to the physical examinations required under the myriad contagious diseases ordinances passed by British authorities throughout the empire from the mid-1850s on. As E. J. Bristow has remarked, "the logic of regulated prostitution everywhere was to prevent disorder, not to stop illicit sex."[26] The small numbers of European women practicing prostitution in Asia, at least according to the police, were cooperative, and since cooperation in this arena was a sign of personal responsibility, it was also represented therefore as an active compliance and not an act of passive ignorant submission. European women *chose* to cooperate while local women, required to do so by their brothel keepers, were attending the examinations for venereal disease out of fear and ignorance, or conversely, not attending out of fear and ignorance.

This contrast also made the individuality of indigenous women effectively disappear. In this picture of a widespread slavery, Chinese, Indian, and other colonized women became a faceless innumerable mass, their personalities sacrificed to male greed.[27] When Henry Champly described the flourishing sexual slave trade he sought out in Hong Kong, he drew a picture of Asians as a throng too dense to enumerate, describing "droves of little Yellow girls . . . made ready . . . for a lifetime of prostitution, on the spot or overseas."[28]

This facelessness of the indigenous woman fostered an important duality by which, on the one hand, onlookers could deplore or even sympathize with her plight, but, on the other hand, she remained lifeless since neither name nor personality was hers. In contrast to the growing interest in criminal exploits in the domestic context where the criminal personality was imagined and described in increasing detail, this erasure of the individual intensified the idea of passivity. The famous criminal, the criminal personality, ran counter to the profile of the enslaved woman; the notorious individual was too active and too colorful an image to invoke in the colonial context.

Resistance on the part of the colonized could thus also be diminished in importance. John Kelley has argued convincingly, in the context of Fiji's indentured Indian laborers, that indigenous resistance was dismissed by discrediting the moral authority of the native voice.[29] Women seen as disorderly or too brutalized to have any semblance of personality, and therefore opinion, would clearly exercise none of the agency or moral power that resistance might imply; their protests, like their names and faces, were muted, blurred, and disregarded.

This racial divide could render even "victims" criminal while contributing to a curious and certainly qualified "rehabilitation" of women who in Europe would have been unequivocally castigated. When local white philanthropists and social purity activists in Bombay petitioned the governor-general of India in 1888 to crack down on the importation of enslaved European women, the government was reluctant to take action. One senior civil servant justified this stand succinctly: "no offence was in these cases committed in India. The women were not under 16 . . . by the time they reached India they had learnt by experience the life they were intended to lead. They can in India always extricate themselves."[30]

That independence of will was racially determined. A British official in Singapore noted that "Chinese and probably Malay women . . . are regarded by the men as inferior beings and treated accordingly and do not exercise any independence of will, so that they have in these cases to be protected against their own weakness of character as well as against the brutality of the men, and of the brothel keepers of both sexes."[31]

Such a statement was as much about British chivalry and civilization as it was about alleged conditions in Southeast Asia. Indigenous women brutalized by a culture of enslavement had neither voice nor moral authority; both their malleability and their acts of resistance were understood to be products of some form of loosely understood slavery. But lest we ascribe this view only to men whose loyalties to the colonial state were strong, or to defenders of the highly controversial legislation where this story began, let me suggest rather that such ideas circulated freely in Britain, as well as among Britons in the colonies, and in many different locations. It was Harriet Taylor Mill, writing on the enfranchisement of women, who echoed the words of her late father-in-law, quoted earlier, when she declared, "in Asia, women were and are the slaves of men for purposes of sensuality."[32]

Significantly, other than in South Africa, the idea of a white slave trade was not applied to women who sought work as prostitutes or who were forced into prostitution in Britain's white settler colonies.[33] Both E. J. Bristow and Donna Guy have pointed out that little concern was ever expressed about a coercive trade in *local* women in those countries where the white slave trade was alleged to be a problem.[34] A white slave trade to a dominantly white country had no meaning as a racial marker, just as the subordination of indigenous women to a local trade had no such currency. In Australia, New Zealand, and Canada, white prostitute women were subject to regulations similar to those that women in Britain experienced.[35] This is not to deny the profound ways in which whiteness operated to signify Englishness and thus civilization, but more to underline the particular historical contexts in which racial difference, as opposed to homogeneity, were dominant at this juncture.

The white slave trade, as it translated to the colonial context, evoked powerful fears—but less for the well-being of women allegedly coerced into paid sex than for the well-being of imperial stability. The translation from passive slave to active business woman and from shrewd manipulation of demand to passive enslavement effected respectively on white and on indigenous women living and working in British colonial possessions is an important phenomenon, one that, as I began by arguing, significantly problematizes our understanding of gender and crime.

Tellingly, the white British criminal woman safely located on *home* soil could be profitably compared to the "ignorant native" and found wanting. Writing of the white slave trade in the Edwardian period, G. Kerschener Knight traced a clear racial degradation through prostitution, heavily influenced by the eugenic theories of the time. "There is no doubt that finding herself the object of contempt and ridicule, the prostitute drifts into recklessness, and the consequence is that her self-respect is gradually eliminated, and she becomes an alien to her race."[36] Half a century earlier, in 1866, an anonymous article in *The Cornhill Magazine* expressed remarkably similar sentiments, long before the rise of eugenics held sway. The author of the *Cornhill* article argued that "[C]riminal women, as a class, are found to be more uncivilized than the savage, more degraded than the slave, less true to all natural and womanly instincts than the untutored squaw of a North American Indian tribe."[37] This association of criminal women with the "savagery" of the uncivilized was perfectly feasible in the domestic context, where it served the rhetorical purpose of separating ruling and subordinate races as well as good and bad women. In colonial contexts, however, such an association would have played dangerously with the overridingly important insistence on the particular and elevated status of white women. Though the narratives of female criminality were effectively racialized in both contexts—at home and out in the empire—the political context demanded in each case was radically and critically different.

This association between the work of female prostitution and the fact of "blackness" has been noted by critics such as Patricia Hill Collins, Sander Gilman, and Anne McClintock, as well as by novelist Lorraine Hansberry.[38] Collins, Gilman, and McClintock trace a growing tendency in nineteenth-century Western culture to class prostitutes and black peoples "within a discourse on racial degeneration," and this was certainly apparent both in the denigration of "eastern" morals and in the treatment of prostitute women domestically. McClintock, however, argues—as does Luise White—that in the colonial setting prostitution allowed black women significant economic control over their own lives.[39]

My reading of how the colonial state made so clear a division on *racial* grounds between white and indigenous women who worked in prostitution destabilizes what I see as an overly optimistic assertion of black female autonomy in this context. That is not to say that indigenous women did not find forms of resistance and independence in this arena—they clearly wielded that power in many instances—but rather to suggest that a picture of uninterrupted optimism and agency is no less misleading than one of an enduring pessimism of victimization. Women did find ways to make an inegalitarian and dehumanizing system work for them economically, politically, and sexually, but that does not, I would contend, dilute the ways in which racial distinction operated to create particular and colonially specific readings of delinquency that shifted suspicion disproportionately away from European and onto colonized women's bodies. In this reading, the disorder of white women—potentially a hugely threatening challenge to the stability of white rule—was tameable by evoking an ersatz notion of professionalism, while Asian lack of agency—already a common theme of colonial commentary—spelled disorder through and within passivity, and on a large scale.

When magistrate Cecil Chapman, writing of his London courtroom, observed that prostitution "is not a sexual offence, but an offence against order and decency in our streets," he might well have been speaking as much of the colonial as of the metropolitan context.[40] Prostitution was a barometer and an index of stability and of the potential for disorder; while prostitution itself was never specifically criminalized by the British, it remained a means of shaping a female delinquency that was different in kind and in character from that of male delinquency, and in ways that fed both the gendered and the racial expectations of a nation deeply committed to colonial rule. Order and decency in the streets had profoundly different meanings in colonial and in domestic settings, and the place of women in that meaning was never color-blind, but there can be no doubt, too, that public order and decency were powerful vehicles whereby the mobility and the choices of women, both British and non-British, could be controlled. The creation of a criminal class of women, sexualized and racialized into an essential if disorderly womanhood, was the necessary corollary of the proper womanhood that was its obverse. Those who continue to consider crime quantitatively and who, thus, dismiss women as anomalous, minor, or otherwise unimportant in our historical understanding of such issues are doomed, therefore, to miss out on a rich vein of resources that point us toward a more complex and more heterogeneously accurate vision of crime and its meaning in greater Victorian Britain. And, in the same vein, those who still choose to read the colonial project as "out there" rather than "back home" might look to this episode for powerful and palpable linkages, not only between "metropole" and "periphery" but between race, gender, and the politics of control.

NOTES

Particular thanks go to Cornelie Usborne and Meg Arnot of Roehampton College, London. Had they not organized a Gender and Crime conference at which I promised to speak, I may never have had the impetus to write this chapter. Antoinette Burton and Debbie Gorham gave invaluable suggestions as I revised the essay, and Doug Peers encouraged me to consider publishing it. I thank all three for their intelligence and their generosity.

1. L. Pike's *A History of Crime in England* (1876), quoted in Allison Morris, *Women, Crime and Criminal Justice* (Oxford, 1987). For the twentieth-century version of this argument, see Freda Adler, *Sisters in Crime: The Rise of the New Female Criminal* (New York, 1975), and Rita J. Simon, *Women and Crime* (Lexington, 1973).

2. Philippa Levine, "Public and Private Paradox: Prostitution and the State," *Arena*, n.s. 1 (1993): 131–144.

3. Susan S. M. Edwardes, "Selling the Body, Keeping the Soul: Sexuality, Power, the Theories and Realities of Prostitution," in *Body Matters: Essays on the Sociology of the Body*, ed. Sue Scott and David Morgan (London, 1993); Anne McClintock, "Screwing the System: Sexwork, Race and the Law," *Boundary* 19 (1992): 70–95.

4. Good examples of this genre include William Logan, *The Great Social Evil: Its Causes, Extent, Results and Remedies* (London, 1871); Baptist Wriothesley Noel, *The Fallen and Their Associates* (London, 1860); James Beard Talbot, *The Miseries of Prostitution* (London, 1844); William Tait, *Magdalenism: An Inquiry into the Extent, Causes and Consequences of Prostitution in Edinburgh* (Edinburgh, 1840).

5. Parliamentary Papers, House of Commons 1880 (118). *Report of the Commission appointed by His Excellency John Pope Hennessy to Inquire into the Working of the Contagious Diseases Ordinance, 1867*, 19.

6. Quoted in A. Copley, "Projection, Displacement and Distortion in Nineteenth-Century Moral Imperialism: A Re-Examination of Charles Grant and James Mill," *Calcutta Historical Journal* (1983): 15.

7. Nickie Roberts, *Whores in History: Prostitution in Western Society* (London, 1992), 253, and Ronald Hyam, *Empire and Sexuality. The British Experience* (Manchester, 1990), both see the white slave trade as a product of the Victorian imagination. Donna Guy, "White Slavery, Public Health, and the Socialist Position on Legalized Prostitution in Argentina, 1913–1936," *Latin American Research Review* 23 (1988): 60–80, argues that the white slave trade was much exaggerated. Lara Marks, "Jewish Women and Jewish Prostitution in the East End of London," *Jewish Quarterly* 34 (1982): 6–10, and Lloyd P. Gartner, "Anglo-Jewry and the Jewish International Traffic in Prostitution, 1885–1914," *AJS Review* 7–8 (1982–83): 129–78; both accept its existence unquestioningly, while Edward Bristow has examined it with great care in his *Prostitution and Prejudice: The Jewish Fight Against White Slavery 1870–1939* (Oxford, 1982).

8. Lord Byron, *The Giaour* (1813), 1, 490; Jerome J. McGann, ed., *Byron* (Oxford, 1986), 220. With thanks to J. C. Aldstadt and Peter Manning for steering me to, and informing me about this poem. Byron's is a complex picture, however, for as Marilyn Butler notes, "Christianity has no spokesmen in the poem but ignorant zealots": "The Orientalism of Byron's *Giaour*," in *Byron and the Limits of Fiction*, ed. Bernard Beatty and Vincent Newey (Liverpool, 1988), 85.

9. See, for example, *The Lustful Turk*, a pornographic novel first published in 1828 and discussed in Steven Marcus, *The Other Victorians* (London 1966), 197–216.

10. Judith Walkowitz also sees a pornographic element in this exposé journalism. See her *City of Dreadful Delight, Narratives of Sexual Danger in Late Victorian London* (Chicago, 1992), 85.

11. *Pitfalls for Women* (London, n.d. [c. 1912–1914]), 25–26.

12. Ann Stoler, "Rethinking Colonial Categories: European Communities and the Boundaries of Rule," *Comparative Studies in Society and History* 31 (1989): 136–37.

13. Oriental and India Office Collection, British Library, London [hereafter OIOC]. L/P&J/6/311. File 2082/1891. Bombay Police Commissioner to Secretary to Government, Judicial Department, 11 Nov. 1891.

14. Fawcett Library, London. National Vigilance Association Records. Box 194. Minutes of Executive Committee, Vol. II, 30 June 1891.

15. Deborah Gorham, "The 'Maiden Tribute to Modern Babylon' Re-Examined: Child Prostitution and Idea of Childhood in Late-Victorian England," *Victorian Studies* 21 (1978): 374.

16. Public Record Office, London [hereafter PRO]. Colonial Office Papers: CO275/34. Proceedings of the Legislative Council of the Straits Settlements, 1888.

17. PRO. CO273/237 (1898). *Report of the Committee appointed by the Governor of the Straits Settlements to enquire and report on certain suggestions made by the Secretary of State for the Colonies as to measures to be adopted with regard to contagious diseases and brothels with a view to checking the spread of venereal disease.* For a different view of the agency of migrant Japanese women working in brothels, see Yamazaki Tomoko, "Sandakan No. 8 Brothel," *Bulletin of Concerned Asian Scholars* 7 (1975): 52–60.

18. PRO. CO 273/140, Minute of W. A. Pickering, Protector of Chinese, 14 August 1886.

19. National Archives of India, New Delhi [hereafter NAI]. Proceedings of Home Department, Judicial Branch. Consultations. July 1873, Nos. 151–205. J. H. Oliver, Deputy Commissioner, Gurgaon to Lt. Col. J. E. Cracroft, Commissioner and Superintendent, Delhi Division, 30 May 1872.

20. Patrick Brantlinger and Donald Ulin, "Policing Nomads: Discourse and Social Control in Early Victorian England," *Cultural Critique* 25 (1993): 38, 39.

21. Joseph Salter, *The Asiatic in England, Sketches of Sixteen Years' Work Among Orientals* (London, 1873), 5, 7, 8. For a discussion of Salter's writings, see Ruth H. Lindeborg, "The 'Asiatic' and the Boundaries of Victorian Englishness," *Victorian Studies* 37 (1994): 381–404.

22. Alec Dixon, *Singapore Patrol* (London, 1935), 209.

23. R.C.H. McKie, *This Was Singapore* (Sydney, 1942), 101.

24. For a discussion of poor whites as a similar group, see Stoler, "Rethinking Colonial Categories."

25. NAI, Proceedings of Home Department, Police. A Series, December 1893, Nos. 50–55. Sir J. Lambert, Commissioner of Police. Calcutta to Chief Secretary, Government of Bengal, 14 July 1893.

26. Bristow, *Prostitution and Prejudice*, 32.

27. Jenny Sharpe has noted a similar tendency in narratives of the Indian "Mutiny" of 1857 whereby "natives" are mostly a fearsome blurry mass, while English women are drawn in sharper outline. See her *Allegories of Empire: The Figure of Women in the Colonial Text* (Minneapolis, 1993), 74–76.

28. Henry Champly, *The Road to Shanghai: White Slave Traffic in Asia* (London, 1934), 147.

29. John Kelley, "Discourse about Sexuality and the End of Indenture in Fiji: The Making of Counter-Hegemonic Discourse," *History and Anthropology* 5 (1990): 45.

30. NAI, Proceedings of Home Department, Judicial Branch, July 1888, Nos. 83–89. J.P.H. to Private Secretary to Governor General, 1 June 1888.

31. PRO. CO 273/139. File 6870. Minute, 28 June 1886. Signature illegible.

32. Harriet Taylor Mill, *The Enfranchisement of Women* (London, 1983), 25. For a discussion of feminists' political use of a rhetoric around slavery, see Antoinette Burton, *Burdens of History. British Feminists, Indian Women and Imperial Culture, 1865–1915* (Chapel Hill, 1994, especially 78–79), and Vron Ware, *Beyond the Pale: White Women, Racism and History* (London, 1992), especially Part II.

33. In his discussion of Transvaal prostitution, Charles vanOnselen continues to use the term white slavery even while acknowledging that European white women

working in the sex trade there were largely there of their own volition. See his *Studies in the Social and Economic History of the Witwatersrand 1886–1914. Volume I: New Babylon* (Johannesburg, 1982).

34. Bristow, *Prostitution and Prejudice*, 203; Donna Guy, "Medical Imperialism Gone Awry: The Campaign Against Legalized Prostitution in Latin America," in *Science, Medicine and Cultural Imperialism*, ed. Teresa Meade and Peter Walker (New York, 1991), 80.

35. Although in Queensland, where a significant aboriginal presence remained, black women were regarded as more promiscuous. See, for instance, Raymond Evans, Kay Saunders, and Kathryn Cronin, *Race Relations in Colonial Queensland: A History of Exclusion, Exploitation and Extermination* (St. Lucia, 1988).

36. G. Kerschener Knight, *The White Slaves of England* (Denham, Buckinghamshire, 1910).

37. "Criminal Women," *The Cornhill Magazine* 14 (July to December 1866): 153. With thanks to Elizabeth Bleicher for drawing my attention to this source.

38. Patricia Hill Collins, *Black Feminist Thought, Knowledge, Consciousness and the Politics of Empowerment* (New York, 1991); Sander Gilman, " 'I'm Down On Whores': Race and Gender in Victorian London," in *Anatomy of Racism*, ed. David T. Goldberg (Minneapolis, 1990); McClintock, "Screwing the System"; Lorraine Hansberry, *To Be Young, Gifted and Black* (New York, 1969).

39. McClintock, "Screwing the System," 84–85; Luise White, *The Comforts of Home: Prostitution in Colonial Nairobi* (Chicago, 1990).

40. Cecil Chapman, *From the Bench* (London, 1932), 107.

Book Review Essay: New Directions in the History of Crime and the Law in Early Modern England

Malcolm Gaskill

Louis A. Knafla, ed., *Kent at Law 1602: The County Jurisdiction: Assizes and Sessions of the Peace* (London, HMSO, 1994). xl + 410 pp. £50.00.

J. S. Cockburn, ed., *Calendar of Assize Records: Kent Indictments, Charles I* (London, HMSO, 1995). viii + 753 pp. £95.00.

In the same way that social history has come a long way since G. M. Trevelyan defined it as "the history of a people with the politics left out," so too the history of crime and criminal justice has progressed since the mid-1970s, when Sir Geoffrey Elton, somewhat casually, imposed a series of limitations upon its potential scope and significance.[1] Indeed, there are strong parallels between the development of the two fields. Between the 1930s and 1950s, social history established for itself an identity distinct from its mainstream political counterpart (albeit one characterized by nostalgia and antiquarianism); then, in the 1960s, its reincarnation as the "new social history" helped to politicize its central concerns; and finally, in a recent, more self-confident phase, it has been repositioned into a wider interpretative context. In other words, goals and perspectives beyond what Trevelyan ever could have imagined in the 1940s have put the politics back in, and many would now argue that the distinction between social and political history is essentially arbitrary.[2] Criminal justice history has followed a similar path, starting life as a cabinet of curiosities, thereafter reborn with a stronger political and administrative bearing from the union of legal history and social history between the late 1960s and mid-1970s.[3] By the mid-1980s, signs were emerging that criminal justice history had gained sufficient stature not just for the statistics of criminality to be *linked* to politics and society via the institutions and offices that created them, but for the whole field to be more fully integrated into the wider historical context that social history since has rejoined. Yet satisfactory integration was elusive, and in 1986 Joanna Innes and John Styles went as far as saying that "the field's potential has not yet been realized . . . because the ways in which historians have attempted that integration have been deficient."[4] A decade on, however, fresh approaches and methods are being tested that promise to make more sense of crime and the law and, beyond that, may cast new light on the broader structures and procedures of politics and society.

This article is divided into three parts. First, it traces some general trends that have emerged in the history of crime and the law in early modern England over the last fifteen years or so. More specifically, it describes and appraises two recently published volumes of seventeenth-century English criminal justice data.[5] Finally, it examines the latter against the background of the former and puts forward some observations and suggestions about new directions for the field, specifically regarding the necessity of proper social and cultural contextualization if historians are to understand what crime and the law actually *meant* to contemporaries. Hence this is an article about criminal justice, but, equally, it concerns the attitudes and mentalities that defined and shaped criminal justice and suggests some ways in which these might be recovered from the past.

THE HISTORIOGRAPHY

There is no need to rehearse twenty years of debate about crime and the law in early modern England, as there are a number of articles in print that do the job perfectly well.[6] The purpose here is to identify patterns in historical research that have become prominent since the mid-1980s, and to see where they might be leading. Perhaps the first point to establish is that interest in the history of law, litigation, crime, deviance, disorder and punishment in early modern England remains strong. At the time of writing, no fewer than fifteen theses listed in the British Institute of Historical Research guide to higher degrees in progress relate to these themes, and undergraduate history courses about crime and criminal justice seem more popular than ever.[7] The output of published work, moreover, is so prodigious that this brief survey cannot hope to be nearly comprehensive. Nor is this due only to volume, but also to the continual subdivision and expansion of the field into areas of interest not easily gathered together under the traditional "crime and the law" heading.

New county studies of crime and criminal justice have become rather rare, perhaps reflecting a feeling that we now have a sufficient number and need instead to concentrate on the issues they have raised.[8] Although the fifteen research projects referred to above mostly have a geographical dimension, they are primarily monographical, focusing on specific interests such as homicide, prostitution, dearth and crime, gender and crime, and the regulation of sexual morality. Indeed, the more recent county studies to appear have a secondary organizing theme, which their authors evidently considered more important than locale. Theft is a good example of this,[9] so too is the relationship between women and the law, which in 1994 produced an unpublished county study and a book of essays covering topics as eclectic as prosecutions for scolding, and war widows seeking pensions through the courts.[10] These new areas also have intersected in a fruitful way. In the aforementioned collection, one of the editors contributed an essay on women *and* theft, and, in turn, recent research into the problem of youth overlaps both subjects.[11] Interest in actions for slander and defamation involving women continues to expand;[12] likewise the wider question of civil litigation by which local disputes might be settled and communal order restored.[13] Female violence also has received due attention, especially infanticide,[14] and although the debate about the decline of violence limps on in its own right, it now extends beyond the interpretation of homicide statistics to the meaning of violence in society in general, including judicial punishment.[15] Allied to punishment is the question of the religious and state ideology it underpinned.[16] Finally, research into rural crime, or "social crime," within a particular county or region remains popular and continues to generate questions and answers about early modern social relationships and cultural conflict.[17]

Expansion and subdivision of the field are natural progressions, but it is important not to allow things to fragment to the point that we can no longer see the whole—a criticism that has been leveled at early modern social history by one of its most committed practitioners.[18] Here questions of context and meaning are crucial: If we cannot occasionally look around while we scrutinize the details, we miss an opportunity to understand the original subtlety and complexity of those details. In 1988, for example, Jim Sharpe argued that "reflecting on the implications of the Reformation on law enforcement might at this stage in the development of the field be a more profitable use of time than constructing the next county's crime statistics."[19] Nor was this an original proposal: Several intensive studies of urban and rural society by historians whose main interest was not crime, had already described contemporary attempts to protect property, contain disorder, and regulate personal behavior.[20] Hence it is in this tradition, as much as that of criminal justice history, that new work is now addressing broad and searching questions of political authority—its institutions and ideologies, how it was exercised and experienced, and whether it was accepted, endured, or resisted.[21] These issues are also linked to the English state, which, though never monolithic, now appears not so much weak as diffuse, drawing its strength from the deployment of central authority at the level of the community.[22] Such lines of inquiry are equally relevant to social, political, and criminal justice history, and it is profitable for our comprehension of the period as a whole that they should be integrated.

This is not to say, however, that criminal justice cannot remain the organizing theme in future work, provided sensitivity is shown toward what John McMullan has called the "structuring processes through time that underpin the relationships between law, property, power, the state and acts defined and managed as crime."[23] For instance, there are still too few studies that explore crime from the perspective of the criminal and within the context of ordinary working lives. Peter Linebaugh's *London Hanged* is a masterly study of economic crime in Georgian London, contextualized in such a way that we cease to see many of the acts he describes as "criminal" at all but regard them instead as normal strategies upon which the proletarian poor depended for survival.[24] Above all, what is needed is a broadly conceived social history of the law in early modern England: a study that examines in detail how and why all manner of people both broke the law and used the law. Recent studies of legal procedure have been helpful in this regard,[25] but still we need research that shows what both formal and informal countermeasures meant in popular and quotidian contexts.[26] We know much about *how* the law operated as it did; now we need to know *why*, or to put it another way, it is time to build on our knowledge of the anatomy of criminal justice with a full investigation of its physiology.[27]

Central to this question are popular attitudes—"that most elusive of issues," according to Jim Sharpe—as difficult to recover as they are essential to understand.[28] Because of this difficulty, historians have tended to assume the existence of attitudes rather than demonstrating them directly. Robert Shoemaker has argued that our limited knowledge of popular attitudes is due to overconcentration on judges and jurors rather than ordinary prosecutors and defendants. By studying misdemeanor prosecutions in London and Middlesex, 1660–1725, Dr. Shoemaker claims to have taken "a step towards a wider understanding of the social significance of the law," and to a degree he has. Yet given his restricted locale and time span, he still is forced to rely on counting data derived from laconic sources such as indictments, which, especially in the absence of suitable qualitative sources, do not allow the membrane of contemporary meanings to be penetrated.[29]

We need to examine what might be called "qualitative contexts of crime and prosecution," which incorporate events at every procedural stage and in every social arena from the moment a crime was committed or detected. Especially important here is pretrial procedure, in particular the meanings of the words, actions, and legal strategies of plaintiffs and witnesses.[30] Only through such contexts can we move away from what E. P. Thompson called "the thin air of 'meanings, attitudes and value,'" and toward an approach committed to examining attitudes in action. In other words, we cannot hope to capture attitudes structurally, but only as a series of contingent and varied choices, deliberations, decisions, and practical responses.[31] As a consequence, we never will be precise; the best we can hope for are tentative suggestions about broad trends over time.[32] Of greatest

importance, however, is that we concentrate on excavating specific meanings, and that we take early modern crime and the law as far as possible
on their own terms rather than imposing the preoccupations of the present
upon the past. As Elton once argued, we must try "to understand a given
problem from the inside."[33] Yet where the positivist Elton would have
drawn the line, but where Dr. Linebaugh breaks new ground, is the need
to use historical imagination—licence even—to breathe life into qualitative
contexts. We must construct actively these contexts for ourselves; we cannot assume them, nor will the sources yield their secrets without them. And
so it is to sources that we now turn.

THE SOURCES

Criminal justice historians wanting to recreate qualitative contexts need
to trawl widely through an ocean of sources and then think carefully about
what they net. There is no space here to discuss the methodological problems of sources essentially elite in production, and they have been discussed
elsewhere.[34] More relevant is the scope of the sources that have become
widely available recently, thus extending the possibilities of research for
students and scholars alike. The last few years have seen the appearance
of numerous editions and reprints of literary sources, including chapbooks,
ballads, rogue literature, newsbooks,[35] and various other editions such as
a collection of assize sermons and an eighteenth-century magistrate's notebook.[36] The printed Old Bailey Sessions Papers now can be read on microfilm, as can several series of eighteenth-century newspapers from London,
Bath, Derby, Ipswich, and elsewhere—still an underused source by historians of crime, and crammed with qualitative information.[37] A collection
of microfiched pamphlets, "British Trials 1660–1900," has further served
these interests.[38] Most useful are microfilmed legal archives, which include
the church court records from the dioceses of Ely and Chichester for the
sixteenth and seventeenth centuries (and earlier), quarter sessions books
and files for the county of Cheshire, and the Northern Circuit assize depositions from 1613 to 1800.[39] For researchers with access to English record
offices, a range of indexes and handbooks, which help make legal archives
intelligible, are now available. These include guides to the central courts of
Star Chamber and Chancery,[40] and the local courts of quarter sessions, the
coroner, and the ecclesiastical authorities.[41] Impressions of the contexts in
which crimes were committed and acted against can be reinforced using
state papers, widely available in printed calendars and now complete in
facsimile form on microfilm.[42] Already, it is possible for anyone, anywhere,
to research a multilayered study of crime in early modern England within
the walls of a single library. The scale and scope of what is available,
moreover, continues to grow.
Dr. Louis Knafla, Professor of History at the University of Calgary, has

been working on the "Kent at Law 1602" project based at the Public Record Office, London, since 1980. This volume—*The County Jurisdiction, Assizes and Sessions of the Peace*—is the first to emerge from those endeavors. The initial idea for the project as a whole was simple: to assess the total volume of legal business for a single county in a single year in the seventeenth century and to make, and make possible, interconnections between different jurisdictions. This broad picture, it was conceived, would include not just the well-known courts at Westminster, the visiting assizes, local quarter and borough sessions, and the ecclesiastical courts, but also an array of less familiar authorities, such as the court of Admiralty, and minor jurisdictions across the county—town and manor courts, for example. In 1983 Knafla set out his proposals in an article that argued that the courts were integrated not just with one another but with society, and that historians' treatment of the records should respect this if they were ever really to understand the law. The task of doing this, he added, had only just begun.[43] The following year, Jim Sharpe concurred, pointing to the problems of saying anything meaningful about patterns of crime from the records of a single court, and suggesting that "The only method by which the problem might be solved would be to study the records of *all* courts in a given area." And yet if Knafla's idea was simple, the task itself seemed, to Professor Sharpe at least, "an undertaking which, without the assistance of a squad of research assistants, would be far too large for the normal historiain."[44] Knafla credits no such squad of researchers, but then again this first volume was fourteen years in the making, and the final goal—a showcase of Kent legal business to enable "thick description" of the law—has yet to be reached. Only then will Knafla's project be, in his own words, "a living, records-based portrait of litigation in action across the various courts of the English legal system."[45]

Appreciating integration between jurisdictions is crucial for reasons of scope and interpretation. In the first place, as Knafla points out, historians frequently suffer from tunnel vision in the archives and consequently overlook the full meaning of cases that appeared in other courts. Then as now, using the law was the art of the possible, and in the first half of the seventeenth century the possibilities were manifold. Take the Court of Star Chamber, for example, where many prosecutions were tactical to the point of fraud, and, argues John Guy, frequently served "to advance a collateral attack by one litigant upon an opponent in furtherance of a wider strategy of litigation undertaken in several courts at once." The true story of so many Star Chamber cases cannot be told, Professor Guy believes, "failing the discovery of parallel litigation in other courts upon the same matter."[46] The second reason concerns inference. Legal and criminal categories observed and cherished by ourselves often had little or no meaning to contemporaries, or, at least, not the meanings sometimes attributed to them retrospectively. These categories, which include distinctions between civil and criminal actions, and sin and crime, tend to impose false dichotomies that can be unhelpful unless we remain sensitive to the grey areas.[47]

Examining the business of the courts in their entirety will provide a better view of individual lawsuits, and more generally, of the criminal law taken on its own terms. Much of this lies in the future. What Knafla has offered us so far is a meticulously assembled compilation of the criminal and administrative business of the Kent assizes and quarter sessions toward the end of the reign of Elizabeth I. He has combed the clerk of assize archives in the Public Record Office and the records of the sessions of the peace held at the Centre for Kentish Studies in Maidstone to produce in a comprehensive and comprehensible manner over 1,600 documentary summaries for around 560 separate legal actions. The classes of record include jail delivery files, commissions of the peace, sessions rolls and papers (including examinations, informations, and confessions), minute books, orders, indictments and recognizances, constables' rolls, and lists of jurors. Over half the records are either indictments or recognizances. The range, quantity, and quality of these records and those to be included in future volumes are of paramount importance. Knafla makes a number of virtues from his choice of Kent and the year 1602: Kent was large and populous, with a diverse topography and dotted with important industrial and commercial centers, and 1602 "lies within the watershed of the 'second formative period' in the history of English law from the 1580s to the 1620s," a period that, moreover, was not disrupted by any great political or pestilential trauma.[48] Yet in the end, as many historians are often forced to concede, neither year nor county was chosen because it was representative of anything in particular, but more because of the coincidental and complementary survival of various types of record. Indeed, ironically, the characteristics identified by Knafla make seventeenth-century Kent rather an *un*representative English county, and 1602 seems no more significant than any other year for which there are good records. This scarcely matters. The incompleteness of so many legal archives means that the existence of records is sufficient justification to proceed.[49]

The significance of Knafla's first volume, as it stands, can be illustrated by choosing an indexed name for which there are a number of references and using it to dip into the text. Thus we learn that on 28 September 1602, magistrates sitting at the Maidstone quarter sessions bound one Robert Bassock, a butcher from Marden, to keep the peace, whereupon a recognizance was drawn up and the fact recorded in the minute book. Early in 1603, he was presented at Canterbury quarter sessions for breaking into William Peak's close at Marden, assaulting him, and stealing oats and peas. The sessions rolls record, however, that Bassock accused Peak of wounding him with a pitchfork and that he and his co-defendants pleaded that the indictment was insufficient at law. The court ordered that a portion of the charge against the accused was inconsistent with the form of the statute, but, regardless, the clerk of the peace set a trial date for May—this time at Maidstone. When the jury failed to turn up on this occasion, the trial was postponed until July, when finally Bassock was acquitted.[50] Here we see how the dryest of documents can combine to revivify real events, and it is worth noting that Knafla himself did not tell the story of Robert Bassock: He simply provided the means to do so between two covers.

Historically, this exercise in reconstruction conveys a sense of the experience of early modern legal procedure: complex, capricious, time-consuming, tiring, and frustrating. Where cases first heard at quarter sessions were passed on to the assizes (and, interestingly, vice versa), this sense extends to the relationship between these two jurisdictions and between two classes of record. For example, 9 out of 120 assize cases listed here were referred from the lower court, and, conversely, sixteen suspects committed at the assizes had their cases disposed of at the sessions of the peace. In addition, Knafla compares the profile of verdicts and dispositions passed at assizes and quarter sessions, revealing findings that are not necessarily surprising but rarely have been demonstrated before. At the county sessions, arraigned criminals were almost twice as likely to confess than at the assizes (presumably because they were not normally facing a capital charge). They were also more than four times as likely to be acquitted and thirteen times more likely to be bailed, remanded, or removed to another court. The most common punishment at the county sessions was a fine (45 percent), whereas at the assizes, it was the noose (36 percent).[51] What cannot be resolved is exactly which jurisdiction was entitled to try what cases and where. By 1600, although it was common for all felonies to pass directly to the assizes, JPs continued to hold rights of jail delivery and drew up their own jail delivery rolls; for example, some cases of witchcraft (a felony) were tried at the Kent county quarter sessions in the 1640s and 1650s. Knafla concludes simply that "the distinction of competence between county assizes and sessions of the peace was not clearly drawn, and that there was a certain fluidity of prosecutions between the two institutions."[52]

Clearly, though, Knafla's book is important not merely as a chunk of administrative history, since, with a little imagination, it helps one to construct the way people across the social order used the law—and indeed were obliged to use the law—as a means of resolving disputes and grievances. Almost literally, it lays a paper chase along which one may follow litigants in pursuit of justice and suspected malefactors as they were moved between constables, magistrates, jailers and courts on a journey, which, for some at least, ended at the gallows. At its heart, therefore Knafla's book draws attention to the exercise of power and the experience of authority. We also learn a good deal about the political culture of later Elizabethan and Jacobean Kent, in particular the network of justices of the peace and their interests. Although the Kent commission of the peace was large, only about thirty JPs were actually operative—a committed, well-educated, and well-connected core, many of whom were also prominent lawyers and politicians. We are also reminded that the most important function of the JP was not the administration of criminal justice but regulation, and that licensing, commerce, debt, weights and measures, rents, taxes, apprenticeship, maintenance of bridges and highways, illegal cottages, poor relief, and so on occupied 38 percent of a sample of presentments from county and hundredal juries. By comparison, what a modern observer would class as crime accounted for only 18 percent of business.[53]

Knafla's book points indirectly to the extent to which the law had expanded from the mid–sixteenth century and the profound impact of this at all social levels. In the year 1602, we learn, almost 3,500 individuals were cited in the records of the assizes and sessions courts at a time when the population of Kent was about 130,000. This means that more than one in forty people was involved in a court case, which, in turn, suggests that perhaps one household in eight had some involvement in a lawsuit in this year alone.[54] One can only guess what proportion of the adult population at some time in their lives became embroiled, even fleetingly, in the law: It must have been just about everyone. Without doubt, when Knafla's project is complete, the full extent of this will be clearer. Obviously, chronological scope will be a drawback in that we will know how many people were engaged in which courts in 1602, but not necessarily in 1603 or any other year. But still, the qualitative sense of the experience of the law in a single county will be rich, unique, and invaluable. We will also be able to demonstrate what this meant in concrete terms.[55]

In some ways there is less to say about James Cockburn's *Kent Indictments, Charles I*, not because of its intrinsic merits (which are considerable), but because the project to which it belongs is already so far advanced and, consequently, well-known and universally admired among scholars in the field. Knafla himself magnanimously regards it to be "one of the major editorial achievements for English legal history in the early modern era."[56] In short, this is the latest addition to a massive collection of abstracts, mainly of indictments, from the Home Circuit assize records for the sixteenth and seventeenth centuries. Between 1975 and 1982, Cockburn devoted two volumes each to the five constituent counties of the circuit (Essex, Kent, Surrey, Sussex, and Hertfordshire) covering the reigns of Elizabeth and James I.[57] In 1976, he added a volume of assize orders for the Western Circuit, 1629–48, and in 1989 returned to the Home Circuit with an edition of Kent indictments during the Interregnum.[58] A seminal general introduction published in 1985 describes both courts and documents and complements Cockburn's own history and guide, already the definitive work.[59] As Knafla observes, among the circuit's indictment files, those for Kent are particularly extensive, and this latest volume is the first of four that, when complete, will form a calendar of all Kent assize business be-

tween the accession of Charles I and the Glorious Revolution. Together
with the Elizabethan and Jacobean volumes, this will be a unique record
of criminal prosecution in a single county covering 130 years of political,
administrative, social, and economic transformation.

Although only part of a whole, like Knafla's *Kent at Law*, Cockburn's
volume is a rigorous piece of scholarship in its own right, which in a
straightforward and concise manner summarizes the business of every Car-
oline assizes for which records survive. Hence the calendar begins with the
Maidstone assizes of July 1625, a time of relative political stability, and
ends in Sevenoaks in September 1648 with all-out war and rebellion (one
of the two annual sessions having been relocated the previous summer due
to the threat of fighting). The entry for each session includes essential administrative details: the judges on the jail delivery commission, the issue of
the precept, the justices of the peace (both those obliged to attend and those
who failed to turn up), coroners, bailiffs (minions of the sheriff who served
writs), constables, and grand jurors. As such, Cockburn's calendar mirrors
local government at every level and, beyond that, the way central authority
worked to maintain order in the localities. Next to the list of constables in
each bundle are the prisoners, their alleged crimes, and abstracts of their
indictments, all of which offer important clues for understanding crime
from the bottom up. Indeed, like Knafla's work, it is the detailed social
historical content of this information for which this book and its companion volumes are perhaps most important.

It has already been mentioned that bills of indictment are laconic sources.
Individual membranes rarely tell us more than the name of accused, occupation, place of residence, offense, date and location of offense, victim
(if applicable), the bill's endorser(s), the grand jury verdict, trial verdict,
and sentence.[60] So, to take a random example, on 22 March 1642, Jeremy
Mayhew, a laborer from Milton, was delivered from Maidstone jail, having
been committed by the mayor of Gravesend for begging using a forged
certificate alleging loss by fire. At his trial, the grand jury found the bill to
be true; he confessed and was ordered to be whipped.[61] That is all we
know, and probably all we can know, given that none of the relevant assize
depositions have survived. Yet even though the deeper meanings of individual crimes and countermeasures may lie beyond our reach, such evidence
can still be of use for building qualitative contexts. Specifically, cases like
Mayhew's still help us illustrate certain broader social developments,
namely the multiplication of the poor in the towns and countryside and
the growing determination of the authorities to deal harshly with those
who sought charity by fraudulent means. The cumulative effect of scanning
without necessarily counting hundreds of similar indictments, moreover, is
the gradual formation of a qualitative sense of criminality and, more importantly, a sense of the wider context in which many marginal people
were increasingly drawn into the clutches of offices designed to serve and

subjugate them. Such contexts do not just concern the experience of ordinary people, but, more dynamically, the exercise of political power at a time when the status quo was being contested. Accordingly, delving deeper beneath the topsoil of Cockburn's calendar reveals that the assizes held in March 1642 was more than just the occasion when Mayhew the beggar got his comeuppance; it was a historical turning point when the gentlemen of Kent announced their famous petition in defense of King and episcopate, thereby antagonizing Parliament and helping to precipitate the Civil War. At one level, then, the contents of both *Kent at Law* and *Kent Indictments* might be used to connect the worlds of the political elite and the marginal poor in their struggle for survival in the first half of the seventeenth century.

The contexts in which crime and the law can be placed—and, indeed, need to be placed—are varied and multifaceted. Indictments may not say much about particular crimes, but they point in many other interesting directions. Reading between the lines, the human activity hinted at in these volumes testifies to changes in every conceivable area of provincial society: the growth and devolution of government, regulatory bodies, and administration (what might be called "state formation"); religious and cultural experimentation, polarization, and fragmentation; an expanding, diversifying, and increasingly mobile population employed in manufacture as well as agriculture; and the quickening of trade, commerce, and the development of markets, credit networks, and channels of communication.[62] It is this richer experience of authority and opportunity, conflict and cooperation, toward which many practitioners of the history of crime could profitably devote more attention. The sheer diversity and interrelatedness of many individual spheres of life including crime and the law, needs to be captured in its entirety, not broken up into less meaningful pieces.

For these purposes, the indexes in both Knafla's and Cockburn's books—arranged by person, place, and subject—are particular strengths and should attract the focused microhistorian and unrepentant source-miner alike. It is unsurprising to discover that larceny was the most common offense, and heinous crimes the rarest. In Cockburn's book there are only four indictments for arson, seven for buggery, seventeen for rape, and ten for witchcraft; Knafla records two cases of arson, no instances of buggery, one recognizance relating to a rape, and one witchcraft accusation. Homicide and infanticide were more common, but, as students of the period are aware, many cases were actually unpremeditated violent affrays and concealed illegitimate births respectively. Turning to larceny, we are reminded that the seventeenth century sustained a culture of opportunity as well as authority and that theft tells us as much about possession as dispossession. Cockburn's index in particular will be of interest to historians of material culture, since the eight pages devoted to stolen goods (there is less detail in Knafla's index) say as much about consumerism as anything else. One notices the twenty-two indictments for the theft of ribbons and bands—the small gifts sneered at by the Essex minister Ralph Josselin at a "strange vaine wedding" he attended in the winter of 1644—and the rest of the entry ("see also falling-bands, garters, hat-bands, neck-bands, ruff-bands, sashes") illustrates the diversity of goods available by the mid-seventeenth century. Small items point to other cultural developments: There are eleven indictments relating to the theft of bibles and one for a prayer book. Ironically, such thefts might have been seen as an encouraging sign by Puritan harbingers of the doom incurred by idolatry and atheism.[63]

Of course, these books are not directly comparable either in themselves or as samples of the series to which each belongs, and therefore to rebuke Cockburn for his lack of tables, charts, facsimile illustrations, and full transcriptions (which Knafla has in good measure) would be otiose. The most damning criticism is that the strength of one is the weakness of the other; namely, whereas Knafla aims at depth within narrow bands of time and place, Cockburn makes accessible the proceedings of the assizes relatively superficially but with great chronological and geographical scope. One positive observation, then, would be that Knafla's book could introduce a new student to the early modern English legal system—procedures, classes of record, forms of words, and paleography (there are facsimile photographs and transcriptions)—before he or she moved on to the greater range offered by Cockburn's series. Their organization—Cockburn's sequentially by sessions, Knafla's by class of record—reinforces this. The advantages of the latter approach are, however, diminished slightly by the inconvenience of having to turn backward and forward through the book in order to make sense of a case—as I discovered when I assembled the short story of Robert Bassock. Ideally, one needs a computer database through which information can be accessed and cross-referenced, thereby cutting a pathway through the thicket of the documents, and providing both breadth and depth at a stroke. But for the moment we must content ourselves with what we have and concentrate on thinking about ways in which it can be deployed to develop existing criminal justice history in a meaningful direction.

CONCLUSIONS

There is, of course, no single direction in which criminal justice history should be taken. What has been offered here is a personal view in three parts: first, the suggestion that existing knowledge might profitably be placed into deeper and richer qualitative contexts to reach hidden layers of meaning; second, the need to exploit a wide and eclectic range of primary sources in order to achieve this; and, finally, praise for the works of Knafla and Cockburn, which make legal records accessible to scholars and students constrained by time or remote from the archives where the documents are stored. It has been argued that although both volumes contain sources most suited to a quantitative approach, by reading between the lines and in bulk, it is possible to develop a qualitative sense of crime and the social contexts in which it was committed and punished. Yet there is more to this than just the importance of revealing a hidden historical dimension of crime and the law, since most historians who undertake such work discover something else in the process: namely that crime and the law provides access to a lost mental world.

Indeed, the subject matter can even be seen as secondary in its importance, given that many symbolic trappings of criminal justice help us to decipher cultural codes. In my book, *Crime and Mentalities in Early Modern England*, I argue that although the reconstruction of qualitative contexts is illuminating for the history of crime; conversely, it can also be used to open windows on the collective psychological landscape of our ancestors. Three crimes—witchcraft, counterfeiting, and murder—form case studies through which broader themes of religious reform, state formation, secularization, and social change are examined from the perspective of popular mentalities. In the same year as the doctoral thesis on which the book was based was completed, a collection of essays on a range of criminal themes was compiled in translation from the Italian journal *Quaderni Storici*. Here similar sentiments were expressed. In their introduction, the editors, Edward Muir and Guido Ruggiero, explained that "the value of criminal records for history is not so much what they uncover about a particular crime as what they reveal about otherwise invisible or opaque realms of human experience." Although all the essays in this collection concern crime, their scope is greater in that "crime opens many windows on the past."[64]

Other studies confirm the growth of this approach, both for criminal justice history and the history of mentalities. In 1989, Ruth Harris used changing attitudes to insanity in the trials of violent criminals to lift the lid on public anxieties about sex, class, and authority in nineteenth-century France. The following year, through suicide in early modern England, Michael MacDonald and Terence Murphy's *Sleepless Souls* shed light not just on a neglected crime but also on broader changes in emotional sensibilities and the secularization of institutions and values.[65] Individual case studies are a popular approach.[66] In 1991, Pieter Spierenburg described his study of early modern prisons as a work concerned primarily with "changes in experience, emotions, and world views," for which prisons offered a way in. More recently, V.A.C. Gatrell's exemplary *The Hanging Tree* (1994), at one level a history of capital punishment, 1770–1868, on closer inspection turns out to be "a history of emotion," which the author was inspired to write after stumbling upon a file of petitions for mercy. "These stories," Gatrell relates, "fired me with a taste for the lived experiences of past people which criminal justice historians have meanly served." As with all such works, however, the findings are suggestive rather than conclusive, and Gatrell considers this "a book to argue with, since in a history of mentalities one achieves no certainty and runs many risks."[67] Recent works on witchcraft also have explored psychological and cultural dimensions, seeking insights into the world view of which witch beliefs were part.[68] Risks aside, the task to which Gatrell refers is essential for understanding both crime and criminal justice, and the society and culture in which they originated.

The history of mentalities, long established in continental historiography, is a relatively new departure for English history.[69] Its novelty is that it seeks a third dimension to history, beyond the traditional political and constitutional approach and even beyond the "new social history" and the subfields it has generated. We need a cultural interpretation of the period that not only suggests what social experience meant to contemporaries—especially the silent majority of the lower orders—but through which an image of a popular mental world might appear. In a way, then, we return to Lévi-Strauss's celebrated proposal that social definitions can only be understood within the cultural contexts in which they were formed—often a context of symbolic meaning—but that if this is observed, these categories reveal dynamic vehicles through which ideas were articulated in that society.[70] Premodern mentalities are often obscure, requiring us to find pathways into this territory so that we may describe not just its outward appearance for ourselves but also its inner meaning to our ancestors. Crime enables us to view mentalities in a proper light, not as a stable intellectual structure but as something dynamic and constantly changing and, most of all, as a twisting thread that leads us to the heart of how power was asserted and experienced. Recommended, therefore, is not just a history from below, even with the politics put back in, but a history from *within*, and there seems every reason for criminal justice history, conceived broadly and treated with sensitivity and imagination, to lead the way.

NOTES

1. G. M. Trevelyan, *English Social History* (London, 1944), vii; G. R. Elton, "Crime and the Historians," in *Crime in England 1550–1800*, ed. J. S. Cockburn (London, 1977), 1–14. For brief but trenchant criticism of Elton, see J. A. Sharpe, *Crime in Early Modern England 1550–1750* (London, 1984), 5–6.

2. Patrick Collinson, *De Republica Anglorum: or, History with the Politics Put Back* (Cambridge, 1989). See also David Underdown, *A Freeborn People: Politics and the Nation in Seventeenth-Century England* (Oxford, 1996).

3. This was something of a bastard birth, however. On the distanced relationship between the parents, see Douglas Hay, "The Criminal Prosecution and its Historians," *Modern Law Review* 47 (1984): 1–29.

4. Joanna Innes and John Styles, "The Crime Wave: Recent Writing on Crime and Criminal Justice in Eighteenth-Century England," *Journal of British Studies* 25 (1986): 3–6, 430–35, quotation at 431. See also Hay, "Criminal Prosecution and its Historians."

5. Louis A. Knafla, ed., *Kent at Law 1602: The County Jurisdiction, Assizes and Sessions of the Peace* (London, 1994); J. S. Cockburn, ed., *Calendar of Assize Records: Kent Indictments, Charles I* (London, 1995).

6. Louis A. Knafla, "Crime and Criminal Justice: a Critical Bibliography," in *Crime in England*, 270–353; Victor Bailey, "Bibliographical Essay: Crime, Criminal Justice and Authority in England," *Society for the Study of Labour History Bulletin* 40 (1980): 36–46; Alfred Soman, "Deviance and Criminal Justice in Western Europe, 1300–1800: An Essay in Structure," *Criminal Justice History* 1 (1980): 3–28; J. A. Sharpe, "The History of Crime in Late Medieval and Early Modern Europe: A Review of the Field," *Social History* 7 (1982): 187–203; Innes and Styles, "The Crime Wave," 380–435; J. B. Post, "Crime in Later Medieval England: Some Historiographical Limitations," *Continuity & Change* 2 (1987): 211–24; John L. McMullan, "Crime, Law and Order in Early Modern England," *British Journal of Criminology* 27 (1987): 252–74; J. A. Sharpe, "The History of Crime in England, c. 1300–1914," *British Journal< Criminology* 28 (1988): 124–37; Malcolm Gaskill and Tim Meldrum, " 'Crime, the Law, and the State' University of Essex/Istituto Italiano per gli Studi Filosofici, Naples, Comparative History Summer School, 6–10 July 1992," *Social History* 18 (1993): 87–92; and the second edition of Jim Sharpe's *Crime in Early Modern England* (London, 1998).

7. Joyce U. Harn, ed., *Historical Research for Higher Degrees in the United Kingdom. List No. 58. Part II Theses in Progress, 1997* (London, 1997). "The History of Crime and Punishment in England," a course taught at Keele University, Staffordshire, has spawned its own textbook: John Briggs, Christopher Harrison, Angus McInnes, and David Vincent, eds., *Crime and Punishment in England: An Introductory History* (London, 1996). The early modern period is covered by chaps. 2–7.

8. To my knowledge, two of the last conventional county-based doctoral theses were completed in the late 1980s: R.A.H. Bennett, "Enforcing the Law in Revolutionary England: Yorkshire, 1640–1660" Ph.D. thesis, University of London, 1988); Sarah Barbour-Mercer, "Prosecution and Process: Crime and the Criminal Law in Later Seventeenth-Century Yorkshire" (D. Phil. thesis, York University, 1989).

9. Robert B. Shoemaker, *Prosecution and Punishment: Petty Crime and the Law in London and Rural Middlesex, c. 1660–1725* (Cambridge, 1991); Gwenda Morgan and Peter Rushton, *Rogues, Thieves and the Rule of Law: The Problem of Law Enforcement in North-East England, 1718–1820* (London, 1998). See also Jim Sharpe, "Social Strain and Social Dislocation, 1585–1603," in *The Reign of Elizabeth I: Court and Culture in the Last Decade*, ed. John Guy (Cambridge, 1995), 192–211; Patricia A. Johnson, "A Study of the Relationship between Crime and Distress in Seventeenth-Century England: With Particular Reference to the North-West" (Ph.D. thesis, University of Central Lancashire, 1995).

10. Garthine Walker, "Women Before the Courts: Gender-Specific Crime in Seventeenth-Century Lancashire and Cheshire" (Ph.D. thesis, Liverpool University, 1994); Jenny Kermode and Garthine Walker, eds., *Women, Crime and the Courts in Early Modern England* (London, 1994).

11. Garthine Walker, "Women, Theft and the World of Stolen Goods," in *Women, Crime and the Courts*, 81–105; Paul Griffiths, *Youth and Authority: Formative Experiences in England, 1560–1640* (Oxford, 1996); Peter King and Joan

Noel, "The Origins of 'The Problem of Juvenile Delinquency': The Growth of Juvenile Prosecutions in the Late Eighteenth and Early Nineteenth Centuries," *Criminal Justice History* 14 (1993): 17–41; Peter King, "The Rise of Juvenile Delinquency in England 1780–1840: Changing Patterns of Perception and Prosecution," *Past & Present* 160 (1998): 16–66. See also Paul Griffiths, "The Structure of Prostitution in Elizabethan London," *Continuity & Change* 8 (1993): 39–63; Tim Hitchcock, *English Sexualities, 1700–1800* (Basingstoke, 1997), chap. 2.

12. Laura Gowing, *Domestic Dangers: Women, Words and Sex in Early Modern London* (Oxford, 1996); idem, "Language, Power, and the Law: Women's Slander Litigation in Early Modern London," in *Women, Crime and the Courts*, 26–47; Tim Meldrum, "A Woman's Court in London: Defamation at the Bishop of London's Consistory Court, 1700–1745," *London Journal* 19 (1994): 1–20; Steve Hindle, "The Shaming of Margaret Knowsley: Gossip, Gender and the Experience of Authority in Early Modern England," *Continuity & Change* 9 (1994): 391–419; Annabel Gregory, "Slander Accusations and Social Control in Late Sixteenth-and Early Seventeenth-Century England: With Special Reference to Rye (Sussex)" (Ph.D. thesis, Sussex University, 1984).

13. C. W. Brooks, "Interpersonal Conflict and Social Tension: Civil Litigation in England, 1640–1830," in *The First Modern Society*, ed. A. L. Beier, David Cannadine, and James M. Rosenheim (Cambridge, 1989), 357–99; Marcus S. P. Knight, "Litigation in the Seventeenth-Century Palatinate of Durham" (Ph.D. thesis, Cambridge University, 1990); Tim Stretton, "Women and Litigation in the Elizabethan Court of Requests" (Ph.D. thesis, Cambridge University, 1994): idem, "Women, Custom and Equity in the Court of Requests," in *Women, Crime and the Courts*, 170–89; and *Waging Law in Elizabethan England* (Cambridge, 1998).

14. Mark Jackson, *New-Born Child Murder: Women, Illegitimacy and the Courts in Eighteenth-Century England* (Manchester, 1996); Laura Gowing, "Secret Births and Infanticide in Seventeenth-Century England," *Past & Present* 156 (1997): 87–115. For comparisons, see: N.E.H. Hull, *Female Felons: Women and Serious Crime in Colonial Massachusetts* (Chicago, 1987); Andrew Finch, "Women and Violence in the Later Middle Ages: The Evidence of the Officialty of Cerisy" *Continuity & Change* 7 (1992): 23–45.

15. J. M. Beattie, "Violence and Society in Early Modern England," in *Perspectives in Criminal Law*, ed. A. N. Doob and E. L. Greenspan (Aurora, Ill., 1985), 36–60; J. S. Cockburn, "Patterns of Violence in English Society: Homicide in Kent 1560–1985," *Past & Present*, 130 (1991): 70–106; J. A. Sharpe, *Judicial Punishment in England* (London, 1990); Randall McGowen, "Civilising Punishment: the End of the Public Execution in England," *Journal of British Studies* 33 (1994): 257–82; Susan Dwyer Amussen, "Punishment, Discipline and Power: The Social Meanings of Violence in Early Modern England," *Journal of British Studies* 34 (1995): 1–34. Philippa Maddern, *Violence and the Social Order: East Anglia, 1422–1442* (Oxford, 1992) explores the meanings of violence in fifteenth-century society.

16. J. A. Sharpe, " 'Last Dying Speeches': Religion, Ideology and Public Execution in Seventeenth-Century England," *Past & Present* 107 (1985): 144–67; Randall McGowen, "The Body and Punishment in Eighteenth-Century England," *Journal of Modern History* 59 (1987): 651–79; idem, "He Beareth not the Sword in Vain": Religion and the Criminal Law in Eighteenth-Century England," *Eighteenth-*

Century Studies 21 (1987–8): 192–211; Thomas Laqueur, "Crowds, Carnival and the State in English Executions, 1604–1868," in *The First Modern Society*, 305–55; Peter Lake and Michael Questier, "Agency, Appropriation and Rhetoric under the Gallows: Puritans, Romanists and the State in Early Modern England," *Past & Present* 153 (1996): 64–107.

17. John Broad, "Whigs and Deer-Stealers in Other Guises: A Return to the Origins of the Black Act," *Past & Present*, 119 (1988): 56–72; Peter King, "Gleaners, Farmers and the Failure of Legal Sanctions in England 1750–1850," *Past & Present* 125 (1989): 116–50; Roger B. Manning, *Hunters and Poachers: A Cultural and Social History of Unlawful Hunting in England 1485–1640* (Oxford, 1993); John Rule and Roger Wells, eds., *Crime, Protest and Popular Politics in Southern England, 1740–1850* (London, 1997), chaps. 8–10. B. J. Davey's *Rural Crime in the Eighteenth Century* (Hull, 1994) deals with North Lincolnshire, 1740–80. "Social crime" was also an urban activity; see John Styles, "Embezzlement, Industry and the Law," in *Manufacture in Town and Country Before the Industrial Revolution*, ed. Maxine Berg, Pat Hudson, and Michael Sonescher (Cambridge, 1983), 183–204; John Rule, "Against Innovation? Custom and Resistance in the Workplace, 1700–1850," in *Popular Culture in England, c. 1500–1850*, ed. Tim Harris (Basingstoke, 1995), 168–88.

18. Keith Wrightson, "The Enclosure of English Social History," *Rural History* 1 (1990): 73–81. In 1987, John McMullan warned of the dangers of "a pettifogging regression as historians exchange ever more liliputian bits of empirical detail drawn from diverse archives in different time periods and places": "Crime, Law and Order," 265.

19. Sharpe, "History of Crime in England," 132. Interesting work has focused on reforming manners: Ronald Hutton, *The Rise and Fall of Merry England: The Ritual Year 1400–1700* (Oxford, 1996), chaps. 3–5; Martin Ingram, "Reformation of Manners in Early Modern England," in *The Experience of Authority in Early Modern England*, ed. Paul Griffiths, Adam Fox, and Steve Hindle (Basingstoke, 1996), 47–88; L. R. Poos, "Sex, Lies and the Church Courts of Pre-Reformation England," *Journal of Interdisciplinary History* 25 (1995): 585–607; Karen Jones and Michael Zell, "Bad Conversation? Gender and Social Control in a Kentish Borough, c.1450–c. 1570," *Continuity & Change* 13 (1998): 11–31. See also Christopher Durston, "Puritan Rule and the Failure of Cultural Revolution," in *The Culture of English Puritanism, 1560–1700*, ed. Christopher Durston and Jacqueline Eales (Basingstoke, 1996), 210–33.

20. Among the best is Keith Wrightson and David Levine, *Poverty and Piety in an English Village: Terling, 1525–1700* 2nd ed. (Oxford, 1995), 113–25, 134–43, 155–57, 177–83, 198–203 (originally published in 1979). See also Ian Archer, *The Pursuit of Stability: Social Relations in Elizabethan London* (Cambridge, 1991).

21. Lee Davison et al., eds., *Stilling the Grumbling Hive: the Response to Social and Economic Problems in England, 1689–1750* (Stroud, 1992); Andrew Wood, "Industrial Development, Social Change and Popular Politics in the Mining Area of North-West Derbyshire, c. 1600–1700" (Ph.D. thesis, Cambridge University, 1994). Chapters 4–6 of Dr. Wood's thesis explore conflicting notions of legality belonging to miners and landowners. See also his "Custom, Identity and Resistance: English Free Miners and Their Law, c. 1550–1800," in *Experience of Authority*, ed. Griffiths, Fox, and Hindle, 249–85. For a study of popular challenges to local

authority, and formal countermeasures taken at law, see Adam Fox, "Ballads, Libels and Popular Ridicule in Jacobean England," *Past & Present* 145 (1994): 47–83.

22. Michael Braddick, "State Formation and Social Change in Early Modern England: A Problem Stated and Approaches Suggested," *Social History* 16 (1991): 1–17; Steve Hindle, "Aspects of the Relationship of the State and Local Society in Early Modern England: With Special Reference to Cheshire, c. 1590–1630" (Ph.D. thesis, Cambridge University, 1992); idem, "The Keeping of the Public Peace," in *Experience of Authority*, 213–248; Keith Wrightson, "The Politics of the Parish in Early Modern England," ibid., 10–46; Joan R. Kent, "The Centre and the Localities: State Formation and Parish Government in England, circa 1640–1740," *Historical Journal* 38 (1995): 363–404; Marjorie McIntosh, *Controlling Misbehaviour in England, 1370–1600* (Cambridge, 1998); "Symposium: Controlling (Mis)behavior: Medieval and Early Modern Perspectives." *Journal of British Studies* 373 (1998): 231–305. Most of Dr. Hindle's thesis deals with disorder and the courts; chap. 5 looks at crime and criminal justice. For a more familiar view of the state, see John Brewer, *The Sinews of Power: War, Money and the English State, 1688–1783* (London, 1989).

23. McMullan, "Crime, Law and Order," 259.

24. Peter Linebaugh, *The London Hanged: Crime and Civil Society in the Eighteenth Century* (London, 1991). Here, crime and capitalism are skillfully intertwined, and a "history of taking" mapped on to a "history of making": ibid., p. xxv.

25. Works that describe legal procedural options in sequence include Cynthia B. Herrup, *The Common Peace: Participation and the Criminal Law in Seventeenth-Century England* (Cambridge, 1987) and J. M. Beattie, *Crime and the Courts in England, 1660–1800* (Oxford, 1986), chaps. 6–8.

26. See Hay, "Criminal Prosecution and its Historians," 17. Garthine Walker is currently preparing a textbook for the Macmillan Press that promises to do just this. Steve Hindle's recent book also adopts something of this approach and announces itself as a study of "the institutional mediation of social relations": *The State and Social Change in Early Modern England, c. 1550–1640* (New York, 2000). Alan Harding, *A Social History of English Law* (London, 1966) is long out of date.

27. This analogy is borrowed from Aron Gurevich, *Medieval Popular Culture: Problems of Perception and Belief* (Cambridge, 1988), xiii.

28. Sharpe, "History of Crime in England," 127. For works that stress both the importance and the difficulty of reconstructing attitudes, see T. C. Curtis, "Explaining Crime in Early Modern England," *Criminal Justice History* 1 (1980): 130; Hay, "Criminal Prosecution and its Historians," 7–8; McMullan, "Crime, Law and Order," 261–62. For some suggestions, see Malcolm Gaskill, *Crime and Mentalities in Early Modern England* (Cambridge, 2000), chap. 1.

29. Shoemaker, *Prosecution and Punishment*, 4–5, 18 and passim.

30. See, for example, Miranda Chaytor, "Husband(ry): Narratives of Rape in the Seventeenth Century," *Gender and History* 7 (1995): 378–407; Malcolm Gaskill, "Reporting Murder: Fiction in the Archives in Early Modern England," *Social History* 23 (1998): 1–30; Clive Holmes, "Women: Witnesses and Witches," *Past & Present* 140 (1993): 45–78. The classic work is Natalie Zemon Davis, *Fiction*

in the Archives: Pardon Tales and their Tellers in Sixteenth-Century France (Stanford, 1987).

31. E. P. Thompson, *Customs in Common* (London, 1991), 7.

32. See Robert Darnton, *The Great Cat Massacre and Other Episodes in French Cultural History* (London, 1984), 30.

33. G. R. Elton, *The Practice of History* (London, 1969), 31. See also the comments made in T. G. Ashplant and Adrian Wilson, "Present-Centred History and the Problem of Historical Knowledge," *Historical Journal* 31 (1988): 253–74.

34. Robert Muchembled, "Lay Judges and the Acculturation of the Masses," in *Religion and Society in Early Modern Europe 1500–1800*, ed. Kaspar von Greyerz (London, 1984), 56–65; Peter Burke, "Strengths and Weaknesses of the History of Mentalities." *History of European Ideas* 7 (1986): 447; Bob Scribner, "Is a History of Popular Culture Possible?" *History of European Ideas* 10 (1989): 177.

35. Arthur F. Kinney, ed., *Rogues, Vagabonds & Sturdy Beggars: A New Gallery of Tudor and Early Stuart Rogue Literature* (1972; repr. Amherst, Mass., 1990); Jerome Friedman, *Miracles and the Pulp Press During the English Revolution* (London, 1993); Barbara Rosen, ed., *Witchcraft in England 1558–1618* (New York, 1969; repr. Amherst, Mass., 1991). In Joad Raymond's compilation *Making the News: An Anthology of the Newsbooks of Revolutionary England 1641–1660* (Adlestrop, 1993), chap. 3 deals with women, including witches, and chap. 7, crime and punishment. Helen Weinstein, ed., *Catalogue of the Pepys Library at Magdalene College, Cambridge*, 2 vols. (Cambridge, 1992–94), contains some useful ballads.

36. Georges Lamoine, ed., *Charges to the Grand Jury 1689–1803*, Camden Soc., 4th ser. (New York, 1992); Ruth Paley, ed., *Justice in Eighteenth-Century Hackney: The Justicing Notebook of Henry Norris and the Hackney Petty Sessions Book* (London, 1991). These are reviewed together by Douglas Hay in *Albion* 26 (1994): 521–24.

37. Research Publications, Ltd., "Law, Crime and Society in Hanoverian England: The Old Bailey Proceedings, 1714–1820, "Early English Newspapers: The British Library's Burney Collection"; and "Eighteenth-Century English Provincial Newspapers." For studies that make good use of eighteenth-century newspapers, see Peter King, "Newspaper Reporting, Prosecution Practice and Perceptions of Urban Crime: The Colchester Crime Wave of 1765," *Continuity & Change* 2 (1987): 423–54; John Styles, "Print and Policing: Crime Advertising in Eighteenth-Century Provincial England," in *Policing and Prosecution in Britain 1750–1850*, ed. Douglas Hay and Francis Snyder (Oxford, 1989), 55–111. See also Owen Davies, "Newspapers and the Popular Belief in Witchcraft and Magic in the Modern Period," *Journal of British Studies* 37 (1998); 139–65.

38. Chadwyck-Healey, Ltd., *British Trials 1660–1900* (1993). This collection is indexed by defendant, plaintiff, victim, judge, women, date, and location of trial, type of crime, and place of publication.

39. Research Publications, Ltd., "Ecclesiastical Authority in England: Church Court Records, c. 1400–c.1660," "Justice and Authority in England, c.1540–c.1800: County Quarter Sessions and Related Records," "The People and the Law: Assize Records for Seventeenth-and Eighteenth-Century England."

40. J. A. Guy, *The Court of Star Chamber and its Records to the Reign of Elizabeth I* (London, 1985); Thomas G. Barnes, ed., *List and Index to the Proceedings*

in Star Chamber for the Reign of James I (1603–1625) in the Public Record Office, London. Class STAC8, 3 vols. (Chicago, 1975); idem, *The Court of Star Chamber and its Records,* forthcoming; Henry Horwitz, *Chancery Equity Records and Proceedings 1600–1800: A Guide to Documents in the Public Record Office,* rev. ed. (London, 1998). For a doctoral thesis that explains the workings of the Court of Requests, see Stretton, "Women and Litigation." Still useful is the *Guide to the Contents of the Public Record Office, Volume I: Legal Records* (London, 1963). For the most up-to-date general guide, see the microfiched *Guide to the Public Record Office* (London, 1999).

41. J.S.W. Gibson, *Quarter Sessions Records for Family Historians: A Select List,* 2nd ed. (Solihull, 1986); Jeremy Gibson and Colin Rogers, *Coroners' Records in England and Wales* (Birmingham, 1988); R. F. Hunnisett, *Sussex Coroner's Inquests, 1588–1603* (London, 1996); idem, *Sussex Coroners' Inquests, 1603–1688* (London, 1998); Anne Tarver, *Church Court Records: An Introduction for Family and Legal Historians* (Chichester, 1995). Older works that remain useful include Brian L. Woodcock, *Medieval Ecclesiastical Courts in the Diocese of Canterbury* (London, 1952); Dorothy M. Owen, *Ely Records: a Handlist of the Records of the Bishop and Archdeacon of Ely* (Cambridge, 1971). On manorial courts, see Mary Ellis, *Using Manorial Records,* rev. ed. (London, 1997); Denis Stuart, *Manorial Records: an Introduction to their Transcription and Translation* (Chichester, 1992); W. J. King, "Untapped Resources for Social Historians: Court Leet Records," *Journal of Social History* 15 (1981–2): 699–704. For the modern period, the standard work is Michelle Cale, *Law and Society: an Introduction to the Sources for Criminal and Legal History from 1800* (London, 1996).

42. Research Publications, Ltd., "The Complete State Papers Domestic: 1547–1625, 1625–1702, 1714–82. "The Complete State Papers Regencies (1716–55)." The most recent published volume is C. S. Knighton, ed., *Calendar of State Papers, Domestic Series, Mary I, 1553–1558* (London, 1998).

43. Louis A. Knafla, "Sin of all Sorts Swarmeth. Criminal Litigation in an English County in the Early Seventeenth Century," in *Law, Litigants and the Legal Profession,* ed. E. W. Ives and A. H. Manchester (London, 1983), 50–67. Dr. Knafla's other books in this area are *Law and Politics in Jacobean England: The Tracts of Lord Chancellor Ellesmere* (Cambridge, 1977); *Crime and Criminal Justice in Europe and Canada* (Waterloo, 1981); with Clive Emsley, *Crime Histories and Histories of Crime: Studies in the Historiography of Crime and Criminal Justice in Modern History* (Westport, Conn. 1996); with Susan Binnie, *Law, Society and the State: Essays in Modern Legal History* (Toronto, 1995).

44. Sharpe, *Crime in Early Modern England,* 52. See also Alan Macfarlane and Sarah Jardine, *Reconstructing Historical Communities* (Cambridge, 1977), 182–88. In 1972, J. H. Baker argued that the volume, complexity, and dispersal of premodern English legal sources were the greatest barriers to their meaningful interpretation: "The Dark Age of English Legal History, 1500–1700," in *Legal History Studies, 1972: Papers Presented to the Legal History Conference, Aberystwyth, 18–21 July 1972,* ed. Dafydd Jenkins (Cardiff, 1975), 1–27.

45. *Kent at Law,* vii. On "thick description," see Clifford Geertz, "Thick Description: Toward an Interpretive Theory of Culture," in idem, *The Interpretation of Cultures* (New York, 1973), 3–30.

46. J. A. Guy, *The Court of Star Chamber and its Records to the Reign of Eliz-*

abeth I (London, 1985), 26. According to one estimate, over half the litigants were involved in suits elsewhere: T. G. Barnes, "Star Chamber Litigants and their Counsel," in *Legal Records and the Historian*, ed. J. H. Baker (London, 1978), 12.

47. As J. H. Baker points out, the distinction between crime and tort was weak before the modern era because a greater sensitivity toward what constituted public order would not allow it: *An Introduction to English Legal History*, 2nd ed. (London, 1979), 411–12. On the relationship between sin and crime in the period, see Martin Ingram, *Church Courts, Sex and Marriage in England, 1570–1640* (Cambridge, 1987), 3 and passim; Patrick Collinson, *The Birthpangs of Protestant England: Religious and Cultural Change in the Sixteenth and Seventeenth Centuries* (London, 1988), 18–19.

48. *Kent at Law*, vii.

49. For a portrait of Kent that is more favorable to the idea of its typicality as a county, see Alan Everitt, *Change in the Provinces: the Seventeenth Century* (Leicester, 1969).

50. *Kent at Law*, 60, 62–63, 65, 98, 112–13, 129–30, 252.

51. These findings are based on the useful pie charts with which Dr. Knafla illustrates his introduction: *Kent at Law*, xxviii–xxix.

52. *Kent at Law*, xxvii. For examples of witches tried at the Kent quarter sessions, see Malcolm Gaskill, "Witchcraft in Early Modern Kent: Stereotypes and the Background to Accusations," in *Witchcraft in Early Modern Europe: Studies in Culture and Belief*, ed. Jonathan Barry, Marianne Hester, and Gareth Roberts (Cambridge, 1996), 257–87; idem, "Witches and Witchcraft Prosecutions in Kent 1560–1660," in *Reformation Kent, c. 1540–1640*, ed. Michael Zell (Woodbridge, 2001).

53. *Kent at Law*, xxii–xxvi, xxxi.

54. The size of Kent's population is taken from Peter Clark, *English Provincial Society from the Reformation to the Revolution: Religion, Politics and Society in Kent 1500–1640* (Hassocks, 1977), 6. The calculation regarding households is based on average household size of 4.75 in a Kent parish in the 1670s: Peter Laslett, *The World We Have Lost Further Explored*, 3rd ed. (London, 1983), 69.

55. On the diversity, complexity and expansion of English legal procedure by the first half of the seventeenth century, see Sharpe, *Crime in Early Modern England*, chap. 2; James Sharpe, "The People and the Law," in *Popular Culture in Seventeenth-Century England*, ed. Barry Reay (London, 1985), 250–51; J. H. Baker, "Criminal Courts and Procedure at Common Law 1550–1800," in *Crime in England*, 28–46; C. W. Brooks, *Pettyfoggers and Vipers of the Commonwealth: The 'Lower Branch' of the Legal Profession in Early Modern England* (Cambridge, 1986), chaps. 4–5.

56. *Kent at Law*, xxvi. Professor Cockburn has done more than anyone to illuminate assize procedure in the early modern period, as the following selection of articles indicate: "The Northern Assize Circuit," *Northern History*, 3 (1968): 118–30; "The Nature and Incidence of Crime in England 1559–1625: A Preliminary Survey," in *Crime in England*, 49–71; "Trial by the Book? Fact and Theory in the Criminal Process 1558–1625," in *Legal Records and the Historian*, 60–79; "Twelve Silly Men? The Trial Jury at Assizes 1560–1670," in *Twelve Good Men and True: the Criminal Trial Jury in England 1200–1800*, ed. J. S. Cockburn and T. A. Green (Princeton, 1988), 158–81.

57. The following volumes were all edited by J. S. Cockburn: *Calendar of Assize Records: Sussex Indictments, Elizabeth I* (London, 1975); *Calendar of Assize Records: Sussex Indictments, James I* (London, 1975); *Calendar of Assize Records: Hertfordshire Indictments, Elizabeth I* (London, 1975); *Calendar of Assize Records: Hertfordshire Indictments, James I* (London, 1975); *Calendar of Assize Records: Essex Indictments, Elizabeth I* (London, 1978); *Calendar of Assize Records: Kent Indictments, Elizabeth I* (London, 1979); *Calendar of Assize Records: Surrey Indictments, Elizabeth I* (London, 1980); *Calendar of Assize Records: Kent Indictments, James I* (London, 1980); *Calendar of Assize Records: Essex Indictments, James I (London, 1982); Calendar of Assize Records: Surrey Indictments, James I* (London, 1982); and *Calendar of Assize Records: Kent Indictments, 1649–1659* (London, 1989). In addition, he has edited a further volume for the years of 1660–1689: *Kent Indictments Charles II* (Woodbridge, 1997).

58. *Western Circuit Assize Orders 1629–1648. A Calendar*, ed. J. S. Cockburn, Camden Soc., 4th ser., 17 (1976); J. S. Cockburn, ed., *Calendar of Assize Records: Kent Indictments, 1649–1659* (London, 1989).

59. J. S. Cockburn, *Calendar of Assize Records, Home Circuit Indictments, Elizabeth I and James I, Introduction* (London, 1985); idem, *A History of English Assizes 1558–1714* (Cambridge, 1972).

60. On the reliability of indictments, see J. S. Cockburn, "Early Modern Assize Records as Historical Evidence," *Journal of the Society of Archivists* 5 (1975): 215–31; and on a specific point of unreliability, see C. Z. Wiener, "Is a Spinster an Unmarried Woman?" *American Journal of Legal History* 20 (1976): 27–31.

61. *Kent Indictments, Charles I*, 423, 427.

62. The best general account of these changes remains Keith Wrightson, *English Society 1580–1680* (London, 1982).

63. *Kent Indictments, Charles I*, 741–8, quotation at 746; *The Diary of Ralph Josselin 1616–1683*, ed. Alan Macfarlane (Oxford, 1976), 29.

64. Malcolm Gaskill, "Attitudes to Crime in Early Modern England: With Special Reference to Witchcraft, Coining and Murder," Ph.D. thesis, Cambridge University, 1994); *History from Crime: Selections from Quaderni Storici*, ed. Edward Muir and Guido Ruggiero (Baltimore, 1994), vii, 226.

65. Ruth Harris, *Murders and Madness: Medicine, Law and Society in the Fin de Siècle* (Oxford, 1989); Michael MacDonald and Terence Murphy, *Sleepless Souls: Suicide in Early Modern England* (Oxford, 1990) (for a critique, see Donna Andrew, "The Secularization of Suicide in England 1660–1800," *Past & Present* 119 [1988]: 158–65). Studies in a similar vein include Martin J. Wiener, *Reconstructing the Criminal: Culture, Law and Policy in England 1830–1914* (Cambridge, 1990); Regina Schulte, *The Village in Court: Arson, Infanticide and Poaching in the Court Reports of Upper Bavaria 1848–1910* (1994). Ulinka Rublack has argued that female criminals and their defenses "open a window onto a community's moral values." "Women and Crime in South-West Germany 1500–1700" (Ph.D. thesis, Cambridge University, 1995), 285.

66. See, for example, Peter Lake, "Puritanism, Arminianism and a Shropshire Axe-Murder," *Midland History* 15 (1990): 37–64; Malcolm Gaskill, "The Devil in the Shape of a Man: Witchcraft, Conflict and Belief in Jacobean England," *Historical Research* 71 (1998): 142–71.

67. Pieter Spierenburg, *The Prison Experience: Disciplinary Institutions and*

their Inmates in Early Modern Europe (New Brunswick, NJ, 1991), 10; V.A.C. Gatrell, *The Hanging Tree: Executions and the English People 1770–1868* (Oxford, 1994), quotations at pp. vi, ix. For works that use judicial processes to explore mentalities, see Robert Bartlett, *Trial by Fire: The Medieval Judicial Ordeal* (Oxford, 1986); Malcolm Gaskill, "The Displacement of Providence: Policing and Prosecution in Seventeenth- and Eighteenth-Century England," *Continuity & Change* 11 (1996): 341–74.

68. Robin Briggs, *Witches and Neighbours: the Social and Cultural Context of Witchcraft* (London, 1995); James Sharpe, *Instruments of Darkness: Witchcraft in England, 1550–1750* (London, 1995); Maurizio Bertolotti, "The Ox's Bones and the Ox's Hide: a Popular Myth, Part Hagiography and Part Witchcraft," in *Microhistory and the Lost Peoples of Europe*, ed. Edward Muir and Guido Ruggiero (Baltimore, 1991), 42–70; Malcolm Gaskill, "Witchcraft and Power in Early Modern England: The Case of Margaret Moore," in *Women, Crime and the Courts*, 125–45; Lyndal Roper, *Oedipus and the Devil: Witchcraft, Sexuality and Religion in Early Modern Europe* (London, 1994), chaps. 8–10.

69. Keith Thomas, *Religion and Decline of Magic: Studies in Popular Beliefs in the Sixteenth and Seventeenth Centuries* (London, 1971), remains the best work on English mentalities in the early modern period.

70. In *The Raw and the Cooked* (London, 1970), Claude Lévi-Strauss aimed to show how "empirical categories . . . which can only be accurately defined by ethnographic observations and, in each instance, by adopting the standpoint of a particular culture—can nonetheless be used as conceptual tools with which to elaborate abstract ideas and combine them in the form of propositions."

Book Reviews

Jocelyn Catty, *Writing Rape, Writing Women in Early Modern England: Unbridled Speech*. New York: St. Martin's Press, 1999. vi + 276 pp., index. $49.00

Crime and sexual offenses have been a popular topic of historical research and writing in Europe and North America. Dominated by scholars of criminology, history, law, and justice studies, it has taken on a life of its own. Largely unnoticed on the landscape of these professions has been the rise in women's literature on the same subject since the mid-1990s. Utilizing legal records as representations of women's contemporary attitudes in early modern Europe, Miranda Chaytor has provided a foundational work.[1] A number of new editions of original women's writings on sexual offenses in the era has contributed to a rich outcrop of literary studies on the subject. Drawing upon some of the threads woven by Kathryn Gravdal for medieval France,[2] and utilizing new editions of contemporary writings for early modern England such as that of Diane Purkiss,[3] the author has produced a book that will be of significant interest to anyone working on the history of crime and sexual offenses in early modern Europe.[4]

What is not here are criminal records and the criminal law. What is here is considerable evidence and insight into the crimes of murder, rape, ravishment, seduction, and suicide, and the contemporary problems of chastity, conduct, madness, resistance, voyeurism, and wantonness. In Part I, "Writing Rape," Catty summarizes the meanings of rape in contemporary writing (chap. 1), rape in romance and prose fiction (chap. 2), Elizabethan poetry (chap. 3), and Renaissance drama (chap. 4). In Part II, "Writing Women," she assesses women reading and writing rape (chap. 5), the translations of Lady Jane Lumley and Mary Sidney, Countess of Pembroke (chap. 6), and the writings of Elizabeth Cary (chap. 7) and Lady Mary Wroth (chap. 8). The conclusion is more an afterword.

Throughout the work, Catty builds upon contemporary women negotiating against the ideological conventions of the period. From the proto-feminist pamphlet *Jane Anger her Protection for Women* (1589) to the works of Rachel Speight, Esther Sowernam, and especially Dorothy Leigh, men's sexual offenses conducted with cruelty and sadism, within male-oriented language and learning, were challenged by women writers. While rape itself was "an accusation easily to be made and hard to be proved,"[5] and seldom reported in the records, it was prevalent in the language and the literature, and a defining element in male-female relations. Catty sees in their texts a "female" perspective (p. 228) of personal resistance that challenged male sexual violence and empowered their utterances. Wedged in the dual position of male property, and keepers or destroyers of male honor, women perceived male conduct and criminal offenses more in political (power) than in sexual (desire) terms.

The most significant contributions of the work for the study of crime and the criminal law are in Part II, especially Elizabeth Cary's "unbridled speech" (p. 153) and Mary Wroth's "liberty to say anything" (p. 182). Cary, in *The Tragedie of Mariam* (1613), makes a sympathetic heroine of a wife who confronts her husband's murder of her grandfather and brother and is accused of infidelity and murdered in resisting her husband's demand that she be killed in the event of his death.[6] For Wroth, the most unconventional writer on the subject of her time, sexual violence was behind courtship and used as an expression of the power relations between men and women. She developed this theme from the rape scenes in Philip Sidney's *The Countess of Pembroke's Arcadia*,[7] where the idea of ravishment contributed to the close involvement between rape and courtship. Mocking the conventional functions of rape, Wroth created new ones to explore female desire and control the narrative of her eight stories of sexual violence.[8] Catty places this within a wider European context by framing it with the sixteen rape stories in *The Queene of Navarres Tales* (1597).[9]

If there is one term that personifies the women's narratives that are explored in this perceptive work, it is what we might term the politics of the age. The role of politics and elites in the study of crime has had a long history. We should not be surprised, therefore, to find that politics informed women's writings on rape and other sexual offenses as it did in the making of royal proclamations and statute law.[10] Thoroughly annotated and clearly written, *Writing Rape* provides a rich tapestry of ideas, although some of the discussions of literary works assume that the reader has a familiarity with them. It will also be useful for its references to contemporary writers on rape and sexual offenses—both original works and modern editions (as cited below), and to the critical literature in the field. One can only hope that the literary evidence will be joined with the records evidence in the continued study of crime and criminal justice.

NOTES

1. Miranda Chaytor, "Husband(ry): Narratives of Rape in the Seventeenth Century," *Gender and History* 7 (1995): 378–407.

2. Kathryn Gravdal, *Ravishing Maidens: Writing Rape in Medieval French Literature and Law* (Philadelphia, 1991).

3. Diane Purkiss, ed., *Three Tragedies by Renaissance Women: The Tragedie of Iphigeneia in a version by Jane, Lady Lumley, The Tragedie of Antonie translated by Mary, Countess of Pembroke, The Tragedie of Miriam by Elizabeth Cary* (Harmondsworth, 1998).

4. For example, see also the new work of Ulinka Rublack, *The Crimes of Women in Early Modern Germany* (Oxford, 1999).

5. Sir Matthew Hale, *Historia Placitorum Coronae: The History of the Pleas of the Crown* (London, 1678), 635.

6. Stephanie J. Wright, *Elizabeth Cary: The Tragedy of Miriam The Fair Queen of Jewry* (Keele, 1996).

7. Jean Robertson, ed., *The Countess of Pembroke's Arcadia (The Old Arcadia)* (Oxford, 1973), and Lady Mary Sidney's revision: Victor Skretkowicz, ed., *The Countess of Pembroke's Arcadia (The New Arcadia)* (Oxford, 1987).

8. *The Countess of Mountgomeries Urania* (1621), and the critical edition of Josephine Roberts, *The First Part of the Countess of Montgomery's Urania* (Binghamton, NY, 1995).

9. Marguerite de Navarre, *The Heptameron*, trans. P. A. Chilton (London, 1984).

10. For example, the recent collection of essays organized by Hilda L. Smith, ed., *Women Writers and the Early Modern British Political Tradition* (Cambridge, 1998), especially Part IV on legal prescriptions.

Louis A. Knafla
University of Calgary

Trevor Dean and K.J.P. Lowe, eds., *Crime, Society and the Law in Renaissance Italy*. Cambridge: Cambridge University Press, 1994. xi + 281 pp., index. £37.50.

As the editors of this excellent volume point out in their cogent and forcefully argued introduction, crime, law, and order in early modern Italy have attracted growing scholarly interest since the publication in 1972 of *Violence and Civil Disorder in Italian Cities, 1200–1500*, edited by Lauro Martines. The bulk of research has, for obvious reasons, been the work of Italians, but a strong interest has persisted within the anglophone world. The publications over the last couple of years of such important books as

J. K. Brackett's *Criminal Justice and Crime in late Renaissance Florence, 1537–1609* and Edward Muir's *Mad Blood Stirring: Vendetta and Factions in Friuli during the Renaissance*, not to mention the latter's co-editing with Guido Ruggiero of a fascinating selection of translated articles from *Quaderni Storici*, bear testimony to the continued depth of interest in this field in Britain and America. The essays brought together in *Crime, Society and the Law* provide still further evidence of the important work that is going on in universities in both Italy and the Anglo-Saxon world.

It is a commonplace that pre-Risorgimento Italian history is beset with a sort of academic *campanilismo*: Strong on regional studies, it is less impressive when it comes to presenting an overall picture. Given this, both Nick Davidson and Catherine Kovesi Killerby deserve credit for offering surveys that are broad in both geography and chronology. Davidson's piece marshals an impressive array of sources in his discussion of attitudes to sexual crime and sin from the fourteenth to the seventeenth centuries. He is at his most interesting when dealing with the way in which sexual offenses were seen as "a threat to the order and stability of the whole of society" for practical as much as moral or religious reasons: "Sexual relations outside marriage led to illegitimate births, confused questions of inheritance, abandoned children and the potential for incest"; adultery offended honor, and offenses to honor led to violence and vendetta (a point made powerfully in Alan Ryder's article on Sicily); homosexuality could aggravate demographic crisis, and so on. I have only one minor cavil with Davidson's article: So bewildering was the terminology employed by the law-makers, theologians and moralists he cites—"sodomia" could mean almost any "deviant" sexual act—that Davidson himself sometimes seems to get confused. What, I want to know, is onanism (p. 77) if not masturbation or coitus interruptus? In contrast to Davidson's exciting survey, Kovesi Killerby's piece on the enforcement of Italian sumptuary laws from 1200 to 1500 is something of a disappointment. Warning at the beginning against the tendency of nineteenth- and twentieth-century commentators to indulge in "too great a reductivism to hidden social and psychological explanations," she never really provides a convincing alternative rationale for sumptuary legislation. Indeed, the article is rather list-like: rich in interesting examples, but distinctly weak on analysis, more questions are begged than answered.

It is perhaps unsurprising that the most convincing pieces in this selection are the less ambitious but more focused essays, concentrating on a particular case, individual, or region. Yet these, too, mirror a general problem with Italian studies. An emphasis on certain areas of Italy has led to the neglect of others. That many scholars have devoted their careers to Venice and Florence is easily explicable, both on account of the greater archival resources and because of the advantages of working within an established historiographical framework. On the other hand, it is disappointing that the consequence of this tendency is very patchy coverage. Of course, a selection such as this cannot hope to be comprehensive, but it is indicative of something amiss that *all* the references in the index to Genoa and Naples combined only equal those for sodomy in Florence. Indeed, on the strength of the contributions to this book, the Florentine specialists seem rather more culpable than the Venetianists. Both Peter Laven and Furio Bianco scarcely mention the *Dominante*, preferring to address remoter regions of the Republic's *Terraferma*. By contrast, when Andrea Zorzi writes critically in his study of the Florentine judicial system that "the historiography of Renaissance Italy, still set in its Burckhardtian mold, has shown an unwillingness to open up other areas of research" he clearly misses the irony of his own remark. It might, incidentally, have been more apposite to substitute the name Nicolai Rubinstein for that of the great Swiss.

Criticisms of excessive emphasis aside, it is only fair to judge the articles dealing with Florence on their own merits, and they are all of an impressively high standard. Zorzi provides a beautifully argued analysis of how Renaissance Florence, in common with many other states in western Europe, witnessed a trend away from face-to-face community control toward the establishment of a more potent state apparatus of public order. In a sense Zorzi's story is continued into the later sixteenth century by Elena Fasano Guarini in "The Prince, the Judges and the Law: Cosimo I and Sexual Violence 1558," in fact a detailed discussion of the duke's treatment of a single rape case. For Guarini, Cosimo's involvement demonstrates his determination to concentrate powers still further in his own hands, defending the "sovereignty of a prince-judge and legislator" against any judicial body that might seek to limit his authority. At the same time, Guarini's case study picks up on themes already addressed by Davidson regarding legal attitudes to rape in the early modern period. These play an equally important part in Daniela Lombardi's "Intervention by church and state in marriage disputes in sixteenth- and seventeenth-century Florence." Rape was an ill-defined concept, since it could be applied to any sexual act outside marriage. Hence the development of what seem to the modern reader oxymorons, such as nonviolent rape and even consensual rape. However, what emerges most clearly from Lombardi's argument is that, for the courts of late Renaissance Florence, the crime was not primarily against the woman: "Female honour was almost a material possession, which a man could rob but also give back [usually through an offer of marriage or the settlement of a dowry]. It did not belong exclusively to the woman, but principally to the men who were supposed to watch over her sexual conduct: her father or brother or husband."

The final article to concentrate largely on Florence is Paolo Rossi's immensely entertaining study of Benvenuto Cellini as criminal and self-

mythologist. As with Vasari's *Lives of the Artists*, Cellini's autobiographical *Vita*, which provides numerous embroidered accounts of his
transgressions, was clearly unconcerned with "the superficial truth of everyday events," but had instead "a much more profound purpose" in ensuring
"everlasting glory for its protagonist." Outlawed from Florence, Cellini
took refuge in Rome, in the employ of Clement VII, where he not only
worked as goldsmith but also helped in the defense of the city during the
dreadful year of 1527. Kate Lowe's article on three alleged conspiracies
against the Pope during the late fifteenth and early sixteenth centuries deals
with Rome in the decades just preceding Cellini's arrival. Where Rossi's
article concentrates on how a talented and rather engaging rogue could
pervert the truth in order to manufacture his own public persona, Lowe's
is about the way in which popes began to pervert the truth in order to
enhance their own power. The three conspiracies Lowe examines appear
to have had little basis in fact. Instead, they were trumped-up charges used
to discredit real or suspected opponents. By the late fifteenth century it had
become clear that one way of curbing the ambition of cardinals was to
accuse them on the skimpiest (or simply fabricated) evidence of plotting
against the successor of St. Peter. As popes realized that they could exercise
their powers arbitrarily in this fashion, acting as both accuser and judge,
it became a good deal easier to cow potential rivals. Moreover, imprisonment and loss of rank, which were used to punish enemies, made benefices
and offices available to be dispensed to supporters and loyal retainers: The
opportunities for patronage opened up by false accusation were legion.

What is very clear in Lowe's article is the complexity of relationships
between different groups competing for power in papal Rome. Much the
same point is made with regard to the Venetian territories by Laven and
Bianco. The 1511 rising in Friuli, which is the subject of Bianco's article
(as well as Muir's recent book) and which was "the largest peasant and
popular insurrection in Renaissance Italy," was not a simple case of the
revolt of the oppressed. The hatred for feudal lords that turned into a brutal
massacre in Udine was generated by a varied cocktail of grievances including encroachments on common lands, the refusal of landowners to compensate tenants for improvements, and the extension of seigniorial
prerogatives. But other issues were also involved: Long-standing feuds, local rivalries, support for the Venetian state, and contempt for imperial sym-
pathizers all played an important role. So did devotion to the most
powerful family in the region, the pro-Venetian Savorgnan, who were seen
as protectors of the poor against the majority of the feudal aristocrats and
urban nobility. The events of 1511, and the subsequent feuds between supporters of the Savorgnan and their rivals, which were to last for much of
the sixteenth century, were not a case of straightforward war between the

"haves" and "have-nots." Similarly any attempt to explain banditry on the Venetian *Terraferma* within the context of a Hobsbawmian model is proved absolutely absurd by Peter Laven's article. It is perhaps inappropriate to dwell too long on this piece since the author is my father. However, in his treatment of the later sixteenth-century outlaws, who often successfully defied the authority of the Venetian state for years, it becomes evident that rather than being "primitive rebels" engaged in some kind of class struggle, they were generally aristocrats, "remnants of a feudal world, haughty, independent, unruly" and resentful of rule from Venice. These robber barons surrounded themselves with armed bravos drawn from a wide social background; they were not romantic Robin Hood figures but bullies, rapists, thugs, and assassins. As Giovanna Fiume has shown in her work on nineteenth-century Sicily, bandits generally prefer soft targets and usually prey on the defenseless. In turn, the poor and vulnerable often see the growth of the state and centralized authority as a blessing, a protection from the arbitrary actions of feudal elites. As the articles in this collection make quite clear, the law frequently might have been a tool for upholding the hegemony of an oligarchy, or the rule of a single family, or, indeed, the dominance of men over women. But it could also protect the weak, a point that too often has been missed by historians of crime and order.

David Laven
University of Reading

Thomas Kuehn, *Law, Family and Women: Toward a Legal Anthropology of Renaissance Italy.* Chicago and London: University of Chicago Press, 1994. xiii + 415 pp., index. $45.95 (cloth); $20.75 (paper).

Since 1980, Thomas Kuehn has developed a singular voice in Florentine Renaissance studies as an interpreter of legal texts. This volume brings together eight of his published articles, together with two new and important pieces. In a brief introduction he confidently defines the singularity of his approach: Legal sources (as distinct from notarial) for Florentine history abound but are not much used by social and political historians; notarial records, which are used, are often read naively; legal historians hardly venture outside the jurisprudential concerns of medieval academic law. Into this gap Kuehn has attempted to place not just his own brand of legal history (one that links doctrine to actuality) but, more recently, legal anthropology (hence, presumably, that awkward "Toward" of the title). The result is a harmonious series of well-crafted pieces, though they do not always make for easy reading, and there are problems with the choice and number of sources.

Typically, Kuehn's articles start with some generally accepted proposition, point out some difficulties, and examine some relevant legislation and doctrinal discussion before taking up a small set of records—a group of notarial acts, some *consilia*, a letter or diary—that reveals the ambiguities and indeterminacies of rules in action. As Kuehn explains: "My desire has been to understand how, or how much, the very sophisticated and complex apparatus of law could serve the interests of litigants and to see how law functioned in a context with other mechanisms of disputing and settling disputes, ranging from fairly formal arbitration to violence"; "mine is an approach . . . that offers a poststructural space for the play of ambiguities." It is indeed dispute, rather than violence or crime, that interests Kuehn: dispute over inheritance between agnates and cognates (chap. 10) or between a legitimated bastard and his female cousin (chap. 7), dispute over possession of a house between owners and occupiers (chap. 3). For the readers of this book, it is violent dispute that will be of interest: chapter 5, in which a knifing in Barcelona and the attempted revenge in Florence leads Kuehn to consider the nature of vendetta, of kin solidarity, and of informal methods of resolving disputes; chapter 4, in which a son reacts to the dishonoring pusillanimity of his father; or chapter 1, which traces some of the contours of arbitration in Florence in the 1420s.

Arbitration and vendetta emerge as key themes of these early chapters, but it is here that Kuehn is at his weakest. He too easily equates Florence with the whole of Italy (as in the title), not aware that Florentine law and practice of vendetta were not typical. His suggestion that arbitration and litigation assisted the decline of vendetta, though possible, lacks proof. He sees litigation as a form of vendetta, and as an increasing substitute for it, though offering no statistical evidence that litigation was more common in the fifteenth century than earlier. His attempts to see nonviolent dispute as vendetta are unconvincing: In one case no evidence is presented (p. 106); in another the evidence is stretched (p. 163). Moreover, the points at issue in vendetta and arbitration were different: Arbitration (on Kuehn's evidence) mainly involved debt and property dispute, not the pacification of violence; violent vendetta was not taken for debt or property, even though vendetta itself was spoken of as debt.

These difficulties regarding violent dispute arise because of Kuehn's choice of source: He prefers extrajudicial sources, such as letters, notarial documents, *consilia*, and nonlegal settlements, to actual trial records. This strange preference, given the exceptional abundance of Florentine judicial records, seems to arise first from the anthropological "insight" that "the form in which a dispute appears in court" is different from "the 'real' substance of the quarrel" (Roberts, quoted p. 96), and then from the historian's difficulty in getting behind the official record (pp. 76–77). Is this adequate? Is it really so difficult to study dispute from judicial sources that the attempt has to be abandoned before it has really begun?

Trevor Dean
University of Surrey, Roehampton

Malcolm Greenshields, *An Economy of Violence in Early Modern France: Crime and Justice in the Haute Auvergne, 1587–1664.* University Park: The Pennsylvania University Press, 1994. x + 262 pp., index. $49.00.

Malcolm Greenshields has given us a revealing and valuable insight into the world of criminal justice and violent crime in early modern France. Nevertheless, *An Economy of Violence* confirms and supplements what is already accepted rather than blazing any startlingly new or innovative trails. Certainly, anyone who has worked in sixteenth- or seventeenth-century French judicial archives can only appreciate and admire Greenshields' skillful exploitation of these fragmentary, difficult to use, and almost illegible documents. In particular, he uses various sorts of documents (reports of the *maréchaussée* and court records in particular) to at least partially compensate for the bias inherent in each.

Greenshields does an excellent job of situating criminal justice and violent crime in its temporal and spatial perspective. The Haute Auvergne in the period under discussion was an isolated and wild place, like many remote and mountainous environments. Barely able to feed themselves, the Auvergnats relied for survival on a precarious subsistence agriculture, transhumant stockraising, and emigration. In this environment lived a hardy and stubborn people, suspicious of outsiders, with the common folk further isolated from the elites by their illiteracy and patois. Temporally, we are in a transition from feudal "privatized" notions of justice to the monopolization of legitimate violence (and therefore of criminal justice) by the centralizing state, a process that was well advanced in other parts of France but was just making inroads into the Haute Auvergne.

Having set the stage, Greenshields then goes onto the core of the work: chapter 3—"Crime: The Varieties of Violence"; chapter 4—"Violence and the Social Order"; and chapter 5—"The Process of Criminalization." Here, the book is valuable for its glimpses into everyday life rather than for any stunning insights. We learn for example, that violence was ordinarily directed downward or at equals in the social order, and rarely upward. Greenshields uses this finding to assert the "vertical" nature of French society, its organization in orders rather than economic classes. Although there was a great deal of antinoble and antielite sentiment and violence (and according to Greenshields, the nobility of the Haute Auvergne were especially predatory), when confronted with an outside threat, such as royal tax collectors or undisciplined and predatory soldiers, rural society showed a significant degree of solidarity. Greenshields neatly escapes the debate concerning crimes against people and crimes against property by the use of "psychic property"—"all that a person possesses, mentally or physically, that can be violated: honor, dignity, space, possessions, and the physical person." Chapter 5, "The Process of Criminalization" is especially interesting and informative, taking the reader through the various stages of criminal proceedings. Greenshields effectively questions the nature of early modern justice as a "relentless inquisitorial process" (p. 207) by showing how individuals were able to work within the system to defend their own psychic property against invasion by a fundamentally foreign culture and process.

In all, *An Economy of Violence* is an interesting and informative work, primarily through illustrating and supplementing our knowledge of early modern French society. I do, however, have several minor criticisms. Greenshields rightly warns that his incomplete and fragmentary judicial sources do not admit of reliable quantification (p. 7). Yet, on several occasions, he does use his figures to indicate a statistical precision that the nature of the sources and the size of the sample do not seem to warrant. We learn, for example, that criminal justice did not grow harsher during this period (pp. 206–7, 236), on the basis of very few numbers of sentences (ninety-six over the whole period 1587–1664). More important, however, is the central conceit of the "economy of violence": "[an] endless round of provocations and retaliations, of affronts and private, violent justice" (p. 2); "a pattern of provocation and riposte, the riposte being a violent informal 'justice' administered by the injured party" (p. 121). That this economy was present in the Haute Auvergne, Greenshields establishes without question. He does an excellent job of describing and explaining the transactions of this economy. What is not clear, however, or at least not as clear as it could be, are the ways in which this economy was unique to the early modern Haute Auvergne. Does not any society operate within such an economy of violence? What would have made the economy of violence described in this book much clearer is a more explicitly comparative approach, showing the ways in which the nature of this economy was similar to or different from the economics of violence in other societies and other times.

Mark Konnert
University of Calgary

Daniel A. Cohen, *Pillars of Salt, Monuments of Grace: New England Crime Literature and the Origins of American Popular Culture, 1674–1860.* New

York: Oxford University Press, 1993. xi + 350 pp., illust., bibliog., index. $44.50.

Andie Tucher, *Froth and Scum: Truth, Beauty, Goodness and the Ax Murder in America's First Mass Medium*. Chapel Hill: University of North Carolina Press, 1994. ix + 257 pp. Notes, illustrations, bibliography, index. $34.95 (cloth); $13.45 (paper).

The history of crime, long the concern of sociologists and legal and social historians, has recently come within the scope of intellectual and cultural historians and literary scholars, reflecting both the new emphasis on popular culture and the history of cultural representation as well as a general fascination with sensational crimes. This attention to crime as a form of cultural narrative is exciting and long overdue, opening up new areas for analytic synthesis and demonstrating how the history of crime and criminal justice explain larger transformations in culture over time. Both of the books under discussion here, Daniel A. Cohen's *Pillars of Salt, Monuments of Grace*, and Andie Tucher's, *Froth and Scum*, represent examples of this new approach, and each, in its own way, tells much about antebellum American culture.

The phrase "pillars of salt" in Cohen's title alludes to the biblical term occasionally used by Puritan ministers to refer to capital offenders and suggests that his work is at once a history of criminals and their crimes as well as a history of the extensive literature about them from the seventeenth to the mid–nineteenth century. It is in establishing this relationship between social history and the history of discourse that the work offers its original and often complex analysis. This thoroughly researched study will surely become a standard reference work on the history of crime literature.

The book opens, for example, with brief descriptions of four capital crimes, each of which occurred at a key historical (and presumably transitional) moment: (1) the killing of a butcher by a drunken courier in a Boston boardinghouse in 1685; (2) a death arising out of a mutinous scene at sea in 1725; (3) the fatal stabbing of a local constable in pursuit of a thief in 1791; and (4) the brutal death of a young woman in a Boston brothel in 1845. Each of these crimes (as well as several others he discusses throughout the book) occurred at a significant point in the evolving literary culture of America, and each was given public voice in a different literary form.

In the seventeenth century, Cohen argues, crimes were chronicled by ministers in the form of execution sermons, a unique invention of New England's leading clergymen like Cotton Mather. Those individual transgressions, which culminated in the public spectacle of the execution, were seen as evidence of God's punishment for widespread social evil. The narrative of these events, placed within the familiar structure of the jeremiad, thus served as the voice of ministerial authority and as a reminder of the power of divine providence. Simultaneously, they were used to promote social and community cohesion.

With time and the decline of Calvinism, the execution sermon gave way to the narratives of criminal conversions, which, by providing a confessional literary role for the felons themselves, focused new attention on the accused. Finally, by the early part of the nineteenth century, these more unified literary forms yielded to a broad spectrum of popular literary discourse, ranging from the published trial transcript to the newspaper account and, ultimately, to the sentimental novel. Accompanying this parade of genres, and giving it meaning, were large shifts in the social understanding and uses of both crime and punishment.

Cohen's account of one particular crime, the death of Elizabeth Fales in Dedham, Massachusetts, at the end of the eighteenth century, provides one of the book's most interesting and suggestive cases. Jason Fairbanks, Fales' beau and a sickly and rather sad young man, was arrested and tried for her murder, and, after a sensational trial, he was convicted and hanged. The highly dramatic case, Cohen shows, was recounted in several distinct forms, bridging the literary styles of both the eighteenth and nineteenth centuries: trial transcripts of the legal proceedings (the prominent Federalist attorneys, Harrison Gray Otis and John Lowell Jr., defended Fairbanks), newspaper reports, broadsides and execution sermons, and, somewhat later, an anonymously published biography sympathetic to the condemned man. Cohen argues that here cultural style (particularly the evolving sentimental tradition) helped to determine how the complicated case was both argued and understood. Events, he shows, including murderous ones, are interpreted within the context of language and literary modes of social discourse.

While Cohen's book concentrates on the period before 1800, ending with the rise of the newspaper and the novel, Tucher's stylishly written *Froth and Scum* uses this same period as the point of departure for a study of the rise of the penny press and, more specifically, the complex relationship between the new newspaper culture and sensational crime. And if the force of the marketplace and the rise of commercial culture form a constant, but sometimes given, subtext in the development of Cohen's history, these two move front and center in Tucher's. Unlike Cohen, who is primarily concerned with transformations in literary genre, Tucher focuses on two specific crimes as a vehicle for a close examination of the newspaper and newspaper reporting in the late 1830s and early 1840s: the ax murder of the prostitute Ellen Jewett in an upscale brothel in New York City in 1836 and the murder of the respectable printer Samuel Adams by his clerk John Colt (the brother of pistol manufacturer Samuel Colt). Both of these crimes, as she suggests, not only happened in New York; they also were (or were made into) stories of New York, the city itself serving as a central, if unnamed, character in the narratives. Thus, through their narrativization in the media, the events she describes may ultimately reveal more about the rise of modern urban culture than they do about the history of crime, let alone criminal justice.

The first case, the sensational death of Helen Jewett, has become the subject of a great deal of scholarly attention.[1] This is at least in part because of the colorful nature of the main characters who were a beautiful and perhaps even poetic prostitute, her madam, her rakish paramour, his able lawyer, and a cast of rowdy young men. The trial was also noted for its theatricality, its unlikely verdict of innocence for the rakish clerk, and, most importantly, the publicity it received from James Gordon Bennett, editor, entrepreneur, and *enfant terrible* on the New York scene. Through Bennett's careful design, the Jewett case not only helped to create a new form of journalism in the pages of the *New York Herald*; it became a central text of urban life.

Tucher provides a detailed history of the case, which she has researched carefully, but the significance of her argument lies in a somewhat more subtle analysis of journalistic objectivity and the relationship between the press and its audience. Truth, she argues, in the context of this emerging journalism, became less an absolute and more a supple and flexible concept; in the hands of Bennett and his competitors for the new urban readership, it became a tradeable commodity. But while the sensational events served the purposes of the pecuniary and jingoistic Bennett, for the new city reader they had a somewhat different meaning. "New Yorkers," she writes, "who chose to buy one penny paper instead of another . . . were choosing an identity, a community and a truth they could understand and accept." Transformed into copy, the story of Jewett and Robinson became a personalized city story that served a variety of purposes for a new urban audience struggling to define itself. "In fact," she concludes, "the destiny of the Jewett story seems to have been to fulfill the personal myth and clarify the personal identity of every last reader who came across it (p. 95).

Although it occurred just a few years later, the Adams/Colt case, Tucher's second example, tells a different tale of journalism and city culture. By 1841 the city scene had changed considerably as radical working-class politics were replaced by the rise of organized parties and dramatic urban growth. Bennett had a reputable and profoundly moral rival in the able reformer, Horace Greeley, who began publication of the *New York Tribune* that same year. And while the Colt/Adams story was lurid and grisly enough (although less sexually explicit than the Jewett death), it told a new and different tale of politics, journalism, and city culture. If I read Tucher correctly here, her point seems to be that by the early 1840s something more dangerous than humbug and deceit overtook the press in its purported quest for truth and objectivity: namely, a new voice of authority. Instead of imagination and popular tradition providing the basis of journalistic narrative, the press now turned to investigation and observation.

But in the name of objectivity and a more straightforward presentation of the news, Tucher argues, not only was the complete story about Colt's guilt or innocence lost (you need to read the book to get all the lurid details), but far more ominously, the press assumed a mantle of quasi-scientific respectability. In short, Tucher says, referring to the newspaper editors of the 1840s, "they replaced humbug with authority," and in the process and to the detriment of all, renegotiated the relationship between reader and paper (p. 187).

It is interesting that these new works use the history of crime and crime literature to such very different ends. It is not so much that they disagree on the specifics of interpretation, or even that their points of emphasis refer to different cultural moments—eighteenth-century New England as opposed to nineteenth-century New York. Rather, their fundamental concerns are different. Cohen seeks to understand the development of literary style against the contested terrain of crime narratives; Tucher, to trace, in these formative years the relationship between audience and text, problems of moral bankruptcy and the abuse of authority in modern journalism. In the end, both of their works serve to reiterate the point that the history of crime, mediated and understood through narrative, provides a very useful vehicle for cultural analysis.

NOTE

1. An earlier analysis of some of the same issues concerning the Helen Jewett case and the early press can be found in Dan Schiller, *Objectivity and the News: The Public and the Rise of Commercial Journalism* (Philadelphia, 1981). The case and its social context has also been written about by Patricia Cline Cohen, who is currently completing a book on the subject. See her "Unregulated Youth: Masculinity and Murder in the 1830s City," *Radical History Review* 52 (1992): 33–52 and "The Mystery of Helen Jewett: Romantic Fiction and the Eroticization of Violence," *Legal Studies Forum* 17 (1993): 133–47.

Amy Gilman Srebnick
Montclair State University

Angus McLaren, *A Prescription for Murder: The Victorian Serial Killings of Dr. Thomas Neill Cream*. Chicago: Chicago University Press, 1993. 217 pp., index. $22.50.

Dr. Thomas Neill Cream, unlike his contemporary Jack the Ripper, did not butcher his victims; he poisoned them. He also was caught, tried, and executed. No doubt it is these differences that have ensured that Jack the Ripper has continued to haunt and excite for over a century, while Cream is all but forgotten. Ripperologists, who are legion, are full of theories about the identity of the killer; they, and most of the authors who deal in murder, revel in the sensational. This is, after all and whatever their protestations, the *raison d'être* for their texts. Angus McLaren, in contrast, following the trend of other recent historians, is more concerned with illuminating the norms of Victorian society and seeks to use Cream's career to cast some further light.

Cream's career was, of course, sensational. He was born in Glasgow in 1850; his family immigrated to Canada when he was four. In 1876, he graduated in Medicine from McGill College in Montreal and was forced into a shotgun marriage by the father of a young woman he had recently made pregnant and aborted. Just over a year later, he may have been involved in the death of his unfortunate wife. By the end of 1881, he was responsible for at least four murders, largely abortion-related, and was embarking on a life sentence in the Illinois State Penitentiary at Joliet. The dubious administration of the prison enabled him to get a limit put on his sentence; this, together with remission for good behavior, led to his release after just under ten years. By the autumn of 1881, he was in London, where he murdered four women and attempted to kill others by giving them pills containing strychnine. But Cream was not just a murderer. He was not averse to a little blackmail, though he appears never to have pressed his demands, and he seems also to have had a fascination for the world of the detective.

At first glance Cream might not seem the best candidate for an examination of Victorian culture and mores. As far as the Victorians were concerned, he was a degenerate. But this categorization was made only after his arrest; before then he appeared to be a respectable medical gentleman, and this provides McLaren with a significant point of entry. Having detailed Cream's career in part one of the book, McLaren focuses successively on a series of topics—prostitution, abortion, blackmail, doctors, degenerates, detectives, women—which contextualize that career and tie Cream closely to the world in which he lived. Cream's murders, McLaren argues, provide "a distorted reflection of acceptable behavior" and consequently broaden our perception of such behavior.

In the second half of the Victorian period there was a generalized misogyny or, at least, a mistrust of women, probably fostered by women's greater bid for autonomy. Prostitutes were denigrated generally as dissolute wretches constituting a menace to society; policemen branded them as unreliable as witnesses. Alone on the street, the prostitute became especially vulnerable; this, and their supposed inversion of respectable womanhood, arguably tempted Cream. At the same time, the police perception of prostitutes as unreliable informants impeded Cream's identification and arrest. Doctors were members of a respectable profession, increasingly ring-fencing themselves and their expertise, and while contemporaries ignored the fact, the Cream affair demonstrated how the doctor/expert, in the privacy of his consulting rooms and with his access to drugs, had as much the power to do evil as to do good.

There is one nagging and rather peripheral query: Is McLaren (and are others) justified in situating the emergence of the serial murderer quite as confidently in Cream's period? The Metropolitan Police do not come out of McLaren's analysis as well as they did out of contemporary judicial and press comment, and rightly so. But might not the development of bureaucratic police and the technical advances of toxicologists and other "experts" have contributed to the ability to link murders and detect such killers? Did not the rise of the popular newspaper press, with its predilection for "orrible murder," similarly contribute to an awareness of the crime and perhaps enable some linkage? Indeed, some of the linkage probably was incorrect; how do we know that the press was right in linking the Whitechapel killings to a single individual? The fact that we cannot pinpoint much in the way of serial murder before Cream does not mean that such offenses did not exist; developments in Cream's lifetime would appear to render the recognition of similarities between different homicides more readily open to discovery. Even in modern Britain, serial murders that may have gone undetected can come to light by accident. Donald Nilson's murders of a succession of young men in the early 1980s—most of whom dwelt in the twilight world of London's transients—only came to light when the remains of one caused a blockage in the local drains. Early in 1994, the inhabitants of Gloucester were appalled to find the police removing the bodies of young women from the basement, walls, and garden of a builder's house in their quiet cathedral city; no one appears to have linked the dead, some of whom had disappeared twenty years before, with a serial killer.

Overall, McLaren's arguments are stimulating and well put. There could have been more evidence drawn from North American sources to support the thesis developed in part two; Cream, after all, murdered on two continents, and most of the discussion here is centered on the English context. But this is an excellent example of what might be gleaned from the detailed interrogation of an incident, from eschewing notions of "rotten apples," and from recognizing that even the most sensational behavior has an historical context.

Clive Emsley
The Open University, Milton Keynes

Eric A. Johnson, *Urbanization and Crime: Germany 1871–1914.* Cambridge: Cambridge University Press, 1995. x + 246 pp., index. £35.00.

Underlying Eric A. Johnson's *Urbanization and Crime: Germany 1871–1914* is a refutation of the general assumption present in contemporary popular culture, as well as in the popular culture of nineteenth-century Imperial Germany, that there was a direct link between urban development in the industrial revolution and an increase in crime concentrated in those urban areas. But of course, it is not just the popular imagination which has seen such links: Politically conservative, Marxist, and many sociological theories also have shared such ideas. By analyzing the wealth of criminal statistics that exist for Imperial Germany in the late nineteenth and early twentieth centuries, Johnson exposes the general shallowness of such conceptions.

The book begins with a general description of the criminal justice system of Imperial Germany and the structure and nature of its police forces, which ranged from municipal watchmen to the tough, military gendarmes. In general, the German judiciary, legal profession, and police appear relatively highly trained, compared to their counterparts in England, for example, and the legal code was both consistent and relatively humane in many respects. However, Johnson also reveals the German criminal justice system to have been both authoritarian and rigid, with the police often overbearing and inclined to focus their energies disproportionately on left-wing political activists and ethnic minorities.

From here Johnson moves on to an analysis of the public perception of crime through its representation in newspapers of various political complexions and in contemporary literature. He detects a clear pattern of political bias in the reporting of crime. Conservative newspapers would often tend to report crime committed by socialists or social "undesirables"; socialist papers had a tendency to emphasize bourgeois crime or police misdemeanors; while liberal papers would generally seek a middle road between the two, reporting the offenses committed by a broader cross-section of society. The papers thus supported their respective political perceptions of society in the way that they reported criminal incidents. It would also appear that while newspaper editors had to be careful about government censorship when reporting crime within the Empire, the sensational reporting of offenses committed abroad was tolerated more readily. In contrast with other European countries, Germany possessed far fewer literary figures concerned with the representation of social hardship in the nineteenth century, such as Dickens, Hugo, Zola, Dostoevsky, and Tolstoy. Although the examples of left-liberal authors such as Max Kretzer and Gerhart Hauptmann can be cited, the more conservative inclination of a majority of contemporary writers meant that they tended to represent crime and misdemeanors in Germany in the form of personal lapses of morality and honor.

The scene set, Johnson moves on to a detailed analysis of the crime

figures. He offers a consideration of the value of the link between modernization and crime, of the shifting patterns of offenses against property and
against the person, and a discussion of crime trends before and after
German unification. Having shown the inadequacy of the simple assumption that urban areas are the centers of crime in modern societies, he stresses
the importance respectively of social attitudes and bias, of political decision
making, oppressed ethnic minorities, gender, demographic change and raw
economic hardship in explaining the crime statistics of Imperial Germany.
For example, there was a popular perception that an ethnic minority, the
Poles, were disproportionately responsible for crime. The editor of a Polish
paper in the city of Herne in 1913 protested that much of the criminality
in his area should be attributed, first and foremost, to "the anti-Polish
system, which the Germans learn . . . the Poles are [constantly] insulted and
ridiculed . . . Taunts like 'damned Polacks' and other such are heard daily
on the street." The importance of hardship in causing crime is illustrated
by the example of Cologne, which had rather low rates of crime in the
1880s but displayed sharp increases by the first decade of the twentieth
century. An explanation for this can be found in the fact that, in this period,
the poorer, working-class industrial suburbs were incorporated with the
old, medieval core of the city, populated by the bourgeois, thus swelling
the population threefold and greatly increasing the proportion of crime-
infested areas.

A major problem with crime statistics is that their reliability, and hence
their value, is always subject to question. Before 1882, the presentation and
publication of crime statistics was the responsibility of the various individual states of the Empire, and they used different formats. After 1882, while
the figures now covered the whole of the Germany in the same format, they
only represented court records. Johnson is careful to clarify the problems
and pitfalls of the statistics, yet the reader is sometimes left with the im-
pression of being bombarded with data in certain parts of the book.

That said, however, the historian has to make the best use of the data
at his or her disposal. In this respect, Johnson has used the wealth of evidence of crime in the period to best advantage and has made a convincing
case that a whole variety of social and economic factors have to be considered in order to understand the nature of crime and policing in Imperial
Germany. It is not satisfactory to make monolithic assumptions about urbanization or modernization, and their effect on crime and society, without
considering the evidence more closely. The book also puts a further nail in
the coffin of the now rather discredited theory of a German "special path"
in history, the *Sonderweg*. While acknowledging a degree of continuity in
the legal positivism of the Imperial period and the authoritarianism of the
Third Reich, Johnson shows how the correct, if rigid, legal practices of late
nineteenth- and early twentieth-century Germany cannot fairly be compared with the legal sham of the 1930s. He also questions the assumption

of a quiescent and socially stable Germany in the Imperial period, pointing to the realities of social tension, the rise of socialism, economic unrest, changing gender roles, rapid urban growth, and population migration in that society. In sum, the book represents another convincing nonhistoricist approach to the analysis of German history by engaging in an empirical study of the workings of the everyday criminal justice system in Imperial Germany, and the perceptions of the origins and patterns of crime within that society.

Carl Wade
The Open University, Milton Keynes

Timothy J. Gilfoyle, *City of Eros: New York City, Prostitution, and the Commercialization of Sex, 1790–1920*. New York: W. W. Norton & Company, 1992. 462 pp., illust., index. $17.95 (paper).

David J. Langum, *Crossing over the Line: Legislating Morality and the Mann Act*. Chicago: University of Chicago Press, 1994. xii + 311 pp., illust., index. $27.00.

Mary E. Odem, *Delinquent Daughters: Protecting and Policing Adolescent Female Sexuality in the United States, 1885–1920*. Chapel Hill: University of North Carolina Press, 1995. xiv + 265 pp., illust., index. $17.95 (paper).

Each of these books makes important contributions to an understanding of changing sexual behavior and values in America in the late nineteenth and early twentieth centuries. Each explores the topic by examining sexual behavior that was or became illegal. Despite the similarity, however, they are sufficiently different so that they can be seen to complement each other rather than to confront directly the same issues. In conjunction with other recent studies, the books highlight the degree to which sexual behavior in America from the Civil War to World War II was more complex, more diverse, and more contested than historians would have guessed just ten or fifteen years ago.

Gilfoyle's central theme is that the redlight districts of New York (and, presumably, other cities) were sites within which various forms of commercialized sex flourished and, therefore, alternative sexual norms evolved and found expression. He provides detailed evidence for the extent and influence of the new sexual culture. At a conservative estimate, some 5 to 10 percent of all New York women in the appropriate age group must have been prostitutes in order to support the districts. The range of institutions within which commercialized sex and titillation occurred included pornography, burlesque shows, concert saloons (the forerunners of nightclubs, offering many types of entertainment), a variety of popular theaters, and a more or less openly accepted gay culture. Although the entertainment activities tended to cluster in recognized sections of the city, they overlapped with residences and businesses. A pedestrian would have been aware of streetwalkers, bright lights, and the crowds of customers on any night. The culture also was displayed publicly in the famous third tier of theaters (where prostitutes watched plays and solicited customers) and in the publicly advertised masquerade balls that brought together men and women from all classes. At the same time, the popular sporting press made celebrities of madams and chronicled the happenings in the city's nightlife.

The great strength of Gilfoyle's book is that, by thick description and by analysis, he places prostitution within a range of commercial entertainment and builds a picture of a culture of recreational sex that emerged over more than a century. The book is divided into two main chronological sections, one from 1820 to 1870 and the other from 1870 to 1920. In each section, Gilfoyle describes the evolving geography of commercialized sex, analyzes the economics and culture of prostitution, explains the growth of various venues for disreputable entertainment, and links these developments to the customers of the alternative culture. He makes concrete the ideas that earlier scholars began to explore in the histories of prostitution and nightlife entertainment. The book is less successful in the analysis of reformers who opposed the sexual culture and the police and politicians who supported or tolerated it. But given the prodigious research and careful analysis of the redlight districts, this is a minor flaw in an important study.

Langum and Odem deal with reform movements that were a reaction to the redlight districts, to the "white slavery" that reformers believed accompanied the districts, and to the sexually oriented youth culture that emerged in American cities as teenagers, no longer under the control of parents, created their own culture of sexual relations. The two books explore the ironies and contradictions in the use of law to police and control sexual behavior in a society of changing sexual mores. And they use the enforcement of law as a prism for examining the complexities of the behavior itself.

Langum chronicles the history of the federal Mann Act from its passage in 1910 until its declining use in the 1980s. This act was a direct response to the reformers' fight against the redlight districts—specifically against the "white slave trade." The act made it illegal to take a woman across state lines for an "immoral purpose." Langum, a professor of law, has written a powerful brief arguing that the Mann Act demonstrates the dangers when government uses coercion to enforce individual morality. He certainly presents a convincing case that multiple injustices resulted from the enforcement of the Mann Act. But, because he does not make a case that the injustices under the Mann Act are necessarily characteristic of any law policing individual morality, the larger case remains unproven. Instead, the book is important as a clear and often incisive study of federal enforcement of a law that, while famous, is relatively unstudied.

Passed during the height of the crusade against white slavery, the Mann Act was drawn with sufficient vagueness that it was soon interpreted to have a broad reach. By 1915, the U.S. Supreme Court held that, when a man and woman crossed a state line and engaged in sexual intercourse, not only could the man be charged for taking her across a state line but she could be charged with conspiring to take a woman (herself) across the line. Because opponents of the law argued that it would become a tool by which women might entrap and blackmail men, this ruling appeared to lessen that possibility by making the woman also guilty. (In fact, blackmail continued despite the ruling.) The most important extension of the act, in place by 1917, stemmed from Supreme Court rulings that the "immoral" purpose could be completely consensual and noncommercial sex. Although the act was passed to fight the interstate trafficking in women for purposes of prostitution, a man and a woman could be prosecuted for going across a state line on a date if they engaged in sexual relations. Langum argues that this extension was a reaction to the new dating behavior among many young girls, who sought a good time with men and in return were willing to have sex. For many respectable persons there was no clear distinction between the new dating behavior and commercial prostitution.

Langum's book, a sophisticated examination of the evolution of federal prosecution, will become the standard source for understanding the uses to which the act was put. While Langum does not examine prosecution in cases involving commercial prosecution, he does analyze in considerable detail the history of prosecutions for consensual sexual intercourse until such prosecutions were finally abandoned in recent years. He also examines how prosecutors selectively pursued some cases in order to harass political radicals or to punish black men whose sexual relations crossed the color line. Among these cases, of course, were the famous prosecutions of Jack Johnson, the African American heavy-weight champion before World War I, and Charlie Chaplin, the movie comedian whose political views angered many Americans during the McCarthyism period after World War II.

Finally, Odem's book looks at the way in which predominantly women reformers reacted to the dangers faced by young women because of the evils of prostitution and more open dating in the late nineteenth and early twentieth centuries. The book has two parts. The first deals with the movement in the late nineteenth century to raise the age of consent; the second deals with the movement in the early twentieth century to create juvenile courts and to adapt them to the control of delinquent girls. In each section, the author analyzes the way in which women reformers defined the problem. Then she examines the reality of behavior revealed when the laws were enforced in Alameda and Los Angeles counties, California. The tensions and contradictions between the reformers' expectations and the behaviors revealed by enforcement provide the central findings of the book.

In the United States after the Civil War, the age of consent for girls, as defined by state laws, varied from ten to twelve. If a man had sexual relations with a girl below the age of consent, he could be prosecuted for rape even if no force was used, but if the girl was above the age of consent, then consensual sex with an older man was not rape. By the 1880s, women reformers saw cities as environments where white slavers recruited young girls for prostitution and wealthy men seduced young girls for their pleasure. On the other hand, they saw the working-class girls primarily as innocent victims. Yet, under the double standard, a girl who was sexually active was regarded as lost, while the man did not lose his status. To protect young girls and to confront the double standard, middle-class women fought to raise the age of consent.

The enforcement of the new laws, however, revealed a different reality from the reformers' vision. Over 70 percent of cases prosecuted for statutory rape involved a consensual relationship of a girl with a male of her own class, often in the context of an ongoing romance. This reflected the fact that working-class girls increasingly were challenging family control and seeking pleasure and companionship. About 25 percent of the cases involved forcible rape—but often by relatives or neighbors. Neither of these patterns conformed to the reformers' image of the innocent girl victimized by the wealthy seducer or the white slaver. In the enforcement of the laws, the women reformers faced another surprise from the men who were prosecutors, judges, and jurors. Often the men, in effect, nullified the law. In court, the girls were asked about their sexual history and whether they had consented—factors irrelevant when the girl was below the age of consent. Officials assumed that girls had a responsibility to control the passions of men—and, when they did not, then they were responsible for the man's sexual behavior. In cases that were clear violations of the law, often the man was either not convicted or only lightly sentenced.

In the early twentieth century, the next generation of women reformers worked to make the newly created juvenile courts into agencies that could deal with the sexual dangers faced by girls. But the reformers now recognized that girls, given the family and urban environment, were becoming part of a youth culture which valued dating and sexual experimentation. In this context, the goal was not to control the seductive male but to reform the family and environment so that girls would be empowered to protect themselves. Reformers also wished to avoid the failure of the previous reform that resulted from male dominance of the justice system. To that end, they often succeeded in assuring that women police officers, juvenile court officials, and judges would be responsible for dealing with girls in the juvenile system.

Again, the author finds the result of the reform problematic. About 63 percent of the girls processed by the Los Angeles juvenile court were charged with sexual delinquency; in contrast, only a small percent of the boys were brought to court for sexual misconduct. Thus, while boys were processed for offenses ranging from truancy to robbery, girls were processed primarily in order to control sexual behavior that was seldom policed in the case of boys. Odem is ambivalent in her attitude toward this outcome. On the one hand, she acknowledges that the reformers correctly recognized the dangers faced by girls under the new sexual codes: possible pregnancy, venereal disease, or involvement in exploitative sexual relations. They had reason, therefore, to control the sexual behavior of girls. On the other hand, the juvenile justice system treated the girls in a coercive manner. Their sexual histories were probed, they were sent to reformatories for "rehabilitation" at a rate higher than for boys, and they were often removed from their homes because their parents were found incompetent by middle-class standards. Thus, the women reformers forced girls into a disciplinary system and policed working-class families. All of this occurred in the context of what was clearly a generation gap. In nearly half the cases, girls were referred to the court by their parents, who sought the court's help in controlling the sexual behavior of their daughters. Reformers and working-class parents shared, at least, a desire to control the sexual behavior of girls.

The three books offer detailed and thoughtful insights into changing sexual patterns in American society. Gilfoyle provides a coherent analysis of the complex commercialization of sex within the entertainment districts of New York. Odem depicts the rise of new dating behavior, developed within a youth culture that was relatively independent of parental control. What is not clear is the degree to which the youth culture derived some of its values from the entertainment districts and the degree to which it was an independent development emerging among young people in their interactions with each other. What all of the books deal with is the complex and contested nature of sexual behaviors and values. There were generational differences, reflected in the male notion that men needed protection from the seductive wiles of 11- and 12-year-old girls. There were generational gaps when some youths became part of a new dating culture over which their parents and other "respectable" adults had little control. There were gaps that reflected class and ethnic cultures that shaped, in part, the sexual norms of many Americans. And, finally, there were the multiple ironies, injustices, and failures that derived from the attempt to use criminal law to police intimate sexual behavior. Examples ranged from the corruption and tolerance of illegal sex within redlight districts to the punishment of consensual sex through the juvenile courts and the Mann Act. These books reflect the distance that historians have traveled in recent years in the exploration of law and sexuality as well as the interesting problems that still remain to be explored.

Mark Haller
Temple University, Philadelphia

Amy Gilman Srebnick, *The Mysterious Death of Mary Rogers: Sex and Culture in Nineteenth-Century New York*. New York and Oxford: Oxford University Press, 1995. vii + 161 pp., illustrat., bibliog., index. $25.00.

In the early 1840s, New York City newspapers sensationalized the death of an attractive young woman. Mary Rogers had been reported missing for three days when men strolling along the Jersey side of the Hudson River sighted her body floating a few hundred yards from shore. According to the New Jersey coroner's report, death resulted from strangulation. The New York City coroner, however, deemed it a death by drowning. In 1842, new evidence revealed that Rogers' death might have occurred in connection with a failed abortion. Public disclosure of this information generated widespread interest in the case and inspired different interpretations of Mary Rogers' identity.

In *The Mysterious Death of Mary Rogers*, Amy Gilman Srebnick leads the reader through the metaphorical landscape of this event. The journey clarifies why and how this case captivated the attention of nineteenth-century New Yorkers and, through representations of the victimized female body, became symbolic of the enticements and dangers of city life. Srebnick's purpose is not to solve the factual mystery of how Rogers met her death. Instead, her inquiry seeks to illuminate the cultural mystery embodied in the Mary Rogers story. Srebnick's approach is informed by new interdisciplinary perspectives that have broadened the scope of history. Here historical inquiry becomes a project in reconstructing meaning. The result is at times a spellbinding account of the historical, the factual, and the imaginative.

Much more of the imaginative than the factual record of Mary Rogers remains available. Srebnick works to overcome this limitation in the sources by tracing Rogers' life through family records and by interpreting her movements within the larger historical framework of rural and urban economic changes. Through this approach to the "historical" Mary we learn of her New England roots and her status as a rural migrant to the city. Unlike most urban working women, Mary Rogers was employed as a salesgirl in a popular downtown tobacco shop. Her employment placed her within the urban and male milieu that formed around entertainment spots and political clubs of the area. Known as the beautiful cigar girl, her presence was on display, poised to bring in a male clientele. Mary Rogers occupied the fringes of respectable society.

Srebnick rules out the possibility that Rogers was a prostitute. Nevertheless, it is difficult to see Mary Rogers as an innocent woman. As Srebnick explains, the appeal of the Mary Rogers phenomenon flowed from the ambiguity of her identity. It was and remains unclear whether she was a simple country girl seduced by the city, whether the city inspired her to use her sexuality as a means of claiming her independence, or whether she was engaged in some other quest or none at all. Without any direct testimony from Mary Rogers herself, we do not learn what she meant to herself, and this is a critical component of the Mary Rogers phenomenon. The paucity of factual knowledge about Mary Rogers allowed contemporaries to fill the void with imaginative stories.

Buried within the saga of Mary Rogers are many New York narratives, including tales of innocence and waywardness. Edgar Allan Poe was perhaps the most well-known interpreter of the Rogers story, and Srebnick devotes an entire chapter to his work. Though of interest in its own right, Srebnick's account of Poe's craft of detective fiction may distract the reader's attention from the central themes of the Rogers' phenomenon. Other writers of the period, as discussed by Srebnick, utilized the Rogers story to work out imaginative moral and social solutions to the central problem posed by urban female sexuality. These narratives integrate the new female identity within larger visions of the city, the republic, and the nation. The ambiguous social status of the woman alone made possible a range of interpretations of the Mary Rogers persona, and a variety of narratives, including stories of seduction, crime and detection, and redemption.

The Mary Rogers phenomenon is the result of the social meanings and literary perspectives that converged in the fabrication of the imaginary Mary Rogers. Srebnick's meticulous research brings together the factors of cultural production responsible for the Mary Rogers phenomenon. These factors include the rise of the city itself as a center of commerce, industry, and print culture and the changing role of women within this urban complex.

The press played a primary role in appropriating the event of Mary Rogers' death by promoting it as a sensational crime of sexuality and violence in the city. Illustrations drawn from the pamphlet literature of the day and reproduced alongside the text convey the melodramatic atmosphere of the case. Srebnick focuses on the activities of James Gordon Bennett, editor of the *Herald*, as she examines the rise of popular journalism and the central place of crime as news in the urban press. In the pages of the *Herald* and other dailies, the body of Mary Rogers served a variety of purposes so far as her death was used to give expression to fears of increasing lawlessness and to argue for police reform and tighter control of abortion.

Srebnick examines the literary and visual representations of the Rogers phenomenon from the different, but related, perspectives of gender analysis and changing socioeconomic relationships. So far as the city's economic growth fed on the increasing employment of women, the working woman became a new and visibly public presence in the streets and thoroughfares of the city. This development in the status of the urban working woman, moreover, took place within the cultural terms of an emerging urban commercialism. Srebnick reveals the formation of a new system of meanings about women, class, and public spaces within New York City in the 1830s and 1840s.

By shifting the focus and displacing attention from the actual event to its public and social representation and meaning, Srebnick defines the central theme of the Mary Rogers phenomenon as the ambiguous status of single women in cities. This ambiguity, as Srebnick's analysis demonstrates, was communicated vividly in the contemporary representations of Rogers as a body. Perceived in life as an object of erotic desire, in death Rogers' body became public property through newspaper accounts and graphic renderings of her as a decaying corpse. The lack of privacy and respect for her body inverted the traditional reverence displayed toward the dead. Srebnick makes powerful use of this analysis by conveying the degree to which public treatment of the victim amounted to a macabre form of symbolic abuse.

The public sexuality of Rogers' identity remains central to an understanding of the link between the Rogers mystery and the larger problem of social control introduced by the new urban woman. Srebnick argues that the key to the new female identity was the combination of public visibility and social isolation of the urban working woman. She was a woman alone, an individual, without the protection of family and male relatives. Srebnick claims that so far as Mary Rogers' sexuality appeared as public and autonomous, it was perceived as both vulnerable to male desire and threatening to the social order. This equivocal aspect of her identity resonated with the concerns and preoccupations of the public imagination during this period.

Srebnick's purpose of discovering a cultural text is fulfiled amply in this study. The book orchestrates a complex vision of how different social currents merged in the creation of cultural meaning. The author's comprehensive treatment of the Mary Rogers phenomenon raises other, more general questions about the rise of female autonomy in connection with the city as a social space. For example, the phenomenon of Mary Rogers may suggest that the woman alone—shall we say the "unsupervised woman"—was as yet ill-prepared to pursue an independent life.

Anne Parrella
Tidewater Community College, Virginia

Jonathan Goodman, *The Passing of Starr Faithfull*. Kent, Ohio: The Kent State University Press, 1996. 311 pp., photographs, illust., index. $17.00 (paper).

The Starr Faithfull case was a sensational one, and the ensuing spectacle that followed her death only contributed to the mystery of her tragic life. As the case that inspired such stories as John O'Hara's *Butterfield 8*, the story of Starr Faithfull, a beautiful yet sullen woman of 25, whose bruised body washed up on New York's Long Beach in 1931, was surrounded with the same type of media frenzy that we have come to expect today. The injuries on her body, which included bruises on her torso and legs, cuts on her face, and the fact that her clothing was undamaged raised a mystery that has not yet been solved.

What the investigators did know was that the cause of her death was drowning, but the question of how she came to such an unfortunate end remained. The three possible alternatives were suicide, drowning, or murder. Elvin Edwards, the district attorney (DA) of Nassau County was convinced it was murder. But who did it? The ensuing investigation of Starr Faithfull's death tried to reconstruct her last days of life and, accordingly, brought light to bear on her sordid affairs, dysfunctional family life, and the counterculture of New York in the roaring twenties and depression-era thirties.

The tale that Jonathan Goodman weaves is a revision of the previous paperback accounts of the case written by contemporary popularists. What Goodman adds to the story is a myriad of newspaper accounts and interviews as well as an alternative explanation for Faithfull's death. Included in this study is a portrayal of Andrew J. Peters, former congressman and mayor of Boston and campaign organizer for Franklin Delano Roosevelt. Peters' connection to Faithfull was sordid and criminal, as he allegedly molested Starr when she was a child, which made him a likely suspect if foul play was her cause of death. As well, there was Dr. George Carr, ship's surgeon on the Cunard Line, for whom Starr professed her undying love. There was also Starr's connection to Edwin Megargee, the New York artist, who on the request of Starr's parents was encouraged to have a sexual relationship with her. Finally, there was Detective Inspector Harold King, who, unlike the DA, was convinced that Faithfull had committed suicide.

To complete this picture, the missing diary of Starr was discovered, bringing to the forefront some of the more sordid aspects of her life, including her hatred for her stepfather and contempt for her mother and sister. To round this off, during the investigation it was discovered that Starr, who was portrayed by her parents as a homebody, was in fact a woman who frequented speakeasies and took hallucinogenic drugs. All in all, it is a story of contradictions, which was played out in the news media as well as the District Attorney's Office.

The personal human drama of the case is well developed by Goodman. His detailed research in fact began in 1971. He also provides an alternative explanation to the officially recognized scenario that led to Starr's death, which was suicide. Where the book disappoints is in its detail. There is simply too much superfluous material included in the text of this book that has little bearing on the story that Goodman attempts to illustrate. The book does provide additional facts regarding the case and presents it with more historical detail than any previous account. For example, the deep context that Goodman provides transports the reader into the dark underside of New York City during the age of mobsters and prohibition. However, the detailed biographies of somewhat minor characters tend to obscure the story at hand, leading to a confused menagerie of individuals who in some way may have had a connection to the Faithfull case in a manner somewhat similar to an exercise in "Six Degrees of Separation."

The Passing of Starr Faithfull can be entertaining and a compelling read for the same reason that it is occasionally awkward. Goodman is the only author who was granted full access to the police dossier, which makes this the most complete account of this renowned mystery. As well, he rounds his account off neatly by using newspaper sources from Great Britain as well as the United States. If a reader is willing to wade through evidence in a manner similar to an investigator, this book can be a useful and constructive exposé of an unsolved case that is full of intrigue and perplexity.

Paul Nigol
University of Calgary

Richard F. Hamm, *Shaping the Eighteenth Amendment: Temperance Reform, Legal Culture, and the Polity, 1880–1920.* Chapel Hill: The University of North Carolina Press, 1995. x + 341 pp., index $22.50 (paper).

Shaping the Eighteenth Amendment is an exhaustively researched and highly focused history of the temperance movement from the 1870s to its culmination in the Eighteenth Amendment and the Volstead Act. In a brief historiographic introduction, Richard Hamm positions his book amidst studies of progressive-era reforms, noting that pre-1970 histories of this reform era in its entirety have given way to contextual analyses of diverse progressive era reform movements. Hamm focuses on the polity: the ways in which the structure and the nature of American government and law from 1880 to 1920 formed and was formed by the prohibition movement. This sets *Shaping the Eighteenth Amendment* apart from studies that explore the social origins, ideologies, and the cultural and symbolic aspects of temperance groups.

The temperance movement was framed by such elements of the polity as federalism, Commerce Clause jurisprudence, and the federal liquor tax. Its history spanned the transformation of the polity from a "state of courts and parties" to an administrative state. Throughout the struggle that culminated in prohibition, temperance forces continuously had to decide whether to press for state or federal action. These choices were in large part shaped by the stance of the Supreme Court at any given time on whether business activity by the alcoholic beverage industry was protected from local interference by the Commerce Clause. As a general welfare state began to emerge in the twentieth century, the most dynamic of the temperance organizations, the Anti-Saloon League (ASL), looked to Congress and to the amendment process to solidify its local gains.

Shaping the Eighteenth Amendment proceeds both chronologically and thematically. The first chapter, for example, begins with the rebirth of the temperance movement in the 1870s. It focuses, however, not on the ideology of the Prohibition Party and the Women's Christian Temperance Union (WCTU) but also on what Hamm labels a "Mosaic" view of law held by these radical prohibitionists. This view was moralistic, formal, and simplistically wedded to the text of statutes as reflections of moral sentiment. The failure of these groups to adapt to the dominant legal ideology of rights and the methodology of constitutional adjudication made the radical drys weak warriors in the legal arena (p. 43).

The book is divided into two parts. Part I, covering the 1880s and 1890s, corresponds to the dominance of temperance activism by the radical prohibitionists and their Mosaic view of law. Part II focuses on the Anti-Saloon League's pragmatic style. Given Hamm's focus on the means used by radicals and pragmatists (rather than on underlying ideologies and motivations), and on their relationship to the polity, the way each group viewed and used law is critical to appreciating the failure of the radical approach and the success of the ASL. The radicals' Mosaic perspective was an ineffective response to the weighty doctrinal support that the wets found in concepts of individual freedom, due process, property rights, and, above all, the linchpin of American federalism—the notion of interstate commerce. Hamm's complete mastery of primary sources allows him to demonstrate, and not simply assert, how the ASL position evolved in reaction to its successes, setbacks, and the counterattacks it faced.

Hamm shows that the key to understanding the ultimate ASL success— the Eighteenth Amendment—depended on two factors in addition to the league's well-known abilities as a political pressure group. First, from "its inception to its demise, the Anti-Saloon League was a law enforcement organization" (p. 141). This gave the league a focus for activity and incremental successes that kept it viable and maintained its support. Next, the league's approach to law was always divided. It pursued an instrumental approach to law by retaining lawyers to enforce liquor regulation (not prohibition). But it also kept Mosaic values alive (p. 140). Early ASL writings reflect the Mosaic view of law as a moral code, and, as the author's nuanced approach shows, the ASL really was not a pressure group designed to bring about legal change through adjudication (p. 140). As its pressure tactics to enforce antiliquor laws spawned legal challenges, the ASL had to shift its response in due process, individual freedom, and Commerce Clause terms dictated by the polity, especially by the Supreme Court.

Thus, when the league achieved considerable success in the second decade of the twentieth century, it was able to shift its focus from local action and regulation to national action and prohibition—the original goal of the radical temperance movement. At that point it had the clout to seize an unusual moment in American history, when war-induced moral fervor was at fever pitch and federal power was at a pinnacle, to push through the Eighteenth Amendment.

In pursuing this theme, Hamm provides ample analysis of books by ASL leaders Howard H. Russell, Wayne Wheeler, and others rather than simply summarizing the league's Mosaic attitude to law. In the portions of *Shaping the Eighteenth Amendment* that are likely to be of greatest interest to constitutional scholars, Hamm delves into the specifics of Supreme Court cases and federal legislation surrounding the Commerce Clause (pp. 56–91, 175–226). The problem, for drys, was that local dry laws were undermined by the system of national commerce embedded in the constitutional scheme. In two decades of fighting this issue, the ASL honed both its pragmatic use of the law and its renowned ability as a one-issue interest group in Congress. For prohibition movement scholars these chapters provide a rich mine of information that helps to explain the ultimate success of the ASL. For constitutional and political scholars familiar with the general development of Commerce Clause litigation, Hamm provides a worthwhile case study of the application of the doctrine to one area, especially as he details how the ASL and the liquor industry turned to Congress and the court to achieve their respective goals. This valuable political history brings out the extent to which the ASL's success was based on contingencies as well as ideologies. For law and society scholars, this book provides a dense account of how court decisions emerge out of the needs of the parties and the shape of legislation as well as on underlying constitutional doctrines.

The federal liquor tax was central to the political journey of the temperance movement from radical to practical, a point most likely to be overlooked in ideological or cultural studies. It was one of the few Civil War revenue measures kept after the war, becoming a mainstay for the federal government. From 1891 to 1916 the tax never fell below 30 percent of the federal government's tax receipts (pp. 95–96). At a time when the departments of the federal government were primitive, the Internal Revenue Office was one of the most developed and efficient bureaucracies, deeply involved in every step of the distilling industry. Internal revenue officials came to admire and support the liquor industry, a posture that infuriated radical drys who saw the tax as a *license* for the alcoholic beverage industry. In contrast to the radicals' tax-abolition position, the ASL pushed for strict enforcement of the tax as a way to burden and ultimately crush the liquor industry. The league fought to use the federal tax to vigorously enforce local dry laws by utilizing federal tax records as evidence of state law violations.

Existing scholarship has established that the Anti-Saloon League's success was due to its role as one of the first single-issue pressure groups. *Shaping the Eighteenth Amendment* provides a significant advance to existing scholarship by showing in detail that the ASL's success depended on a strategic understanding of the polity that allowed it to advance its agenda. This required the ASL, as part of its law enforcement agenda, to play close attention to the minute details of the legislative process as it shepherded bills through Congress while simultaneously pursuing a litigation strategy shaped by larger Commerce Clause concerns.

Hamm has thus succeeded, up to a point, in his larger goal of exploring the relationship of the polity and reform movements. Although *Shaping the Eighteenth Amendment* compares prohibition to other progressive-era reforms, it is not a general synthesis of the reform-polity relationship. Future studies of progressive-era reforms will have to consider Hamm's polity-reform thesis, which may indeed pave the way to a new synthesis for an understanding of the progressive era.

Shaping the Eighteenth Amendment is not for the neophyte. It assumes knowledge of the forces behind the temperance movement while it focuses on the means used to advance prohibition. More accessible studies that cover broader time periods[1] or provide explanations for the prohibition phenomenon in the context of the progressive era[2] give the general reader a more easily traversed overview of the temperance movement. Its detailed analysis of Commerce Clause cases is unnecessarily tedious for readers seeking a general understanding of the prohibition phenomenon and may be formidable for readers unfamiliar with constitutional law. For specialists in law and politics, progressive era history, or the prohibition movement, however, *Shaping the Eighteenth Amendment* provides a significant advance in scholarship.

NOTES

1. Jack S. Blocker Jr., *American Temperance Movements: Cycles of Reform* (Boston, 1989).

2. Joseph R. Gosfield, *Symbolic Crusade: Status Politics and the American Temperance Movement* (Urbana, Ill., 1963); and James H. Timberlake, *Prohibition and the Progressive Movement, 1900–1920* (Cambridge, Mass., 1963).

Marvin Zalman
Wayne State University

Dorothy Harley Eber, *Images of Justice—A Legal History of the Northwest Territories as Traced through the Yellowknife Courthouse Collection of Inuit Sculpture*. Montreal and Kingston: McGill-Queen's University Press, 1997. 223 pp., bibliog., index. $39.95.

One of the impressive growth areas within the corpus of Canadian legal history has been that concerned with the meeting ground of aboriginal peoples and Euro-Canadian legal systems. Indeed, some of the most thought-provoking research in the field has explored the contested relationships involving aboriginal notions of order and corresponding methods of dispute resolution, arrayed against those imported by explorers, fur traders, settlers, and the rising wave of newcomers to the region now known as Canada. Through this work we have come to understand not only the complexities of legal interactions between natives and non-natives, but we have begun the process of reconstructing the diversity of the various legal orders that have historically functioned in Canada.

Although there has been an impressive expansion of research dedicated to unraveling the legal relations between aboriginal peoples and Euro-Canadians, the emphasis in this work has been uneven. For example, with a few notable exceptions, neither the northern section of the Canadian provinces nor the territorial north have received a great deal of legal historical attention. This is not to say that these northern reaches have been unstudied but, rather, that much of the work has involved celebratory accounts of mounted police daring do, case studies of notable or infamous crimes, and present-minded criminological or anthropological investigations. Insofar as the north has been concerned, theoretically grounded legal historical inquiry has been the exception rather than the rule.

The recent publication by Dorothy Harley Eber, entitled *Images of Justice—A Legal History of the Northwest Territories as Traced through the Yellowknife Courthouse Collection of Inuit Sculpture*, is an illuminating example of the current state of legal historical writing on northern Canada. This handsome volume, containing as it does, black and white photographs of Inuit carvings housed in the Yellowknife courthouse, contains fourteen case descriptions of notable trials and legal proceedings that occurred between 1955 and 1970. Two additional cases from the early 1990s also are included, in part to document the changes in northern Canada since 1970. A brief history of the Northwest Territories Supreme Court opens the book and the epilogue explores how, in the aftermath of the various trials, the carvings came to be made.

For those unfamiliar with the legal historical events of these years, there is little question that the case descriptions in *Images of Justice* offer captivating human dramas. There is the famous story of Kikkik, the Ennadai Lake Inuit woman who was tried for a double murder and child abandonment in 1958 in the wake of unimaginable personal hardship and deprivation. Or the 1962 "billion dollar duck" trial involving Michael Sikyea, who was charged with shooting a wild duck contrary to the Migratory Birds Convention Act. Also included is the wrenching case of Shooyook and Aiyoot, who were tried for murdering Soosee, Aiyoot's deranged mother, in July 1966. Presented within the context of their times as well as subsequent history, these and the other case studies offer valuable insight into the complexities of law and culture contact in Canada's north. Indeed, for bringing these cases together and adding updated information on the lives of the various participants since the trials, Eber has provided a useful tool for those wishing to explore and expand upon northern Canadian legal history.

While useful, Eber's work cannot be credited with being particularly novel, nor does the work offer an analysis of the deeper issues that these cases involve. For example, in the 1956 case of *R. v. Kaotak*, a trial alleging that Allan Kaotak had murdered his father, Eber noted that Judge Jack Sissons recognized that assisted suicide, the central issue of the case, clashed "with accepted southern values" (p. 42). This clash of values, representing as it did the larger conflict between indigenous and non-native ideals, remains central to the imposition of southern Canadian legal norms and processes on northern Canadian indigenous peoples. Consequently, exploring the nuances of this meeting of law-ways should have occupied the central interpretative thrust of this book. Indeed, even the respective autobiographies of Justices Sissons and Morrow acknowledged, at some level, that cultural biases colored their individual views from the bench. Yet other than periodically acknowledging the issue, Eber fails to explore this basic aspect of northern Canadian legal history.

Further, while she has done a considerable service in bringing these cases together, it must be admitted that Eber has not actually expanded our understanding of the cases or their meaning for all northerners. Indeed, the vast majority of the information in this book is to be found in Sissons' and Morrow's autobiographies. We need to begin asking more penetrating questions of these cases and the legal colonialism they represented. We also need to press beyond the assertion that by their actions and their activism, Sissons and Morrow symbolized a pivotal point in northern Canadian legal history. This may very well be true, but such accolades tell only one small part of the story. After all, no matter how well intentioned and conscientious these two men were in the performance of their official and unofficial duties, and how much they endeavoured to tailor the law to the northern circumstances, they still represented the imposition of southern Canadian legal values in the north. The time has come to start exploring these other realties of northern Canadian legal history.

Eber's epilogue, in which she details the process whereby the carvings came to be made, acquired by Sissons and Morrow, and then eventually donated to the Yellowknife courthouse, also raises an assortment of questions that is left untouched. Through some method or other, Sissons and Morrow solicited all of the carvings. None were the independent creation of Inuit artisans who, pursuing cultural and artistic expression in response to the various trials and legal proceedings, attempted to depict or capture the deeper meaning of these events. These carvings were, as Eber notes, primarily a means of obtaining funds for the purchase of supplies or food-stuffs (p. 192). Although this genesis does not detract from the artistic beauty or character of the various carvings, it does suggest that these works might not provide insight into a cultural or artistic reconciliation with the arrival of white Canada's system of law and order. As such, the link be-tween these carvings and the deeper meaning of the cases they represent may, in fact, be tenuous.

Therefore, despite the claim of its title, Dorothy Harley Eber's book, *Images of Justice—A Legal History of the Northwest Territories as Traced through the Yellowknife Courthouse Collection of Inuit Sculpture*, is not, in terms of the late 1990s, a legal history of the Northwest Territories. Rather, at its core, it is a handsome repackaging of fourteen prominent cases that have been detailed previously in the autobiographies of Justices John Sissons and William Morrow. This is not to suggest, however, that Eber has done nothing new with this book. In fact, she has provided a useful if brief history of the Northwest Territories Supreme Court and, in retelling the case histories of the trials and legal proceedings, Eber has pro-duced an interesting effort in connecting material, artistic, and legal history in the Canadian north. Finally, for those who are unfamiliar with the ju-dicial careers of Sissons and Morrow, and the prominent cases of their respective tenures, *Images of Justice* offers a readable entrée while, at the same time, bringing these cases together between the covers of a single book. While these contributions are not to be dismissed easily, the sub-stance of the cases that compose the heart of this book deserve a closer, more penetrating look so that we can finally begin researching, writing, and unraveling the legal histories of northern Canada. Essentially, we have yet to capture the image of justice in the land of the Inuit.

Jonathan Swainger
University of Northern British Columbia, Prince George

Steven Greer, *Supergrasses: A Study in Anti-Terrorist Law Enforcement in Northern Ireland*. Oxford: Clarendon Press, 1995. xvi + 309 pp. bibliog., index. $55.00.

Jackie Goodman was a budding supergrass.[1] On 14 March 1982 in Bel-fast, the Royal Ulster Constabulary (RUC) arrested Goodman, allegedly an operations officer for the Irish National Liberation Army (INLA), the violent republican group separate from the more famous IRA, the Irish Republican Army. Two days after his arrest, in return for immunity from prosecution, Goodman turned informer against his INLA colleagues. For the next six months, the detained Goodman (and his wife) gave statements to police. He and his wife were moved around a lot: to ten hotels in Ulster, then into army barracks, then to East Sussex in England, then to West Sussex. The Goodmans allegedly were promised a house and jobs in England, Canada, New Zealand, or South Africa, plus £30,000 in a bank account, if Jackie would go to trial. But Mrs. Goodman, homesick for Belfast, finally left him in mid-September, and ten days later, with telephone reassurances from the INLA that he would not be killed if he retracted, Goodman recanted, was released by the police and left England, rejoining his wife in Belfast. Fourteen of the people he had named were released from jail. Most were subsequently rearrested on the testimonies of other supergrasses.

Steven Greer's book is about the men who, unlike Jackie Goodman, fulfilled their promise to give evidence against former colleagues. A law professor at the University of Bristol, Greer has published a dozen articles (in legal journals) and two books on topics related to the present work.[2] Greer's *Supergrasses* is a history of the supergrass trials in Northern Ireland in the 1980s; it is more legalistic, thorough, and up to date than Andrew Boyd's popular account, *The Informers: A Chilling Assessment of the Supergrasses in Northern Ireland* (Dublin, 1984). Greer has produced his book without cooperation from the Director of Public Prosecutions for Northern Ireland, who declined to be interviewed, and without being granted access to any of the supergrasses themselves. The author's principal sources are published and unpublished accounts of the trials and appeals, government reports, newspapers, and a wide array of secondary literature. *Supergrasses* does presuppose considerable knowledge of the Northern Ireland problem. Greer does not discuss in any detail the paramilitary activities that called into being the supergrass system, so the reader is well advised to look elsewhere for the context of political crime and violence.[3]

Supergrasses evolved out of British security policies in the 1970s. Intelligence gathering was initially chaotic and competitive among the MI5, MI6, army, and RUC Special Branch and was only marginally improved by the creation (1973) of the Special Military Intelligence Unit (N. Ireland). To break the cycle of violence, at this stage largely from the IRA, the British authorities resorted to "psy ops" ("psychological operations"),[4] interrogation techniques used in Kenya and Malaya,[5] and special nonjury "Diplock courts."[6] In the absence of testimony from witnesses (sympathetic or intimidated), the key to convictions was extorting confessions from those arrested, which of course led to charges of psychological and physical abuses during interrogations.[7] The continuing IRA successes—most sensationally, Lord Mountbatten's assassination in August 1979—produced the appointment of Sir Maurice Oldfield, head of Britain's MI6 (1973–78), as Security Coordinator for Northern Ireland. Oldfield initiated a two-pronged policy of "taking out" (selective assassinations) and "turning" (getting so-called "converted terrorists," or CTs, to inform on their accomplices). If in the Diplock courts confessions had not produced the necessary results, then the "turning" of accomplices—men like Jackie Goodman—would have to serve the purpose.

Greer's piecing together of the evidence reveals that the height of the supergrass era was 1981 through 1983. Over those thirty-six months, twenty-seven supergrasses (eight "turned" loyalists and nineteen republicans) produced nearly 600 arrests. Not all were prosecuted but those who were included top leadership in Protestant (Ulster Volunteer Force, or UVF) as well as republican (IRA, INLA) groups. At five big trials in 1983, the year of ascendancy eighty-five people were tried and sixty-six convicted (a 78 percent rate); of the convictions, twenty-eight (42 percent) were on uncorroborated supergrass testimony.

The British could be savagely nonpartisan. In *Rex v. Graham* (1983), a trial of sixteen UVF members, fourteen were convicted, eleven solely on the testimony of supergrass Joseph Charles Bennett, a 36-year-old n'er-do-well with a long criminal record. Bennett had agreed to testify for immunity from prosecution, safe passage to a new location, a new job, and bankrolling for a new life. At the trial, before pronouncing guilty sentences on the others, Justice Murray noted that a person with Bennett's "appalling" record "would not . . . scruple at perjury if it suited him," since Bennett had a history as "a ruthless and resourceful criminal whose criminal acts extended to the use of his dead father's police uniform to carry out daring armed robberies" (p. 65).

British authorities dosed the same medicine to suspected republican terrorists. *Rex v. Donnelly* (1983), an IRA trial, Greer describes as "nothing short of a public spectacle. The thirty-eight defendants sat in rows around three sides of the courtroom, guarded by a score of prison officers and more than seventy policemen, two of whom were armed with M1 carbines" (p. 71). The trial, the biggest in Irish criminal history, was to an "astounding" degree characterized by camaraderie, knowing glances, and whispered jokes between witnesses and police and prosecutors. *Rex v. Donnelly* fills 70,000 pages, lasted eight months, cost more than £1 million, and produced prison sentences totaling 4,022 years. Of the 34 defendants convicted, 8 were solely from the testimony of supergrass Christopher Black, a 28-year-old semiemployed laborer/machinist who had joined the IRA in 1975. In his summation, Justice Kelly described Black as follows: "Throughout I was conscious of his bad character, his perjury, the motivations and benefits that preceded him to the witness box, the possible motivations while there, the inconsistencies and omissions revealed and indeed all of the infirmities that that cross-examination exposed. . . . But at the end of the day . . . my conclusion was that . . . he was one of the best witnesses I have ever heard" (p. 75). Black himself had been declared immune from prosecution.

The Graham and Donnelly trials were two of thirteen terrorist trials, 1980–91, involving supergrasses. Over that decade, a total of 245 people were tried and 145 (59 percent) convicted, sixty-nine of them on uncorroborated supergrass testimony. The tide began to turn in 1984, when thirty-five defendants in *Rex v. Robson*, an IRA/INLA trial, were all acquitted, overriding supergrass Raymond Gilmour's testimony, which Justice Lowry pronounced "entirely unworthy of belief" (p. 136). In 1985, the trial *Rex v. Steenson* brought convictions for *all* 28 INLA defendants, 24 on supergrass Harry Kirkpatrick's controversial testimony, but essentially from the mid-1980s the tactic of "converted terrorist" testimony was being discredited rapidly. There was only one supergrass trial after 1985, and the ten convictions in that 1991 IRA trial resulted from substantive evidence that corroborated informer Sandy Lynch's testimony.

Steven Greer argues convincingly that if the rise of the supergrasses resulted from Northern Ireland's crisis in governance c.1979–81, the fall was because of the conflict the supergrass trials posed to British common law. The beginning of the end can be traced to the Gifford Report (1984)[8] and the British government's own report on human rights in Northern Ireland (1985).[9] Both reports declared legally unacceptable the explosive combination of uncorroborated supergrass testimony in a nonjury trial setting, especially when immunity from prosecution or early release was associated with that testimony. Also faulted by the reports were the long delays in bringing prison defendants to trial and the length and size of the trials. Apart from the legal criticisms, there were numerous reasons for the end of the supergrass era: the decline in paramilitary violence; the frequency of supergrasses' retractions of testimony (by February 1984, Stanley Smith was the seventeenth supergrass to retract); highly unfavorable public opinion polls (in 1985, only 26 percent of Northern Irish Protestants and 6 percent of Catholics supported the supergrass system); and, perhaps most serious of all, the frequent quashing of convictions by the Northern Ireland Court of Appeal (by 1987, 66 of 75 appeals had reversed convictions; including appeal decisions, the overall conviction rate 1983–85 was thus only 24 percent).

Greer argues that a number of lessons can be learned from the supergrass era. While he strongly favors the restoration of jury trials, Greer recommends several legal reforms on the assumption this will not happen in the near future. There must be no further prosecutions on uncorroborated testimony. Corroboration itself must be "clear and compelling," and silences in police custody and refusals to testify in court should not be construed as guilt, notwithstanding the Criminal Evidence (N. Ireland) Order 1988.[10] There must be no grant of immunity from prosecution to any prospective witness. Any sentencing discount should take into account the witness' own criminal record. Although some relocation assistance is appropriate, no large sums of money should be available to witnesses.[11]

Toward the end of his book (in chapter 10, "Distant Cousins"), Greer discusses how other nations have used accomplice testimony to secure judicial convictions. In England in the 1970s, supergrass trials targeted London's organized crime; significantly, the trials were by jury and required corroborative evidence.[12] Early on, the granting of immunity from prosecution was abandoned in favor of prior trial and sentencing of the supergrass before he "squealed" on his accomplices. Greer also offers some instructive comparisons to quasi-supergrass practices in the United States (specifically, the Witness Protection Program), Italy, Germany, Spain, and France where organized crime or political fringe groups—small minorities in society—were targeted.

Northern Ireland is, of course, a very different place from the above *nations*. In this tumultuous province within the "United" Kingdom, disorder stems from an endemic political problem. Whether from the Protestant UVF or Catholic IRA, strong communal feelings collide against British government rule. It was the very weakness of Britain's authority that led to suspension of trial by jury. Greer's basic thesis is that in an attempt to restore order and restate its legitimacy, the British government sacrificed due process to what he calls crime control. But Diplock courts and supergrasses alienated first the Catholic community, then the Protestant working-class community, and finally even the legal community. By the mid-1980s, the supergrass system had so discredited itself that "either the system had to be destroyed or the judiciary in Northern Ireland had to relinquish any credible claim to impartiality, independence, and rationality" (p. 275).

To those affected, it is cold and belated consolation that even in wartorn Northern Ireland due process can eventually prevail. But should there be a recrudescence of political violence, there is no telling how Britain will respond. Her recent imperial history, from Malaya to Kenya to Ulster, does not inspire immediate confidence. In the current era of quiescence and ongoing dialogue involving London, Dublin, and Belfast, Britain must seize the day and negotiate a political settlement of the problem that triggered the supergrass excesses. The bottom line, suggests Greer, is that the British government will be hard put to govern effectively until it comes up with a credible answer to the Northern Ireland question.

NOTES

1. The origins of this word are unclear. Speculation includes "snake in the grass," "grasshopper" (Cockney rhyming slang with "copper," from early 1970s London trials), or a then-popular song, "Whispering Grass." Of course, the word can have had multiple derivations.

2. The books are S. Greer and A. White, *Abolishing the Diplock Courts: The Case for Restoring Jury Trial to Scheduled Offences in Northern Ireland* (London,

1986), and S. Greer and R. Morgan, eds., *The Right to Silence Debate* (Bristol, 1990).

3. For a beginning, see J. B. Bell, *The Irish Troubles: A Generation of Violence, 1967–1992* (New York, 1993); P. Bishop and E. Mallie, *The Provisional IRA* (London, 1988); J. Darby, *Conflict in Northern Ireland: The Development of a Polarised Community* (Dublin, 1976) and *Intimidation and the Control of Conflict in Northern Ireland* (Dublin, 1986); M. Dillon, *The Dirty War* (London, 1991); W. D. Flackes and S. Elliott, *Northern Ireland: A Political Directory, 1968–88* (Belfast, 1989); S. Nelson, *Ulster's Uncertain Defenders: Loyalists and the Northern Ireland Conflict* (Belfast, 1984); J. Darby, ed., *Northern Ireland: The Background to the Conflict* (Belfast, 1983); and S. Wichert, *Northern Ireland Since 1945* (London, 1991).

4. The brainchild of a young brigadier stationed in Belfast. See Frank Kitson, *Low-Intensity Operations: Subversion, Insurgency, Peace-Keeping* (London, 1971).

5. C. Andrew, *Secret Service: The Making of the British Intelligence Community* (London, 1985); J. Block and P. Fitzgerald, *British Intelligence and Covert Action: Africa, Middle East, and Europe Since 1945* (London, 1983).

6. So named for Lord Diplock, chair of a British House of Lords committee, whose Report (December 1972) recommended suspension of jury trial and an array of new police and army powers.

7. See A. Jennings, ed., *Justice Under Fire: The Abuse of Civil Liberties in Northern Ireland*, 2nd ed. (London, 1990); J. McGuffin, *The Guineapigs* (London, 1974); M. Urban, *Big Boys' Rules: The SAS and the Secret Struggle Against the IRA* (London, 1992). See also the British parliamentary reports on interrogations in Northern Ireland, the Parker Report, Command Paper 4901 (Her Majesty's Stationery Office [HMSO], 1972), and the Gardiner Report, Command 5847 (HMSO, 1975).

8. Lord Gifford, a Labour peer, was privately commissioned by the London-based civil liberties organization, the Cobden Trust, to investigate the use of supergrasses. He published his findings in a terse, brutally critical book, *Supergrasses: The Use of Accomplice Evidence in Northern Ireland* (London, 1984).

9. *Tenth Report of the Standing Advisory Commission on Human Rights for 1983–84*, HC 175 (HMSO, 1985).

10. See Greer and Morgan, *The Right to Silence Debate*.

11. The Secretary of State for Northern Ireland, Mr. Douglas Hurd, informed the House of Commons on 26 February 1985 that the cost to U.K. taxpayers for "providing protection for people who had given evidence against former accomplices in terrorist organizations" (Greer and Morgan, 269) had in the period 1978–84 come to a total of £1.3 million.

12. See M. O'Mahoney, with D. Wooding, *King Squealer: The True Story of Maurice O'Mahoney* (London, 1978).

Stanley H. Palmer
University of Texas, Arlington

George Robb and Nancy Erber, eds., *Disorder in the Court: Trials and Sexual Conflict at the Turn of the Century*. New York: New York University Press, 1999. 329 pp., index. $25.00.

W. F. Yeames' celebrated genre painting "Defendant and Counsel" graces the cover of *Disorder in the Court*. First exhibited at the British Royal Academy's summer show in 1875, the painting depicts a young woman in her soliciter's office staring soulfully out of the frame while her advocate gazes at her with tense anticipation. The tableau's very ambiguity sparked a national debate as to the unidentified woman's crime and circumstance. George Robb and Nancy Erber argue that this incident was symbolic of a turn-of-the-century mindset, or *mentalité*, that desired a single truth or narrative during an age when rapid industrialization, the women's suffrage movement, and colonial unrest were blurring the traditional boundaries between the public and the private.

Disorder in the Court consists of eleven accounts of high-profile and sensationalized cases of spousal violence and homicide, divorce, and public homosexuality that served to "rend the façade of bourgeois sexual orthodoxy" in England, France, and the British Empire (p. 8). Drawing upon police archives, coroner's inquests, magistrate's courts, and newspaper coverage, the authors share a mission, on the one hand, to reveal the debates (or discourse) surrounding the trials and the degree to which they were manipulated to serve political and public agendas, and on the other, to shed light on aspects of working-class and homosexual culture that allude capture through traditional historical sources.

A majority of the volume's contributors explore how private acts of marital discord and violence sparked public debates on imperial and patriarchal privilege in law and society. Antoinette Burton's "Conjugality on Trial: The Rukhmabai Case" and Ginger Frost's "A Shock to Marriage?: The Clitheroe Case and the Victorians," for instance, detail how different meanings were attached to two women's denial of their husband's conjugal rights in the 1880s. While Rukhmabai's case enhanced demands for legislation against early child marriage in India, it also provided the British government with a new justification for imperial rule in the face of burgeoning Indian nationalism: If Indian men could not control their women, perhaps they were unfit for self-government. In England, by contrast, Emily Jackson's case became a watershed in married women's legal rights when the judiciary denied her husband a proprietary interest in her body. Yet, as Frost argues, the Clitheroe case also enhanced conservative fears that two pillars of English society, the institution of marriage and the common law itself, were under attack. In a similar vein, George Robb's account of the English "Dreyfuss" case demonstrates how the conviction of Florence Maybrick—a proven adulterous—for poisoning her husband gave American and English feminists a *cause célèbre* to contest the double standard of sexual morality and deep-seated anxieties about the New Woman in the 1890s.

Just as policy-makers perceived the "new woman" as symbolic of societal chaos, so they also interpreted the emergence of a distinct homosexual culture at the turn of the century as evidence of national decadence and decay. Contributions by William Peniston, Morris B. Kaplan, Nancy Erber, Nicole Albert, and Anne Summer Holmes explore the meanings that were attached to cases of aristocratic liaisons with youths of the French and English working class and the suppression of literary representations of lesbianism in *fin-de-siècle* Paris. The trials that resulted from these cases served to reproduce existing assumptions that associated homosexuality with criminality; thus, they effectively kept homosexual culture on the margins where policy-makers deemed it should remain. The authors' exploration of the public reactions to the cases reveal, however, that they provided an ideal forum to criticize class privilege in the justice system and society. The popular and radical presses, for instance, held up aristocratic homosexuality and the courts' lenient treatment of offenders as direct proof that the ideal citizen was bourgeois, heterosexual, and masculine.

Disorder in the Court's greatest strength lies in the fact that it will appeal to both the general public and to scholars from diverse fields and disciplines: postcolonial studies, the history of crime, gender, class, and sexuality, and poststructuralist literary criticism—to name but a few. Although it can be argued that high-profile trials derived from unique and sensational circumstances are indicative of nothing, the volume's chapters highlight the trial as a meeting-place, both figuratively and literally, of law, culture, and society. As the editors argue:

social and sexual behaviour are regulated simultaneously by the state and the community, the one chiefly through legislation and the courts, the other mainly by the force of public opinion. Each of the cases in this collection demonstrates the interplay of the two realms. (P. 2)

Given the authors' focus on the turn-of-the-century obsession with gendered behavior and its international context, the book's underlying premise could have been strengthened by an exploration of high-profile sex crimes against women that crossed race and class boundaries. But despite this minor deficiency, *Disorder in the Court* stands as a testament to the value of the legal record for research in the social sciences and humanities.

Lesley Erickson
University of Calgary

Index

About the Editor and Contributors

LEE BEIER is Professor of History and Chair of the History Department at Southern Illinois University, Normal. He has written widely on the history of the poor, vagrancy, and the poor laws in early modern England, and has contributed books, articles, and chapters on this topic. His most well-known work is *Masterless Men: The Vagrancy Problem in England, 1560–1640* (1985). He is currently engaged in a study of the poor and the problem of criminality.

TREVOR DEAN is Professor of Medieval History in the History Department at the University of Surrey, Roehampton. Recent publications include *Crime, Society and the Law in Renaissance Italy* (1994), edited with Kate Lowe, and a study of *Crime in Medieval Europe* (2000). His interests focus on vendetta and disputes arising from marriage in late medieval/Renaissance Italy, and he is currently researching a range of further crimes in late medieval Bologna including insult and theft.

CLIVE EMSLEY is Professor of History and co-director of the European Centre for the Study of Policing at The Open University. He has published second, revised editions of the popular *The English Police: A Political and Social History* (1996), and *Crime and Society in England 1750–1900* (1996), a major study of *Gendarmes and the State in Nineteenth-Century Europe* (1999), and has co-edited with Richard Bessel, *Patterns of Provocation: Police and Public Disorder* (2000). He is currently working on several aspects of policing the state in modern Europe.

DAVID ENGLANDER was Senior Lecturer in European Humanities Study, and Co-Director of the Charles Booth Centre at The Open University. His recent books include *Mr. Charles Booth's Inquiry: Life and La-*

bour of the People of London Reconsidered (1993) and *A Documentary History of Jewish Immigrants in Britain, 1840–1920* (1994). Tragically, he passed away in the spring of 1999, after this chapter was written.

LESLEY ERICKSON is a doctoral candidate in History at the University of Calgary. She had published "The Interplay of Ethnicity and Gender: Swedish Women in South-eastern Saskatchewan," in *Other Voices*, ed. David de Brou and Aileen Moffat (1996) and is working on several case studies of women as victims of violent crime in the Canadian west.

MALCOLM GASKILL is Fellow and Director of Studies in History at Churchill College, University of Cambridge. He has recently contributed to volumes of essays on women and crime and on witchcraft and belief and has published *Crime and Mentalities in Early Modern England* (2000) and *Hellish Nell: Last of Britain's Witches* (2001). Currently he is working on the Great War and manifestations of the supernatural, to be followed by a book on the Matthew Hopkins East Anglian witch trials in the 1640s.

MARK HALLER is Professor of History and Criminal Justice at Temple University. He has published numerous articles on the history of gambling, vice, bootlegging, loansharking, and other illegal activities in American cities, as well as several prominent works on law and the Constitution. He is the co-editor with Allen Freeman of the recently reissued *The Peoples of Philadelphia* (1998).

LOUIS A. KNAFLA is Professor Emeritus of History at the University of Calgary. Recently he has authored *Kent at Law 1602: The County Jurisdiction* (1995) and co-edited with Susan Binnie, *Law, Society, and the State: Essays in Modern Legal History* (1995), and with Clive Emsley, *Crime Histories and Histories of Crime* (Greenwood, 1996). He is currently working on the courts of Star Chamber and Chancery in the late sixteenth and early seventeenth centuries and a study of "living on the edge" in early modern England.

ANDREA KNOX is Lecturer in Early Modern History and Women's Studies in the History Division at the University of Northumbria. She has published "Magical and Prophetical Women in Sixteenth and Seventeenth Century Ireland," *Quidditas* 21 (spring 2002) and book chapters on "Barbarous and Pestiferous Women," in *Women, Crime and Deviance in Scotland since 1400*, ed. Yvonne Brown and Rona Ferguson (2002), and "Women of the Septs," in *Historical and Cultural Representations of Irish Nationalist Women*, ed. Louise Ryan and Margaret Ward (2002). She is currently involved in research on Irish female immigration to Spain in the seventeenth century.

MARK KONNERT is Associate Professor of History at the University of

Calgary. He has published a major study of French towns on the middle ground of the Reformation: *Civil Agendas and Religious Passion: Chalons-sur-Marne during the French Wars of Religion, 1560–1594* (1997). His research interests include France during the Wars of Religion and urban history and religious violence in the early modern era.

DAVID LAVEN is Lecturer in History at the University of Reading. He is currently completing a book on the Austrian government of northern Italy in the early nineteenth century.

PHILIPPA LEVINE is Professor of History at the University of Southern California. Her major study is *Feminist Lives in Victorian England: Private Roles and Public Commitment* (1990), and she has written numerous articles on Victorian prostitution, labor, Marxism, and feminism. She is currently completing a study of venereal disease, prostitution, and the sexual politics of race 1860–1918.

PAUL NIGOL is currently articling with a Calgary law firm. He has a book chapter in press on "Private Law in the Hudson's Bay Company, 1670–1870" (2002). Research interests include legal pluralism, the history of colonial legal systems, and policing in North America.

STANLEY H. PALMER is Professor of History at the University of Texas at Arlington. He is the author of the monumental study *Police and Protest in England and Ireland 1780–1850* (1990). He continues to work on the comparative role of the police in Ireland and England.

ANNE PARRELLA is Professor of History at Tidewater Community College. Her major work is *Violence in Northern France: A Social Historical Analysis of Murder, 1815–1909* (1983), and she has published "Industrialization and Murder: Northern France, 1815–1904," *Journal of Interdisciplinary History* (spring 1992). Her research interests include theories of violence and historiography.

ANTONY SIMPSON is Reference Librarian at the John Jay College of Criminal Justice and a member of the doctoral faculty of the City University of New York. He has published a number of articles addressing relationships between law, value systems, and social change in eighteenth- and nineteenth-century England. His most recent book is *Information-Finding and the Research Process* (1993).

AMY GILMAN SREBNICK is Professor of History at Montclair State University. She is especially interested in cultural history and interdisciplinary studies and is the author of *The Mysterious Death of Mary Rogers: Sex and Culture in Nineteenth-Century New York* (1995). She is currently working on the history of crime discourse.

JONATHAN SWAINGER is Associate Professor of History at the University of Northern British Columbia, Prince George. He has published numerous articles on extradition in nineteenth-century Canada, lawyering in Red Deer, Alberta, and crime and criminal justice in the Peace River country of Alberta and British Columbia. He has recently published *The Canadian Department of Justice and the Completion of Confederation, 1867–78* (2000) and is currently writing a history of crime in the Peace River area.

ARVIND VERMA is Associate Professor of Criminal Justice at Indiana University, Bloomington. He served formerly with the Indian Police Service as Superintendent of the elite Indian Police Service in Bihar until 1990. Managing Editor of *Police Practice and Research: An International Journal*, and consultant to the Bureau of Police Research and Development, India, his recent publications include "Construction of Offender Profile Using Fuzzy Logic," *Police Studies* (1997); "Maintaining Law & Order in India," *International Criminal Justice Review* (1999), and "Organized Crime in India," *Kanagawa Law Journal* (2000). He has a forthcoming article, "A Topological Representation of the Criminal Event," in *Western Criminological Review* and an edited book on *Organized Crime: A World Perspective* (2002). Current research interests include policing, research methods, and criminal justice in India, fuzzy logic, GIS, and mathematical analysis of criminal justice data.

CARL WADE is a postgraduate student in History at The Open University. He is preparing a doctoral dissertation on crime and criminality in mid–nineteenth-century Berlin and has interests in European policing.

MARVIN ZALMAN is Professor of Criminal Justice at Wayne State University. He has had articles and chapters published on the president's 1967 Crime Commission, drug asset forfeiture policy, assisted suicide law and policy, civil rights and criminal justice, and a critique of selected political science analyses of the Supreme Court, and numerous edited works on crime, criminal justice, and sentencing. The third edition of his popular *Criminal Procedure: Constitution and Society* (1997) will be published in 2002.